MARRIAGE: EAST AND WEST

Books by David Mace:

DOES SEX MORALITY MATTER?
COMING HOME
MARRIAGE COUNSELING
MARRIAGE CRISIS
MARRIAGE: THE ART OF LASTING LOVE
WHOM GOD HATH JOINED
HEBREW MARRIAGE
YOUTH LOOKS TOWARD MARRIAGE
SUCCESS IN MARRIAGE

Marriage:

EAST AND WEST

BY

David and Vera Mace

Robert

Garden City, New York

DOUBLEDAY & COMPANY, INC.

1960

Permission to quote from the following copyright material is gratefully acknowledged. In a few instances exact ownership is obscure. If for this reason, or through inadvertence, any rights have not been acknowledged, it is hoped that the owners will pardon the omission.

The Broader Way by Sumie Seo Mishima. Copyright © 1953 by the John Day Company. Reprinted by permission of the John Day Company, Inc., publisher. *Daughters of Changing Japan* by Earl Herbert Cressy. Copyright 1955 by Earl Herbert Cressy. Used by permission of the publishers, Farrar, Straus & Cudahy, Inc. *East Wind: West Wind* by Pearl S. Buck. Copyright © 1930 by Pearl S. Buck. Reprinted by permission of Harold Ober Associates Incorporated. *The Good Earth* by Pearl S. Buck. Copyright © 1931 by Pearl S. Buck. Reprinted by permission of Harold Ober Associates Incorporated. *House of Exile* by Nora Waln. Copyright 1933 by Little, Brown & Company. Used by permission of Little, Brown & Company and A. M. Heath & Co. Ltd. *A Marriage to India* by Frieda Hauswirth Das. Reprinted by permission of the publisher, The Vanguard Press. Copyright, 1930, by Vanguard Press Inc. *My Boyhood in Siam* by Kumut Chandruang. Copyright © 1938, 1940 by Kumut Chandruang. Reprinted by permission of the John Day Company, Inc., publisher. *Nectar in a Sieve* by Kamala Markandaya. Copyright © 1954 by the John Day Company. Reprinted by permission of the John Day Company, Inc., publisher. *Chinese Women Yesterday and Today* by Florence Ayscough. Reprinted by permission of Houghton Mifflin Company. "Christianity and Sex" from *Sex and Religion Today*, ed. Simon Doniger. Reprinted by permission of Simon Doniger. *The City of Two Gateways* by S. D. Nanda. Reprinted by permission of George Allen & Unwin Ltd. *Dream of the Red Chamber* by Tsao Hsueh-chin, translated by Chi-chen Wang. Used by permission of Twayne Publishers, 1958. "Greater Learning for Women" by Kaibara Ekken (introduction by Shingoro Takaishi) in *Women and Wisdom of Japan*. Reprinted by permission of the Wisdom of the East Series and John Murray Ltd. *History of European Morals* by W. E. H. Lecky. Reprinted by permission of A. C. A. Watts & Company, Limited. *Home Life in China* by Mary I. Bryson. Reprinted by permission of the American Tract Society. *Home Life in China* by Isaac T. Headland. Reprinted by permission of the Macmillan Company of New York and Methuen & Co. Ltd. *Lamps in the Wind* by Eleanor McDougall. Reprinted by permission of Edinburgh House Press. *The Long March* by Simone de Beauvoir. Reprinted by permission of World Publishing Company, Librairie Gallimard, Weidenfeld & Nicolson and André Deutsch Ltd. *Mother India* by Katherine Mayo. Reprinted by permission of Harcourt, Brace & Company. *The New Face of China* by Peter Schmid. Reprinted by permission of George G. Harrap and Company Limited. *Poems by Indian Women*, ed. Margaret Macnicol. Reprinted by permission of Y.M.C.A. Publishing House, Calcutta. *Purdah: The Status of Indian Women* by Frieda Hauswirth. Reprinted by permission of Routledge & Kegan Paul Ltd. *Sex Problems in India* by N. S. Phadke. Extract reprinted by permission of the publishers, D. B. Taraporevala Sons & Co. Private Ltd. *Sinhalese Village* by Bryce Ryan. Reprinted by permission of University of Miami Press. *Springtime in Shanghai* by Mabel Waln Smith. Reprinted by permission of Christy & Moore, Ltd. *Suttee* by Edward Thompson. Reprinted by permission of George Allen & Unwin Ltd.

To
SHEILA and JAGAN
in Whom
West and East
Meet
and Are One

Contents

Preface

The justification for writing this book is that, to the best of our knowledge, no similar volume exists—at least in the English language. This puts us in the comfortable position of knowing that, though it may well be criticized, it will not be compared unfavorably with its competitors!

Our hope is that this small study of ours will fill a gap. As we have moved back and forth between East and West, we have become aware of a complex of misunderstandings that exist on each side about the other's culture. In certain areas the misconceptions have become acute and present a serious threat to mutual trust and co-operation. One of these areas, we believe, is that of the relationship between men and women.

This is a field so vast that no one could possibly possess all the qualifications necessary to speak authoritatively about it. We certainly make no claim to do so. But we have at least given the subject careful consideration and tried to learn what we could from four separate visits to Asia and the reading of about 90 books. This means that we know something more about it than the average reader does. We can lead such a reader by the hand and carry him a little further than he was when he started. We can raise in his mind some questions about marriage in the changing world of today—questions not remote and academic, but often very personal and deeply concerned with the future happiness of mankind. And we can indicate where he can turn for further knowledge if he desires it.

We wish this book to be judged, therefore, not as a work of scholarship, but as an impressionistic picture painted on a very broad canvas. We believe such a picture is needed by many people who have neither time nor inclination to consult scholarly works. We do not claim that the picture is accurate in every detail. Though we have striven to avoid errors, both of fact and of interpretation, we cannot hope to have succeeded entirely. We do, however, believe that the picture we have given is on the whole a true one.

To make the picture as vivid as possible, we have ranged widely in our search for illustrative material. We have made use of novels and poems as well as of technical works, travel records, and volumes intended for public enlightenment. Wherever possible, we have allowed the authorities, and the people with firsthand experience—both ancient and modern—to speak for themselves. In this way we have tried to convey feelings as well as cold facts, atmosphere as well as information.

We have not been concerned about reaching conclusions so much as with presenting the facts and discussing them. Naturally we have a few opinions and convictions of our own, and they will be obvious to the reader. But the purpose of the book is to ask questions, and to put these questions in their right context, rather than to answer them.

When we began this study, we had to decide what we meant by East and West. Both terms are loosely used. When we speak of the West, we mean European culture together with its products outside the continent of Europe. That is clear enough. But when we speak of the East, we do not mean all of Asia. We found this too large, and too complex, to be treated as a single cultural unit. So we had to limit it to something reasonably manageable in size and reasonably uniform in pattern.

We felt it best, for example, to omit those cultures, largely Moslem, which are found in what we call the Near East and the Middle East. All of Asiatic Russia was also omitted. Our study was therefore confined mainly to the three great civilizations of India, China, and Japan, and the cultures outside of these countries that are essentially derived from them. These make up the vast bulk of the population of Asia; and their cultures, being of considerable age, have deeply influenced their own and each other's ways of living.

In terms of Eastern religion and philosophy, our interest has been focused mainly on the Hindu, Buddhist and Confucian traditions. We recognize that Islam has some strongly established positions in the areas we have studied. But, rightly or wrongly, we formed the impression that its influence has been relatively recent and peripheral. So we have decided, not without reluctance, to give Moslem marriage patterns only incidental attention.

Another problem we had to face was how to make effective contrasts between East and West when both are in a state of movement and change. Both have traditional marriage patterns from which they are moving away. An accurate comparison between the two cultures as they exist today would see them both as transitional. We decided that our objectives would best be met by placing side by side the very old and the very new, and so sharpening the contrasts that we wished to make. We therefore chose deliberately to emphasize not the process of change itself, but what seem to be the respective ends of the continuum.

In the East, therefore, we have portrayed the traditional marriage patterns of the three great civilizations—the point of departure of the transition now in progress. In the West we have gone to the opposite extreme and portrayed, as far as possible, the results to date of the transitional process. This device has its disadvantages, as we are fully aware. But we justify our choice on the basis that the detailed stages of the transitional process are not our primary concern. What we are concerned with is the broad direction in which marriage patterns are moving, and we believe that this will be best seen by looking in turn at each end of the process of movement.

We have written primarily for people without specialized knowledge, either of marriage or of the East-West culture contrasts. We have therefore adopted a style of writing designed to make the book interesting and readable. Our material is based on personal observation during three extensive visits to the East; on the knowledge and experience of Asians from many countries; and on our reading of the books listed in the bibliography. We wished to avoid the use of footnotes, which are distracting. Yet we desired to acknowledge the many sources from which our material came. We have tried to compromise by putting the references separately at the end of the book. We assume that most readers will not bother to look them up. But they are there for those who wish to do so.

Now a word about our joint authorship. This book is a product, as it should be, of the thinking together of a married couple. The division of labor has been based on our diversities of gifts, and our separate contributions need not be enumerated. In recording a few personal experiences that happened only to one of us, we have recounted them, to avoid confusion, as though we had both been involved.

In conclusion we wish to thank the many people who have helped to make this book possible. It is practicable to name only a few of these—Dr. Glora Wysner and Dr. Irma Highbaugh, of the International Missionary Council; our Chiengmai delegates representing eleven Asian territories; Lady Rama Rau, Dr. Sushila Gore, and Mrs. Avabai Wadia, of India; Dr. Frank Price and his assistants, Mr. John Ma and Miss Lucy Ann Dunlap, at the Missionary Research Library, New York; Dr. and Mrs. Floyd Shacklock, formerly of Japan, now of New York; and Mr. Clement Alexandre, of Doubleday. To these, and a host of others, our good friends, we express our gratitude.

Prologue

TWENTY ASIANS AT CHIENGMAI

The sun sank slowly, like a ball of fire, over the rim of the far-thest rice field. The harvesters, weary of the long day's toil, slackened their pace, straightened their aching backs, and began to trudge contentedly homeward. As the train from Bangkok chugged its way northward through the sea of golden-yellow grain, across the skyline the silhouettes of men, women and children in their broad-brimmed hats, of lurching ox wagons, of tapering, feather-topped palms, grew dim and dissolved into the swiftly gathering darkness. Suddenly in the railroad train the lights came on, the outside world vanished, and the attendant appeared through the sliding doorway with a tray bearing two cups of sickly sweet, lukewarm tea.

A railway journey in Asia is an experience of unhurried leisure. The arrival in each station is an event. Crowds swarm in and out of the train, vendors of endless varieties of food and drink skirmish hopefully along the platform, shouting their wares. Passengers descend, walk, talk, brush their teeth, perform their ablutions, replenish their water supply. Officials move tentatively about, with or without any discernible sense of purpose, fraternizing with the amiable, and arguing vociferously with the recalcitrant. Curious children gaze and gambol and get in everybody's way. Finally, after what seems an interminable delay, a sense of the train's impending departure somehow communicates itself to the milling multitude. The passengers find their way back to their compartments, the vendors pack up their unsold wares, the officials become purposeful, and the lookers-on realize that the show is over. Slowly the train begins to move. The last stragglers nonchalantly clamber on board, the doors slam, the engine picks up speed, and all is calm until the next station is reached, when the whole performance is repeated.

When we had drunk the insipid tea, our bunks were made ready, and we stretched out for the night. Eddying dust soon settled on the clean white sheets. Flying insects, infiltrating through the tattered window screen, scorched themselves on the lights overhead and fell writhing in the dust. The train lurched and rumbled on through the sultry night. Soon, we reassured ourselves, we would be clear of the plain and climbing into the mountains. Then it would be cooler. There would be fewer flies. And fewer stations.

Drifting fitfully between sleeping and waking, we thought of the proud city of Bangkok that we had left behind—*Krung Thep*, the City of Angels, the Thais call it. And we thought of Chiengmai —the "New Town"—five hundred miles north among the mountains. Once it *was* a new town. But that was long, long ago. The ancient capital of Thailand's Northern Kingdom, it has stood guard through the centuries behind its massive walls, now crumbling to dust, and defied invaders across the great moat where now the ducks swim idly and the water buffaloes wallow in the soft, oozing mud. Our journey would take some twenty hours. Tomorrow Dr. Chinda would meet us at the station and take us to his home for lunch. Then we would look over the buildings and make our plans. We fervently hoped Chiengmai would come up to our expectations.

Drowsing, we reviewed the long course of events that had led up to this journey into the mountains of northern Thailand.

*   *   *

The interior of the church was in darkness. With hands joined in a wide circle, the two hundred delegates waited. In each hand was a small candle. The wax grew soft and malleable in the warm night air.

At the far end a light appeared. Someone carried a taper to Dr. Charles, and lit his candle. He held it steady while his neighbors to right and left ignited their wicks over the flickering flame. Slowly the lights increased in both directions, creeping round the circle as each used his neighbor's candle to light his own. Shadowy forms took more definite shape, features became recognizable as the lines of light moved steadily on. In the silence we thought of the crowded days we had spent together. Scanning the faces we saw the characteristic lineaments of the Eastern races—of India and Ceylon, Burma and Thailand, China and Japan. Eleven countries had sent representatives to Manila to study family life in Southeast Asia. Tomorrow the delegates would scatter and return to their homes.

The line of light moved steadily on. The circle of faces grew wider. Almost all of them were Asian faces. Just an occasional Westerner was included, as a consultant. Otherwise, this was an Asian conference. It was about Asian family life—something no Westerner can know, except from the outside.

The invitation to the Manila Conference had come to us unexpectedly. Half of the year 1954 had been spent in a strenuous trip round Africa, helping to develop marriage guidance services to meet the rising threat of family disintegration. To this work we had begun to devote ourselves, back in our native Britain, soon after our own marriage in 1933. We had said we were willing to go anywhere to work in the cause of making marriage and family life happier and more stable.

The lighted candles were now twinkling like a galaxy of stars. The dim outline of the church was becoming clearer. We held our candles expectantly, waiting for the light to reach us.

Less than three months after returning from Africa we had set off again on the long flight to the Philippines. Our plane had come down over Tokyo at sunrise. Earlier that year, we had first set foot on the Asian continent—away at the Western end of it, in Aden. The vast area between Aden and Tokyo was to us, before November 1954, mysterious and unknown. But it seemed to beckon us. Asian faces were, to us, friendly faces.

The circle of light was now swiftly closing. Expectantly we waited. The hundreds of candles gave the church a festive air. Still the delegates stood in silence. No one could move, the ceremony could not proceed, until the line of light was complete and unbroken—a perfect circle; like a wedding ring, the symbol of endless devotion.

It seemed to us, that night in Manila, symbolic that we, of all those hundreds of delegates, should close the ring of light. It was as if we had a part to play that enabled the conference to be completed, and its purposes to be fully achieved. We did not know what that part was then. But later it became clear.

*   *   *

Irma Highbaugh was made aware, in her work as a missionary in western China, that the people she tried to serve needed help in their family relationships. The breaking down of the old patterns was leading to confusion. Nothing stable was taking their place. Western influence was in part responsible for the giving up of the old ways. Representing the West, she felt vaguely uneasy about what was happening. She wanted to do something to make amends.

On her furloughs, instead of resting, she worked. She studied family life. She learned about the new techniques with which the West was striving to meet its growing problems of marriage breakdown, of juvenile delinquency, of family disorganization. By persistent effort, by diligent use of her furloughs, she completed the requirements first for her M.A., then for her Ph.D. degrees. She was now equipped to serve China at the point where she felt the need was greatest. She could teach the Chinese about marriage counseling, about family life education. She could train the pastors, instruct the parents, guide the youth.

Then the Communist armies swept victoriously across the land. The missionaries had to leave. Irma Highbaugh was ready to serve; but the door was closed.

She could not believe that she had toiled and studied and prepared herself to no purpose. In other Asian countries there were the same needs, the same problems. What she could not do for China she could do elsewhere.

Dr. Glora Wysner is the only woman staff member of the International Missionary Council with full executive status. With a woman's insight she saw that Irma Highbaugh's frustration could become fruition. She planned a program to promote new emphasis on family life throughout the Christian churches of East Asia. She created the organization, and found the money, to send Irma Highbaugh campaigning into country after country.

The program was a success. In Japan, in Korea, in Thailand, in Indonesia, in Ceylon, the people came in crowds. Religion that concerned itself with the daily life of the home, that helped to improve family relationships, was the kind of religion that touched human need at a vital point. The movement grew. In country after country the churches set up organizations to foster better family life.

The Manila Conference was organized to bring together Asian Christians who were part of this growing movement. They set up a committee with Dr. G. P. Charles, the Tamil pastor of St. Gabriel's Church in Rangoon, as chairman. They drafted plans for the extension of their work—for the training of professional leaders, the holding of conferences, the publication of literature.

But in all this planning there was one great weakness. There was plenty of enthusiasm, but no trained leadership. Irma Highbaugh had behind her many years of disciplined study and training in the West. These Asian leaders had had no similar opportunities. Many of them were ignorant, untrained, poorly equipped, often confused.

So the Manila Conference passed a resolution, asking the International Missionary Council to find ways and means to provide the East Asian churches with better trained native leadership. Some time later, we received a request from Dr. Glora Wysner, asking us if we would assume the responsibility of carrying out this training program.

As we considered this request, we remembered how the circle of light could not be completed till we had done our part. Was this a symbol? We did not know. But we accepted the invitation.

*   *   *

In 1956 we went to Australia. For four months we traveled from state to state, visiting the marriage guidance centers, holding public meetings and professional conferences; and finally reporting our conclusions to Mr. Menzies, the Prime Minister, in his office in Canberra.

This task completed, we flew to Singapore. Our plans for the training of the Asian Christian leaders had taken shape. As a first step, we would hold a three-month Study and Training Institute, and bring together picked people from twelve countries. It was important to find the right place to hold this. It must be central for countries stretching across the continent from Japan to Pakistan. It must be in a country that would exclude none of our delegates on political grounds. It must be reasonably pleasant and secluded, with a tolerable climate. And it must provide a building where our group could live and work together for a three-month period without interruption.

This proved to be a tall order. We made inquiries in Singapore, throughout Malaya, in Bangkok, and southern Thailand. We followed up every suggestion that was made. All to no purpose. Our time was running out. We were due within a few days to start a program for the Indian Government.

When our spirits were at low ebb, someone asked if we had considered Chiengmai. We hadn't even heard of it! As we made inquiries, it sounded hopeful. A twenty-hour train journey from Bangkok was involved. There were planes—but not when we could travel. All right, we would go by train, and fly back.

Chiengmai exceeded our wildest hopes. It had everything. Back home later we called it our Shangri-la. A fertile plain ringed with mountains; a dry and bracing climate, in contrast with Bangkok's enervating heat and humidity; a friendly community, with considerable missionary enterprises—schools, hospital, leper colony, and a theological seminary. To crown it all, the seminary had a vacation covering the exact three-month period we had planned for our Institute! And it had all the accommodations and facilities we needed!

*   *   *

In February 1958 snow fell in Thailand for the first time on record. It fell only in the high mountains. But in Chiengmai the nights were so cold that we had to collect extra blankets for our delegates—especially those who had come straight from the Equator.

No one complained. We had come prepared to work hard, and to live a strictly disciplined life. The program was tough. We ourselves found it so. Asians in general do not easily adapt to closely timed schedules. Yet for our purpose everything had to be strictly scheduled. It speaks volumes for our group that they accepted it, day after day for twelve long weeks, with unfaltering loyalty.

They came from eleven territories—Japan, Korea, the Philippines, Taiwan, Hong Kong, Thailand, Burma, Malaya, Ceylon, India, and Pakistan. There were twenty in all—eleven men and nine women. All were picked leaders, of graduate status, and professionally qualified.

Living a close community life with our twenty Asians had a deeply pervasive effect on us. The Asian food we shared with them was an unmitigated hardship—before the end our reactions against the inevitable dish of rice became intense! At every other point, we found ourselves slowly undergoing a process of assimilation. This was obviously accelerated because our delegates were of such high caliber. Our discussions with them were intellectually stimulating to the point of being exciting. We began to see old truths from completely new angles. With gentle persuasiveness they laid bare prejudices in us of which we had been unaware, and tenderly exposed stupid foibles we had never before recognized as such. They readily admitted that we were challenging them; but no more, we had to confess, than they were challenging us.

In this atmosphere many of our Western institutions and traditions took on a new light. Some were enhanced and made us feel proud of our heritage. Others looked pitifully threadbare and shamed us. What went deepest was our increasing awareness that, after all our world travels and four visits to Asia, we had still preserved intact an unconscious attitude of superiority that we now saw to be wholly unjustified by the facts, and quite obnoxious. We had regarded it as an unassailable presupposition that the West is better than the East. Actually it was merely an unexamined prejudice.

It was a startling fact that in those three months in Chiengmai we lived closer to these Asians than we had ever done for a similar period with any Western group. We were deeply involved with them in a total experience of group living, and at the same time were personally involved with each of them in a counseling relationship. We have asked ourselves what would have happened if we had gone through a similar experience with a Western group. We seriously wonder whether any Western group could have remained intact throughout such a test. Asians seem to have a greater capacity for involvement and interdependence than we have.

Out of all these experiences there came an awareness that we must re-evaluate our whole Western philosophy of marriage and family life. Seen through Eastern eyes, much that we had taken for granted showed grave deficiencies. At the same time, many Eastern institutions took on new meaning and significance when viewed from the point of view of the Asian.

During our many hours of discussion we tried to take notes. These in the end ran to a hundred closely written pages. We had hoped to summarize them in time to include the material in the printed report of the Chiengmai Institute. But we had to give up this idea. Many of the issues were too subtle and complex to be categorized. Much of what we had learned needed to be thought out at leisure, so that its full implications could be understood. Sometimes we could not grasp the relevance of what we had been told, and wanted to check our facts with the findings of other observers. Our Chiengmai group repeatedly warned us that they were not necessarily, in relating their individual experience and observation, speaking for their cultures as a whole. We therefore put our notes away for closer examination later.

*   *   *

On the bumpy little airfield we clustered together under the wing of the ancient DC-3, seeking shelter from the scorching midday sun. Over toward the west rose the mountain, crowned with its Buddhist temple, three thousand feet up, to which we had climbed one Saturday. Eastward the trim rice paddies stretched to the edge of the town—the "new town" that was old a thousand years ago.

Many Thai friends had come to see us off. We chatted and sang gaily together. But our heartiness was forced. It covered a deep sadness—the sadness of our final farewells. Never again on this earth would our little band be assembled together in one place. We had lived in a fellowship so close that its termination was for us like the dying of a part of ourselves.

Now the plane was ready. One by one we climbed aboard and took our seats. The motors spluttered and roared. The waving figures on the airfield below became tiny specks, then melted into the landscape.

It was all over. Two years of planning and preparation. Three months of learning, training, studying. Chiengmai, which had wrought in us such depths of new experience, would henceforth be only a name on the map of Asia. The circle of light in which we had lived together was broken and scattered.

Yet each of us held in his hand a tiny candle. Our circle of light was broken. Yes—but only in order that new light might be shared with others. Our delegates had pledged themselves, before they parted, to initiate training programs in their own countries within twelve months. Each would go back and from his candle start a new circle of light.

And we, who had gone to Asia to take the light to these others, what would we do? We would go back to the West. But not with complacency. Not with empty hands. We, too, had a candle—a new candle whose light had been kindled in the East. And now we had to take that light to the West. So the light from the East and the light from the West could mingle, and together make a greater light than either could make alone.

MARRIAGE: EAST AND WEST

Chapter 1

THE REIGN OF THE PATRIARCH

Sou-mai was wrapped in the robe of apple-blossom silk which was her marriage-bed nightdress. She held the child against her breast. I saw her smile as her husband came near to her. Before he took the child she offered, or looked on its face, he put on her pillow, as thanks-gift, a gold hairpin such as each mother of a son wears in her nape knot. In his wife's pin he had set an oblong of clear green jade.

Then he took the child in its warm wrappings of rosy satin in the palms of his two hands. He knelt to his own mother. He knelt to his wife's mother. He carried his son through every court in the homestead, making the new Lin's arrival known, with ceremony, to all the Family —men, women and children—and to the God of the Hearth. Standing under the lamp of continuous life, he told the glad tidings in the Hall of the Ancestors.

Then he gave his son back into his wife's keeping for the "three days of quietness" when her own mother and her serving woman were the only persons permitted to enter the court of her dwelling.[1]

Here is the supreme drama of life in the East. The details may vary widely. Nora Waln is describing an old-fashioned, aristocratic Chinese family, where ceremony was of great importance. In a peasant home, the same occasion would have been more simply celebrated. But with or without the trimmings, we are here at the very heart of Asian family life.

Nothing that a man ever achieves—wealth, honor, fame, even sainthood—is more profoundly significant than the event in which he becomes the father of a son. This is the fulfillment of his destiny—religious, social, personal.

Nothing that a woman ever achieves is remotely comparable to the proud moment when she gives her husband a male child. This is her shining hour of glorious triumph. The Chinese character for

"good" is compounded of the two characters for "woman" and
"boy." A woman with a son is as good a thing as can possibly be
imagined.

In the birth of a first son the life of the family is renewed. The
torch is handed on for another generation. The continuity of the
line is assured. This is a moment of profound human satisfaction
and of divine blessing.

Failure to produce a son is the greatest disaster that can over-
take any married couple. Of the three unfilial acts, says Mencius,
the most serious is to leave no descendants. This is the supreme act
of ingratitude to a man's parents. In no way can he do them
greater damage. The Sanskrit word for a son, *putra*, means literally, one who saves from *put*, or hell—the hell for parents who
have no sons.

All other duties must therefore yield place to the all-important
obligation to beget an heir. In the thirteenth century Lin Fu-yi,
at eighteen years of age, was commanded by the Emperor Kublai
Khan to go north from Canton to Peiping, to use his skill in working on the canal system. A command from the Emperor was never
questioned. Yet when it was made known that he was the only
son of a father who had "plucked the flower of life" (died), he
was allowed to delay his departure till it was certain that his bride
had conceived. When the child turned out to be a girl, an order
was secured releasing him to make the long journey home in order
to beget another child. Again a daughter was born. A second order was secured, and he returned home again. This time his wife
bore a son. He never returned to Canton. His obligation to the
family was at last fulfilled.[2]

From early childhood, a boy knows that life's greatest goal is
to have a son. From early childhood, a girl knows that unless she
marries and gives her husband a son, her life will be without
significance.

So, in the Hindu marriage ritual, the bridegroom prays:

"Oh God of Fire from whom emanate all good actions, bestow
upon us abundance of sons.

"Oh God of Indra, bestow upon my wife worthy sons and all
glory. I pray to you that ten sons be born to me."[3]

*   *   *

From the Fertile Crescent, lapped by the gentle waters of t..
tideless Mediterranean, to the rocky eastern shores of Nippon,
where the great Pacific breakers crash in foaming surf—nearly six
thousand miles of land mass inhabited by well over half of the
world's population—the patriarchal family reigns supreme. For
full four thousand years of recorded history it has held undisputed
sway. The odd and fascinating family patterns of some island peoples and hill tribes—polyandry, matrilineal descent, matrilocal
marriage, and the like—have captivated the anthropologists. But
these are, by comparison with the patriarchal family system, of
little account in the great stream of human culture. They are like
ephemeral bubbles on the surface of the moving waters. They
are the oddities produced by gene mutations. The hereditary pattern that has dominated the human family, that has been passed
down through countless generations, in East and West alike, is
solidly, unvaryingly patriarchal. It is impossible to comprehend
human culture and human history without grasping clearly this
central fact. Patriarchalism has shaped, and has been shaped by,
all the great civilizations that have been the cradle, the nursery,
and the home of man.

What is patriarchalism? It is the authority, the rule, the dominion of the male as father. In marriage that is patriarchal, the husband is the head. If, as usually happens, it is also patrilineal, the
children take their father's name. If it is also patrilocal, the son
takes his bride into his father's home, which becomes her home
also.

Why this dominance of the male? Because he was stronger? Because he was believed to be more intelligent and resourceful?
Because he had seized the money and the power? All these reasons have been given, and all are valid. But these are not the basic
reasons. Again and again, discussions of male dominance seem to
have missed the essential point. The real reason is biological. Today it is known to be bad biology, inaccurate biology. But only
our modern scientific knowledge has brought this to light. Ancient
wisdom found its own interpretation logical and obvious.

When we find life good, we want it to continue. Even if it is
not so good, we do not desire it to end. We crave for the continuity of the things we value, first our life, then our cherished
possessions—land, home, the fruits of our toil, our creative achieve-

he inexorable demands of nature insist that personal
, we still wish to live on in our children—those who
eness, and are flesh of our flesh, bone of our bone,
blood.

sees in his son the continuation of himself into the
future that he must personally relinquish. Therefore he wants
sons. And to get sons, he needs a woman. The process of reproduction is like the ageless miracle of the harvest. The grain of
rice is planted in the earth. It lies buried out of sight for a time.
Down in the darkness, it draws sustenance from the soil. Then,
in the fullness of time, it emerges and becomes fruitful, multiply-
ing itself as new grains of rice.

So it is with a man. He plants his seed in the woman. This is
the ancient language of reproduction—the seed planted in the soil.
The seed is the whole gelatinous mass of the seminal fluid. Ancient man knew nothing of the sperm and the ovum. This knowledge belongs to the era of the microscope. For him the seminal
fluid was the substance that grew into the child—drawing sustenance from the womb of the pregnant woman, absorbing the
blood that issued periodically from the womb when there was no
child there. The woman's body nurtured the seed, as the soil
nurtured the grain of rice. But the seed was the man's seed and
the child was the man's child. It was his ongoing spirit, his
continuing life.

To the Eastern mind, therefore, the difference between the man
and the woman was a basic difference, a fundamental difference
of function. The woman could never be as important as the man,
any more than the soil could be as important as the seed. By her
very nature she was secondary, auxiliary. This is the very root of
all the discrimination between man and woman that has charac-
terized the history of the East, and, in earlier times, of the West
as well. This explains everything. No other explanation does so.

Patriarchalism is the enthronement of man as father. As father
he is the bearer of the torch of life. It is passed on, that precious
torch, from generation to generation—through the medium of a
womb. To have a womb you need a woman. A woman is, supremely, a womb, as a man is, supremely, the bearer of the seed
of life. That is their destiny. Their destiny decides their function.
Their function defines their relationship.

*   *   *

In the shady land of ghosts the ancestors dwell.

When Sou-mai's husband had carried his infant son triumphantly through the courts of the homestead, and proclaimed his birth to the members of the family who dwelt there in the flesh, he then made his announcement to the unseen members of the family group—the household gods, and the ancestors. To them, the news was even more welcome than to the others.

What the ancestors do in the spirit-life is not made clear in detail. But their main preoccupation is not in doubt. With loving care and anxious concern they brood over the continuing life of the family. And their major interest is in the arrival of sons to continue the line. This is their main topic of conversation when they get together with other spirits, the ancestors of other families. Those whose descendants are bringing forth a goodly crop of boys have great prestige. Any hapless spirit whose current heir is without a son is in a pitiable state—he knows no peace and he withers like a flower cut off from its roots. For if an ancestor's line dies out, he has lost his continuity on earth. His name is forgotten, his land and goods are devoured by strangers. He leaves the abode of the spirits and becomes a lost, wandering ghost.

The ancestors are thought of as being in every sense members of the family, except that they live on the other side of the veil. "Never in the House of Lin or of Wong," Nora Waln tells us, "have I heard anyone speak of any ancestor as dead. On all feast days they send him, by fire, gifts symbolic of wishes for good fortune in Heaven. On all days he is very much alive on the lips of his family, who speak of him as having a keen interest in all their affairs."[4]

In the old aristocratic families, the stories of the ancestors are not allowed to be forgotten. "Our family history is long," Su-ling explains, "but there are none among our clan who do not know its principal events. It is the custom here to have the family genealogy committed to memory by each child during the first year in the schoolroom; for the Family to repeat the genealogy aloud in unison in the Hall of Ancestors at each family anniversary; and for each Family Elder to gather the homestead women and children about him for the relation of family incidents, axioms, and life stories."[5]

In simple peasant homes where life is a relentless struggle against famine, pestilence, and disaster, there is no room for ancestral halls and little time for storytelling. But the ancestors are not forgotten. They are remembered at the family altar. In Buddhist and Shinto homes this is a small shelf or shrine, located at some central point in the house. On tablets of wood are written the names of the deceased, with the dates of their death. Family members are expected to bow to the altar, to light incense sticks at appropriate times, to make offerings of rice and tea on special occasions. On anniversaries and religious festivals, special rites are observed. At times of crisis the ancestors and the household gods are implored to intervene. In these ceremonies, the male head of the household, usually the son of the most recent ancestor, assumes the role of priest, and offers the sacrifices.

The worship of ancestors seems to lie behind all the great patriarchal civilizations. There are traces of it in the Old Testament, showing that it was a feature of early Semitic family life. Undoubted evidences are found in the Hindu family. In China and Japan it has survived down to our own time.

In Roman society ancestors were worshiped along with household gods. At a patrician wedding the approval of the unseen members of the family, who dwelt in the spirit world, had always to be sought. Bride and bridegroom took part in the sacramental eating of a special cake that had first been offered to the gods. The wedding cake in our modern marriages is said to be a direct survival of this ancient custom.[6]

*   *   *

"So Wang Lung sat, and so his age came on him day by day and year by year, and he slept fitfully in the sun as his father had done. . . . But still one thing remained to him and it was his love for his land. . . . When Spring came each year he must go out on to the land; and now although he could no longer hold a plow or do anything but see another drive the plow through the earth, still he must needs go and he went. . . . In the dawn he went out and with his trembling hands he reached and plucked a bit of budding willow and a spray of peach bloom and held them all day in his hand. . . . He came to the enclosed place upon a low hill where he had buried his dead. He stood trembling on his staff and he looked at the graves and he remembered them every one. They were more clear to him now than the sons who lived in his own house. . . . And he looked carefully and he saw the place where he would lie below his father and his uncle and above Ching and not far from O-lan. And he stared at the bit of earth where he was to lie and he saw himself in it and back in his own land forever."[7]

The patriarchal family was rooted in land tenure. The land was life. It yielded season by season the means of sustaining life. It provided the only earthly possession that moth and rust could not corrupt, that thieves could not steal. So long as the family kept its land, the future was assured. So long as its members gave their labor to cultivate the land, it yielded its fruits in due season. Land was security. Land was survival. And when life came to an end, the land, like a patient and compassionate mother, gathered tired bones and weary flesh into its embrace.

The land gave the family stability and continuity, and this pleased the ancestors. But sharing the land called for co-operation and harmony among the family members. Discord could be disastrous. The work could not be done if the workers were constantly disagreeing. The labor of all was needed if all were to prosper.

At this point the ancestors made their contribution. They held the family together in a common loyalty. Fear of their wrath, and of the powers they could invoke, prevented factions from breaking out, and enabled the family members to live peaceably together.

All families in the East did not own land. Peasants were often tenant farmers. Artisans lived by their craft. But the core of patriarchalism is the family that owns land. Uprooted from the land, the patriarchal family loses its stability.

* * *

The patriarchal family existed in many forms. Where there was enough land or wealth to sustain all, the *extended family* was the desired pattern. In theory this meant that the patriarch and his wife, all their sons and their wives, their grandsons and the wives of such as had them, and even their great-grandsons, would live together in one large community. The greatest blessing a man might enjoy was to see his house extend to five generations before he died. It was a blessing rarely vouchsafed.

An extended family could be a large group. In addition to family members it might include servants, apprentices, employees, lodgers, and visiting guests. The Lin family home in North China, where Nora Waln lived, and which she has so vividly described in *The House of Exile*, comprised a total of eighty-three persons. We have ourselves been guests in such a home. The dining area was like a public restaurant, the kitchen like that of a hotel, with its staff of cooks and kitchenmaids. At night, when the children had gone up to bed, their shoes lay in dozens at the foot of the stairs, of all sizes and shapes—some tidily placed together, others carelessly thrown down.

Traditionally, this kind of home was run as a *joint family*. This means that there was no individual ownership of property. The family resources were owned in common. All contributed what they had to give, in skill and labor and service. Each was entitled to what he needed, so far as the family resources were able to provide it. "All for each, and each for all" was the motto.

A family community of this kind required efficient organization. There had to be rules. Someone had to exercise authority.

That someone was the patriarch, or family elder. He was usually, but not necessarily, the oldest male in the family. But he must be old enough, and experienced enough, to command respect. The patriarch might be a tyrant. He had a good deal of power—though seldom, in the East, as much as the *potestas* of the Roman patrician, who could sentence his own children to death without outside interference. The patriarch might be benign and kindly, and often he was. Rulers in every sphere of life vary a good deal, in their personalities and in the methods they employ to keep order.

What was essential was that he should have undisputed authority. "As the Emperor should have a father's love for his people, so a father should have a sovereign's power over the family," says an old Chinese maxim. In various ways the prestige of the patriarch was emphasized. This was especially true in Japan.

"As a means of emphasizing through external impressions the mental attitude of filial obedience, the head of a family (generally the father) enjoys markedly privileged treatment in everyday life. The family head does not do with his own hands even trifling things—or rather is prohibited from doing such things because it is thought to compromise his authority. He must be served in everything by his wife, children or others subject to his patriarchal power. For instance, he should get his wife or servant to hand him anything which is right under his nose. The family head must be better fed and must not eat the same things as other members of his family (especially children), for it impairs his authority as such. When entering or leaving his house, he should be treated with special ceremony. In his house the head's room must be one fit for his authority. In all other trifles of everyday life the head of a family should enjoy special treatment becoming his position as absolute ruler. A parent's, especially a father's, position is majestic and supreme."[8]

Under its undoubted head the extended family became a hierarchy. The patriarchal system creates within the whole family group a complex balance of dominance and submission, authority and obedience. We see this particularly at three levels—the authority of the in-laws over the junior couple; the authority of the husband over the wife; the authority of the parent over the child. In other, less clearly defined relationships the guiding principles usually were that a junior is subservient to a senior and a woman subservient to a man.

When chickens are closely observed, it is evident that in every group living together there is an established "peck order," ranging from the self-assured boss, who can bully any other bird in the yard with impunity, right down to the scrawny and miserable individual who is pushed around by everyone else. Every time a new chicken is introduced into the group, it has to establish its place in the peck order by a series of encounters with the old-timers.

The patriarchal family likewise has its peck order. "Peck" is not an inappropriate word. The old Chinese penal code allowed a senior relative to hit a junior relative as hard as he liked, without risk of penalty as long as he did not draw blood.

The order is not, as in the case of the chickens, based on individual valor. It is defined by the person's place in the group. The rules are clearly understood by all, and each knows his place and has to accept it. There is no such thing as competitive "getting ahead"—at least so far as recognized status in the family group is concerned. Individual worth can be recognized and rewarded in other ways, but the rules that determine the hierarchy are sacrosanct. Only for very strong reasons, in very unusual circumstances, can they be set aside.

The security that the patriarchal family offers is therefore purchased at a price. That price is the severe limitation of individual aspiration. Ambitious and rebellious persons are doomed, unless they have the good fortune to inherit positions of power and prestige, to suffer acute frustration. Fortunately the age-old philosophy of the East, embodied in its religions, does not encourage ambition or rebellion, but inculcates resignation and acceptance.

As the family, so goes the community. "The state," said Plato, "is the family writ large." Society in the East was based upon the same kinds of hierarchical systems as we find in the patriarchal family group. In Japan, for instance, the whole nation was conceived of as one large family, with the Emperor as the Arch-Patriarch to whom complete filial obedience was due from all. A rigid social system kept individuals in their appointed stations, vigorously discouraging any movement up or down in the scale. The most rigid of all was the caste system in India.

Through the interplay of family and society in the maintenance of a hierarchical order, life in the East has been kept stable through long ages. Within this order each individual has had his role assigned to him according to the circumstances of his birth and the rules of succession, and not on the basis of individual merit. This concept stands in complete contrast with the principles that govern society today in the West.

*   *   *

The extended family has been, for the vast majority of people living in the East, the theoretical ideal. The principles that govern its operation have been the basis of the teaching of the lawmakers and the sages—of Manu, of Confucius, and of many others. These principles have deeply affected the life and thought of nearly all East Asians.

Yet the idea that all Eastern people live, or have lived, in such families is quite mistaken. Olga Lang, studying census returns used for taxation purposes, estimates that during typical periods of Chinese history the average family could not have consisted of more than six to eight persons.[9] So large extended families must have been only a small minority. Most of them were found in the wealthy aristocratic class—the gentry—and among well-to-do farmers.

The obstacles have been formidable. The first is poverty. Joint ownership of land, property or wealth becomes unworkable when the resources are inadequate to provide for the entire group. Even desperate expedients like infanticide, the selling of surplus daughters, and the sending of surplus sons into the army or into servile labor—even such measures have not always sufficed. When there is not enough to support everybody, the family must break up and some members seek their fortune elsewhere. "Land in Garhural was at first measured by acres, then by rods, then by poles, then by yards and feet, till they all left the village and are today distributed all over the country as domestic servants."[10] The same excessive subdivision of the land may be seen in Japan today. Similarly, it is forcing young people to leave the ancestral family and look for work in the cities.

Often severe family quarrels would break up the group. The ideal was complete harmony. The story goes that this was achieved by the famous Ch'en family, in the Chinese town of Chiang Chou, whose seven hundred members all lived together without a trace of discord. Even the family dogs were so well behaved that if one was late for dinner the other ninety-nine politely awaited his arrival before beginning to eat![11]

Needless to say, this ideal was seldom achieved. The famous Chinese classic, *Dream of the Red Chamber*, describes an aristocratic homestead and portrays a dismal sequence of intrigues and quarrels. S. C. Dube's careful study of family relationships among Indian villages tells a similar story.[12]

Brothers often quarreled among themselves, and finally set up separate establishments of their own. Or a son, rebellious and strongly desiring independence, would take the costly step of breaking with his family, forfeiting his rights and privileges, and taking his wife and children to begin life over again in a new community.

Under these pressures, the extended family has often shredded away until all that was left was the *stem family*. This means that only those in the direct succession remained in the patriarch's home—the first-born in each generation, together with the children who were as yet unmarried. The eldest son was bound to remain and take care of the family property, to assume responsibility for the care of his aged parents, and to perform the ancestral rites. If he abdicated, another son would be appointed in his place. Sometimes, however, the property was divided up among all the brothers, the eldest receiving a double portion.

When the extended joint family became unworkable, the resulting situation was handled in a variety of ways. If the brothers separated, they might continue to live in the community, on good terms with each other—better, perhaps, than if they had stayed in the same household! Each, except the eldest, would live alone with his wife and children. This small unit would constitute the *conjugal family*. As the sons grew up, this new family unit might develop into an extended family, or a stem family, according to the circumstances.

These varying family patterns have, in the long history of the East, been fluid and interchangeable. All can coexist without disruption of the patriarchal system of which they are varied expressions. The father in each case is the head of the family. What varies is merely the size and structure of the group over which he exercises his authority.

The patriarch acts as family head in the making of all major decisions. His approval is required for marriages and divorces, for adoptions, for the expulsion from the family of recalcitrant members. He is responsible for the family property and for the payment of family debts. He must see that the family fulfills its obligations to the state, to the community, and to all who have legitimate claims upon it.

Sometimes a *family council* helps the patriarch to deal with a complicated problem. It may merely make suggestions which the family head accepts or rejects, or it may have power to act on the basis of a majority decision. In Japan the powers of the family council are legally recognized—as was the case in Louisiana until 1934—and in the event of serious disagreement an appeal may be made to a court of law.

*   *   *

While disagreements and quarrels were not lacking in the Eastern family, the members always closed ranks to meet a threat from the outside. Their common kinship put them under obligation to stand by one another in times of trouble. A wrong done to one was a wrong done to all. A kinsman in trouble must always be given succor—this was a sacred obligation.

"Wang Lung's uncle returned suddenly without explanation of where he had been and what he had done. He stood at the door as though he had dropped from a cloud, his ragged clothes unbuttoned and girdled loosely as ever about him, and his face as it always was but wrinkled and hardened with the sun and the wind. . . . He sat himself down, then, and he drew a bowl and chopsticks to him and he helped himself freely. . . . Wang Lung knew very well that now his uncle would never be driven forth again, now that he knew Wang Lung had wherewith to feed him. And Wang Lung thought of this and thought of his uncle's wife with great fear because he saw that they would come to his house and none would stop them.—And he was exceedingly angry and the more angry because he must bury it all in his heart and answer with smiles and welcome his relatives."[13]

Regardless of a man's feelings, the duty of hospitality must be performed. Therefore, in the East, none but those who have violated the law and put themselves outside the pale need ever be destitute. In a society where the joint family functions there is no need of orphanages or asylums, of social or welfare services. The needy go to their kin and are received. After the great fire of 1842 in Hong Kong, it is said that not one of the victims needed to seek charity. All were taken in and tended by their relatives.[14]

We knew a man in Bombay whose dream it was to become a lawyer. He began to attend law school, taking an evening job to support his family. Then a kinsman died, leaving a widow and six children. No other relative was able to help. Without hesitation, this man abandoned his personal plans. Now he carries a daytime job as well as an evening one and supports both families. It never occurred to him that his own ambitions mattered in the least in comparison with his family obligations. "For the family, sacrifice the individual" expresses good Hindu philosophy.

The obligations to help a kinsman may run to unreasonable lengths. In one of the Liao-chai stories, Mr. Chu finds himself con-

demned after death to be a wandering ghost. He is not unduly
disconcerted. He reflects that his maternal cousin works as a secretary in the office of the king of the underworld. With such influence at court, he is sure he can get his relative to arrange for
him to be reborn into a nice family, and so get back to earth!

The members of the patriarchal family stand together because
they are knit one to another by strong bonds of kinship. They are
of the same seed, grafted to the same stem, the same blood flowing in their veins. Above and beyond all other differences, their
final obligation is to the unity of the family.

*   *   *

The position of privilege goes always to the first-born son. He
is given the best food, the best room, the most expensive presents.
He is destined for an important role, so it is proper to foster in
him a sense of self-importance.

After him, in order, come the other sons. Then come the daughters, in order of birth—but all of lesser importance than the youngest boy. The proper priorities must be carefully observed. E. H.
Cressy describes the taking of baths in a Japanese family. Father
has first turn; then the eldest son, followed by other sons in order;
then the mother, followed by the daughters in order; and finally
the servants.[15]

Girls do not bear the seed and are therefore not true members of
the family. They are not part of its stem. They grow out of it, but
only to be detached later and grafted on to another family stem,
which it is then their duty to support and build up. They are birds
of passage, nurtured in the family until they are ready to fly away.
If food is short, they get only the pickings. If space is congested,
they double up to make more room for the permanent family
members.

As the children reach the age of marriage a process of inter-
change goes on among the family's female members. One by one
the brides of the sons come to live in the parental home. One by
one the daughters leave to go to the homes of their bridegrooms.
So the Eastern mother keeps her sons and loses her daughters.
The places vacated by the daughters are taken by her daughters-
in-law. They come as strangers into the family just as she herself
once did years ago.

My mother is spinning her spinning wheel,
    For whom do you spin, my mother?
For whom do you put the spools in your basket?
    We, the daughters will be going away for ever
To homes of our husbands.
    For whom do you spin now?

For whom do I spin, my daughter?
    For whom do I put the spools in the basket?
You, my daughters, shall leave me for ever,
    You shall go to the other lands.
I spin these spools for the brides of my sons,
    For them I put the spools in the basket
Brides of my sons who will come to this my home,
    Their home.[16]

Normally all girls marry in the East. So, in the course of a generation, all of the women born into a family leave it, and all of the women who become established members of the family are those who entered it first as strangers. This is the patriarchal system. The family continues, generation by generation, as an endless line of males, passing on the seed from father to son, from father to son. The women's function is a secondary one—to receive the seed, to nurture it, and thus to build up the family of their husbands and their sons.

The family assumed the duty of finding wives for its sons, and husbands for its daughters. Marriage was a family concern, because it was the means by which the family's future was assured. Individual wishes were not ignored, but they could not be allowed to clash with the interests of the family. Care was exercised in matching brides and bridegrooms, because much was at stake. The couple themselves, however, had little choice in the arrangement of their marriage. In China their signatures were not even required on the certificate, which was an agreement concluded between the family elders!

There is no evidence to prove that this system has led to more conflict in marriage than any other method of bringing husband and wife together. The East has certainly had its share of truly happy marriages.

*   *   *

One factor in fitness for marriage was emphasized above all others—the chastity of the bride. By contrast, there was little inquiry into the sexual past of the bridegroom. This "double standard" has been bitterly attacked in the modern West as an evidence of unjust discrimination against the woman.

The explanation is simple when we remember the all-important function of the woman—to give her husband sons. A man wanted sons above all else, but he wanted his *own* sons, not those of some other man! The womb in which he planted his seed must not be contaminated by any alien seed. This might lead to falsification of the family line, which would bring down upon all concerned the curse of the ancestors.

A man, therefore, was entitled to exclusive rights over the sexuality of the woman he married. He must be able to rely upon her completely in this respect. A girl who would consent to have sex relations before marriage rendered herself unfit to be any man's wife. She proved herself incapable of the self-control needed to guard her integrity. What she could do before marriage, it was reasoned, she could also do after marriage. Her husband would never be able to trust her out of his sight. He could never be certain that the children she bore were his, and truly of the family seed. Such a wife would be worthless for the fundamental purpose a wife existed to serve.

So the bride must be chaste as a guarantee that as a wife she would be faithful. A wife who committed adultery betrayed her husband in the gravest possible way. Not only did she betray him, she betrayed the family also. She forfeited all her rights and privileges, and rendered herself useless.

The man's situation was entirely different. He was the bearer of the seed, and he could plant it where he willed. He needed a wife to bear him sons in the family line. But if he begot other children besides, he was entitled to do so. If he knew them to be his, he was of course required to assume responsibility for them. The patriarchal principle holds that all a man's children are legitimate, regardless of the owner of the womb in which they are nurtured. His seed is his, wherever it is planted. Thus a man's children by a slave girl are entitled to his care and protection as much as his children by his wife—though they would not be accorded the same rank and status.

If the woman concerned is a harlot, however, he is not normally responsible for any children she may bear. The fact that she is sexually available to many men means that the paternity of her children cannot be established, and the responsibility therefore cannot be laid upon any one of them.

A man in the East does not, therefore, wrong his wife by having sex relations with another woman. The functional difference between them makes what would be heinous for her harmless for him. He can give her the life-giving seed just as effectively, if he also distributes some of it elsewhere. There are times—when she is pregnant, for instance—when she has no use for it. What he does with another woman need not interfere with discharging his duty to raise sons by his wife, and cannot falsify the family line. It therefore does not violate his integrity as a husband. Technically he cannot be unfaithful to her in the sense that she can be unfaithful to him. The difference is not one of discrimination between the sexes. It is biological.

In practice, however, the man does not have unlimited sexual freedom. In a society where every woman is expected to marry, sexual license would have disastrous consequences. A man may not be sinning against his wife in having relations with another woman. But he is very definitely sinning against the woman and her husband or potential husband. If she is married, he is doing to another man the worst thing that any other man could do to him. He is conspiring with another man's wife to cheat him, to rob him of his exclusive sexual rights over his wife, and to endanger the integrity of his family line. This makes the adulterer as guilty as the adulteress, but for a different reason. The woman has violated her own marriage. The man has violated another man's marriage.

If a married man has sex relations with a woman who is not married or betrothed, he does not wrong her husband, because she has none. Yet he wrongs her, in that he renders her unfit for marriage. He wrongs her father and her family by bringing disgrace upon them; and he wrongs the prospective husband who might otherwise have had her as his wife, by removing her from the marriage market.

Though in the East the basis of sex morality is different from that in the modern West, it is logically derived from the principles that govern the patriarchal family. Its demands upon the woman are absolute—not because of discrimination, but in accordance with the biological concept of functional difference. While its demands upon the man are theoretically very light, in practice his behavior is more strictly controlled than is that of the Western man.

*   *   *

Historically the patriarchal family has been a magnificent institution. It has given the East stability and order for four thousand years. It has given purpose and direction to the life of the individual. It has defined and shaped the life of society. Sometimes its demands are harsh. Always the self-interest of the individual must be sacrificed to the welfare of the group. It is intolerant of variety and stubbornly resists change. When its rigid rules are broken it can be ruthless and implacable.

Yet it has given great benefits to its members. Life in the extended joint family could be rich and good. Consider what it has to offer.

In such a family group you are unlikely to feel lonely or rejected. You are secure among your own kith and kin. You have no worries about personal finances or personal property, because you possess neither. There is no fragmentation of life; old and young, men and women, live together in a fully rounded community. As the years pass there is little change to disturb or uproot you. Life is placid, and events follow their logical and predictable course. You are accepted for what you are. Provided you contribute your quota of labor, obey the rules, and are reasonably co-operative, no harsh judgments will fall upon you, no unreasonable demands will be made. You are not encouraged to compete, to strive to get ahead. Your role is to accept your appointed place and to live the life for which you are destined. This is your fate, and it is of no use to challenge it. So the years peacefully pass. When old age and infirmity approach, there is nothing to dread. With increasing years come increasing honor. In the bosom of the family you will be provided for and protected. When death finally comes, you will take your place with the ancestors in the abode of spirits.

In our modern Western culture, some would say that life offers them decidedly more than this. On the other hand, some would have to admit that it offers them decidedly less.

Chapter 2

CHANGE OF MODEL IN THE WEST

The largest available hall in the Y.M.C.A. building in Colombo, the capital of Ceylon, was crowded to capacity. The title of the lecture was "Marriage in the Modern World." This was one of a number of meetings at which we were scheduled to speak during a visit to the "Pearl of the East."

The audience listened attentively. They were keenly interested. At the conclusion a dark-skinned gentleman in flowing white robes climbed onto the platform. From the ample folds of his garment he brought out some crumpled pieces of paper. Smoothing them, he read out many facts and figures from the United States—divorce rates; figures about juvenile delinquency and sexual crimes; data from the Kinsey Report about premarital and extramarital sex relations. Each new fact was given due emphasis.

When he had finished, he folded up the papers.

"Ladies and gentlemen," he said, "that is how they are living in the part of the world from which our lecturer comes. Do you think that people who behave like that have anything to teach us about how to conduct our family relationships?"

It was an embarrassing incident. But it was also a revealing one. The gentleman in the flowing white robes was speaking his mind. He was speaking not only for himself, but for many other Asians too. The fact that he violated the traditional code of courtesy to visitors revealed the depth of his feelings. Asians do not often speak in such plain words.

But this is how they feel. The Asian who is a guest in the West will not say so. Even in the East, he will not say so when speaking to a Westerner. But among themselves, Asians express their real feelings. And one of their strongest feelings is the horror with which they regard the "mess" we have made of our family life in the West.

In Calcutta we conducted a two-day seminar for professional leaders in the community. We told them about our programs of marriage counseling and family life education. They listened attentively, asked many questions. On the second day a small group of them took us aside.

"We are very interested in what you have been saying," they told us. "These programs you have described are very good. We need these services for our people. But we are afraid to take over the Western ways."

"Why?" we asked innocently.

"Because," they replied, "if we copy the West, we are afraid we may be contaminated by their immorality."

They spoke almost naïvely. They did not mean to offend. They were genuinely puzzled. But to us, the words they used were full of significance. Contamination by our immorality. That was what they feared. And this was India, of whose sexual customs Katherine Mayo had written in searing words. The East shrinking away from the contaminating touch of the West!

The picture of the West that has been built up in the Eastern mind is very complex. It is compounded of many elements. These we tried, as we gained the confidence of our Asian friends, to disentangle. First, Hollywood movies. Then, the morals of Western men in uniform, and of some not in uniform. Then, our sex-ridden magazines. Then, the Kinsey Report.

Especially the Kinsey Report. It would not surprise us to learn that Alfred Kinsey's name is more widely known, beyond the frontiers of the United States, than that of any contemporary American. The name of Kinsey seems to have penetrated where Western influence is otherwise negligible. And with it, a garbled, twisted picture of Western men and women living in the depths of moral depravity.

Here are two Indian assessments. One describes a man who expressed the belief that "the West was incredibly immoral and that there was no such thing as a chaste white woman. He based his observation largely on the fact, shocking to him, of seeing white women in indiscriminate society with men, in witnessing their disgraceful modern dances in the dance-halls of the hill stations, and in watching American films with their sensational sex content, the very worst of which are sure to be shown, even in small towns. Then the retaliating answers to an American book accusing India had served to acquaint him with the darkest side of American life. He quoted Judge Lindsey as incontrovertible proof of typical American licentiousness and sex degeneracy."[1]

The other is a comment from an Indian woman, the Rani of Sangwar: "You, masahib, and your beautiful daughter did not indulge in the vices of Western women. You did not run about half naked, showing your legs and your back to any man who happened to be around, as in this country even the lowest dregs of the whores would be ashamed to do. You did not practice Western dancing, as the vice of rubbing your bodies against a strange man's is being misnamed."[2]

We shall not begin to understand the East today until we recognize the contempt and disgust with which many Asians view what they consider to be our standards of man/woman relationships. They have a mental picture of the United States as a land of lecherous men, shameless women, sex-mad youth, and children beyond all control. Unfortunately, among those who hold this view are some who have visited the West.

* * *

Kansas City is a community with many institutions of which its inhabitants have good reason to be proud. It might well be regarded as a typical city, exemplifying the American way of life.

Invited to participate in a program in this community a few years ago, we asked for the marriage and divorce statistics for the preceding five years. We discovered that, during those years, for every two couples who went to church, synagogue or justice of the peace to be married, one couple already married went to court to be divorced.

These figures surprised us. They surprised even more the worthy inhabitants of Kansas City to whom they were quoted. Indeed, they could scarcely believe that the statistics were true. As one lady remarked, "Well, I suppose when people get married it's all done in public and everybody knows about it. But when

people get divorced it's all done privately and only those closest
to the couple get to know."

The Kansas City figures just quoted are about twice those of
the United States as a whole. This is no reflection on Kansas City.
Urban areas generally have the highest divorce rates. The rate for
the United States as a whole is one divorce for every four new
marriages.

This sounds more reassuring. But it compares badly with rates
elsewhere. Professor James Bossard has discovered that half of all
the reported divorces in the entire world are granted in the
United States.[3] One out of two in the entire world!

Of course, many divorces are never reported. When an African
tribesman sends his wife back to her parental home, this doesn't
become a statistic.

But all broken marriages are not recorded in the United States
either. Husbands and wives desert each other, drift apart. In 1951
the Federal Census Bureau made a count of the husbands and
wives who were living apart because of marital discord. The official figure was one and three quarter million![4]

And what about the remainder? Those who *do* stay together—
are they happy?

This is very difficult to estimate. Several studies have been attempted to find out. Clearly people are not going to admit they are
unhappy unless they really are. Any figure arrived at in such an
inquiry is likely to be an underestimate.

Yet the average proportion of acknowledged unhappy marriages among couples living together, as shown by four different
studies, is about 20 per cent. And an additional 15 per cent, three
of the studies reveal, are only moderately happy. Total—35 per
cent, or over one third of the functioning marriages, not entirely
happy.

These are rough indications only. But they add up to a picture
that could justify Eastern cynicism. First, one quarter of all marriages are written off as total failure. Then a million and a quarter
additional husbands and wives are in such bad trouble that they
are living apart. Finally, only two thirds of the remainder are
really happy.

It doesn't require aptitude in higher mathematics to arrive at
the conclusion to which these figures lead us. The conclusion is

that *the average married couple in the United States today have less than a fifty-fifty chance of being happy in their life together.*

* * *

At Chiengmai there were long and earnest discussions about the state of family life in the West. We made no attempt to conceal or defend our predicament. We gave our Asians the full facts and figures. The library included the two volumes of the Kinsey Report that had so far appeared, and they were closely studied—especially by the delegates from the Philippines, where these volumes are banned.

The note that was sounded in our earlier discussions was that of criticism. The fact that we welcomed frank opinions, and discouraged polite evasiveness, was readily accepted. Our delegates spoke of the evil effects upon their people of many of our Western influences, of their pride by comparison in their own strong and stable family life.

Then came the questions. *Why* were things so bad in the West? Had it always been so, or was this something new? This led to the realization, new to many of our delegates, that in the West also the patriarchal family was once supreme.

This is true. The three great ancient civilizations that are the roots of Western culture—the Hebrew, the Greek, the Roman—were all completely patriarchal in their family life. Never in any comparable human culture was the position of the father stronger than in ancient Rome. The *patria potestas* literally gave him the power of life and death over his children.

Roman law, which became the basis of legal systems in most European countries, was based on the same hierarchical family system as that of the East. When Japan decided in 1898 to create a new legal system, it took over the Napoleonic Code, which was based on the laws of ancient Rome, and found that it almost perfectly fitted the conditions of Japanese patriarchalism.

Throughout the Middle Ages, the family system of the peasants and gentry in Europe was little different from that of the great Asian civilizations. Until as late as 1870, in a country as enlightened as England, a wife could not legally own property in her own right. All she possessed, until the passing of the Married Woman's Property Act, was legally reckoned as belonging to her husband.

Once they saw this clearly, our Asians narrowed down the scope of their inquiry. Why was it, they now asked, that in comparatively recent times the West had broken away from the tradition it shared with the East and set up new and dangerously unstable patterns of family life?

Gradually, as they examined the question, a picture emerged that, while it was familiar enough to us, took on new meaning as we saw it through Eastern eyes.

We saw the world divided roughly into two major camps, based on two major ideological concepts of human society. The first concept held that the way to make society work successfully is to create hierarchies—to put the majority of the people under the domination of a few leaders who would run their lives for them, tell them what to do, and see that they did what they were told. To try to run either the family or the community on any other basis than this authority-obedience, dominance-submission pattern would, it was believed, result in chaos and disorder. In one form or another, this is the concept of society that has been basic throughout human history, in East and West alike.

The second concept, however, challenges this. It declares that the best way to make human society work successfully is to give to each individual the maximum amount of personal freedom, autonomy and self-determination that he is able to handle responsibly, and to increase his freedom progressively as he learns to accept more and more responsibility for himself. It is this daring doctrine upon which the Western world of today has staked everything. One of the phrases used at Chiengmai was "the great gamble the West is making"—the gamble of operating a culture, and the family life upon which that culture is based, on the principle of the freedom of the individual.

When the Asians spoke of it as a gamble they meant that there was no certainty that it would succeed. Already it has led to chaotic disruption of family life. Can a society go on taking that kind of punishment without disintegrating? Time alone, they concluded, would provide the answer.

But once they had seen clearly the ideas, and the ideals, that were behind our great Western "gamble," their criticism gave way to admiration. For they perceived that at the root of the whole concept lay a belief in the sacred worth of the individual.

This resulted in a changed attitude in our Asian group toward some of the defects in Western culture that had troubled them. They now saw the chaos and confusion in our family life not as ruin and disaster, but as the price we were having to pay for our tremendous venture in seeking to create a society of men and women free to find themselves and to be themselves.

Finally, they wanted to know by what processes all this had come about, and whether these same processes might not already be at work in the East also. Since it was now clear that East and West had started with almost identical family patterns, was it possible that the difference between East and West was simply that the West had traveled further along a road that the East in its turn would soon be treading too?

*　　*　　*

In human history there have been innumerable minor social changes. But there have been only two major mutations.

The first came when simple nomadic peoples, hunters and food collectors, discovered that they could live better by settling down and cultivating the land. When this happened it brought about basic changes in the life patterns of the people concerned.

The second change came when agrarian peoples, their lives deeply rooted in the land, began through scientific knowledge to gain new and vast power to manipulate the natural resources around them. By the use of this new power, they were able to tear up their roots and create for themselves fantastic new living patterns that have led us into the industrial, the scientific, and now the atomic age.

Of these two major changes, the second is by far the most significant. The first affected only small numbers of people at a time and progressed slowly. It began somewhere in the dawn of human history, and it has not yet been compassed by some peoples living at the present time—the Bushmen of the Kalahari Desert in South-West Africa, the aborigines of the Australian interior, and others.

We are passing now through the second change. It began in England about two hundred years ago. It has already involved about half of the human race, and seems likely with rapidly accelerated speed to involve the other half. It is changing our way of life so radically that it is as if we were all being caught up in a vast net, lifted off the planet on which we have lived hitherto, and put down on a new planet where we have to adapt ourselves to profoundly different conditions. The result is that, right in the vortex of the process of change as we now are, it is hard to retain any sense of security or stability. Everything around us is in a state of movement.

This is having a profoundly disturbing effect upon all our established human institutions. Someone has remarked that whereas, before the Industrial Revolution, the quality of an institution that guaranteed its permanence was stability, now the desirable quality is flexibility, adaptability. Consequently institutions that were strong under the old order are found to be weak, unable to survive, under the new. One institution for which this is particularly true is the patriarchal family. Its magnificent, rock-like strength and inflexibility become, under the new conditions, the very cause of its doom. Resistant to change, it proves, in an era when all is changing, incapable of survival. Unyielding, it cannot bend and so ride out the storm. With dogged but fatal resolution it plants itself in the path of the storm and is pounded to pieces.

This, in greater or lesser degree, is happening all over the world today. If you were to draw a map of the world to show, by depth of shading, those areas where urbanization and industrialization have been furthest advanced, you would also be drawing a map to show the extent to which, in the areas concerned, the patriarchal family is in decay.

The evidence is overwhelming that the patriarchal family cannot ultimately survive in the new kind of industrial society that is coming into being in the modern world.

*   *   *

The old-fashioned rural family in the West was remarkably self-contained. With or without the aid of neighbors, the members built their own house and made their own furniture. They found their own water supply and disposed of their own sewage. The labor of man and beast provided all the power they employed. They grew most of their own food, and the women members made most of the necessary clothes and furnishings. They organized their own recreation, undertook most of the education of the children. Men, women and children worked together in a co-operative enterprise to cultivate the land and to provide what was needed for the well-being of the group. Tasks too large or too complex for the family alone were carried out with the help of other families nearby.

The family was an economically sound producing unit. A man without wife and children was at a great disadvantage, and usually he had to join up with a family group. Wife and children all played their part in the organized labor that made the life of the home run smoothly.

The coming of industry changed all this. Families left their land to live close to the factories and mills. At first, men, women and children all contributed their labor, as had been their custom. But abuses led to legislation preventing child labor. Women, unable to combine factory work with child-bearing and home duties, gave homemaking priority. The man became the sole breadwinner of the family. His wife and children, formally his co-workers, now became his dependents. All their needs had to be met out of his wages.

Increasingly, what the family had provided for itself had to be bought outside the home. Building and furniture-making became specialized trades. Food and clothes were bought in market and store. Water, then gas, finally electricity were piped in by utility companies which billed the family. Standards of living improved, and yesterday's luxuries became today's necessities. Machines were invented to perform routine household tasks, greatly increasing comfort and convenience, but costing money to provide and maintain. The family, previously an economically sound producing unit, became an economically unsound consuming unit. A man's wife and children became a burden to be borne. The more children he had, the heavier the burden. The man without wife and children, who could spend all his wages on himself, now had the advantage.

The family's unity was becoming seriously undermined. The men went out of the home to work. With the rapid growth of towns and cities, they had to travel farther and farther from home. With the coming of compulsory education, the children were out of the home for most of the day. The woman was cut off from her husband's life and labor. Increasingly freed from household chores, she had leisure time to enjoy.

The co-operation of neighboring families also declined. They had little need of each other's help. In the impersonal life of the city people split up into special interest groups, and often scarcely knew their next-door neighbors. Increasing mobility of families (one in five moves every year in the United States today) made for more and more superficial involvements with each other. Modern cities became places where a person might, in the midst of crowds, feel completely alone.

Not knowing one another, people ceased to care what others thought of them. Freed from the social pressures that had imposed the morality of the group on the individual, men and women often became careless of their family obligations. Unhappy husbands and wives sought escape in extramarital adventures. The public censure of divorce was weakened. Young people could no longer be closely supervised, and the chaperone became an anachronism. The old conventions concerning the relations between men and women were considered old-fashioned, the taboo on discussion of sex was swept away.

The popularization of scientific contraception coincided with the decline of the old morality. Women, released from unremitting household toil and the burden of rapidly successive childbirth, demanded social and economic emancipation, and equal rights with men—including rights to sexual freedom.

During all this time the economic burden of maintaining a family became heavier and heavier for the husband and father. Finally it reached the point at which he could no longer shoulder it. The standard of living the family aspired to could be reached only if the mother also contributed her labor outside the home. This ended her isolation from the life of the workaday world. It also carried the process of change full cycle. The home, once the place where the family members lived a close, self-contained life together, anchored to the land that provided for their needs, now became the place to which they returned periodically, from pursuing their separate individual enterprises, for food, rest, and sleep.

Early in this transitional process the power and authority of the father began to wane. His inability to provide alone for the family's needs, his long periods of absence from the home, the growing independence and freedom of wife and children, with their many outside associations—these made him a person of greatly diminished importance. The father in the West today, as one American sociologist put it, is no longer an august and commanding figure—he is "a sap and a dope."

In broad outline, this is the process, extending over roughly two hundred years, that has brought the patriarchal family to irretrievable ruin and collapse in the West.

*   *   *

The widespread disintegration of our family life has not been accepted with complacency. A few Jeremiahs have interpreted it as the impending collapse of an institution that was rotten anyway. George Bernard Shaw described our traditional family as "an Augean stable, so filthy that it would seem more hopeful to burn it down than to attempt to sweep it out."[5] But most people were filled with consternation at the thought of family life coming to an end, and considered that this would mean the end of our culture too.

These observers interpreted the collapse of the patriarchal pattern as the demise of the family institution. This is not surprising, because we have never in our cultural heritage known any other kind of family pattern. So the gloom spread. One writer even worked out an approximate date when the family would probably have ceased to exist. Someone else wrote a book entitled *Can the Family Survive?*

It was the American family sociologists who began to challenge this pessimism. Chief among them was Ernest Burgess of Chicago. He and others began to stress the fact that what was happening in the West was not that the family was collapsing, but that it was undergoing a change of pattern. The institution of the family was too precious and fundamental to be dispensed with. But in the new cultural order, a new family system was required. What was happening was that the new system was taking shape.

The phoenix was a legendary bird which had this in common with old soldiers: it never died. Or rather, its death was also a process of rebirth. The old bird perished in a funeral pyre—from the ashes of which a new phoenix arose to take the place of the old. Its death was a process of renewal and rejuvenation.

So it was, said Burgess and others, with our Western families. The patriarchal pattern, pounded and beaten by the titanic forces of our vast cultural change, was indeed dying. But its death agonies did not spell doom and disaster. They were at the same time the birth pains of a new family system, more appropriate to the new life of the new age.

The family and society are, and must be, inextricably interdependent. The family shapes the personalities of those who will shape the society. The values and standards of the society are introjected through its citizens into the living patterns of the family.

What the Industrial Revolution did was to set the individual free. The hierarchical system in which he had lived, with its inflexible authority/submission patterns, collapsed like the walls of a prison shaken by an earthquake. From the ruins the prisoners walked out and were free to go where they wished and to do what they chose.

The grim, impersonal world of industry did not, it is true, seem at all like freedom in its early days. As we look back on England in the early nineteenth century, the life of the workers looks more like slavery than liberty. Yet it does stand for personal freedom— even if it is only the freedom to choose the location and form of one's enslavement. When industry develops, and the smoking factories go up, the people leave the land and flock to the towns. The mills may be dark and satanic, as Blake described them. Yet a man sees them as the way to a better life, a channel leading to ultimate freedom, if he can but contrive to navigate it.

Increase of individual freedom in a society spells disaster for the authoritarian family. A power system can only be sustained in the family if it is supported by the community. Once an individual defying family authority can gain support from outside, or can leave home without becoming a fugitive, the absolute power of patriarchalism is broken. And, once broken, that power is in decay. Partial power is very difficult to exercise. It generally leads to instability and, in time, to the end of the power system.

Not only does a free society corrode and undermine an authoritarian family system. It is also hindered in its growth by such a system. Life in a hierarchical family ideally trains and equips people for life in a hierarchical society. But in a society that grants to individuals the liberty and the opportunity to define and seek their own personal goals, authoritarian families produce social misfits. The personality trained to obey orders without question lacks the initiative and flexibility to exploit opportunity and to enjoy freedom of choice. The patriarchal family system cannot serve a free and fluid social system. It becomes a hindrance, a drag on progress, an anachronism. In the end, it has to go.

*   *   *

The new pattern emerging in the West has been called the _democratic family_. What this means is that it tries to reflect, and to inculcate, the values enshrined in the new concept of human society to which the West, in its "great gamble," has committed itself.

Democracy may be a misleading word, with many meanings. What it means as a description of a family system can be roughly spelled out in four words—freedom, independence, equality, and fulfillment.

1. The heart of the idea is _freedom._ We have seen that the freedom of the individual is the basic distinguishing feature of Western culture today. To inject this idea into a hierarchical family system is to plant a time bomb under the floor.

When the bomb goes off, the immediate result is wild disorder. When a wife refuses any longer to obey her husband, or to submit to his authority, the marriage becomes a battlefield. When children rebel against parental domination and demand the right to immature self-expression, discipline collapses in the home and the community is filled with young delinquents. When young people will no longer have their marriage partners chosen for them, but insist on making their own selection, all the confusion born of ignorance, inexperience and emotional unbalance combines to vitiate the choice.

The new pattern cannot, however, be judged on these, its immediate, consequences. Freedom is a heady wine, and large draughts play havoc with the system unaccustomed to it. The hope is that, when family and society alike learn how to match freedom with a mature sense of responsibility, these first explosive results will diminish, and a new and higher order of human relationships will emerge.

2. The desire for *independence* is the natural corollary of attained freedom. In the Western family of today, it shows itself in the rebellion against family ties and obligations, in particular the rebellion against in-law domination.

Under patriarchalism, family continuity was paramount. The young married couple had to conform to the family traditions and give unquestioning obedience to their elders. This often led to conflict. Such conflict could be resolved only in one way—the youngsters had to sacrifice their wishes to the senior generation.

In the modern West they refuse to do this any longer. The young couples of today refuse to live with their in-laws. They refuse to allow their in-laws to dictate to them, to tell them how to run their homes or how to raise their children. Maintaining the family traditions has become far less important than keeping up with the peer group. The mobility of population has scattered families widely, and in many instances the links between relatives have grown tenuous and have perished.

Much has been lost in this process. The conjugal family of the West today has no roots, and withers easily in adversity. It has no anchorage in the past, and no tried principles to guide its affairs. The old solidarity has gone, leaving the aging couple lonely and purposeless in an unheeding world where the bonds of kinship hardly matter any more.

3. The principle of *equality* derives inevitably from the philosophy of Western democracy. The assertion that all men are created equal under God is written into the American Constitution.

The interpretation that this makes men and women equal in human society has been somewhat grudgingly conceded. But with insistent pressure from the female section of the community, it is being increasingly accepted today. Only the last stronghold of religion doggedly refuses to accord to women the right of entry to positions of high leadership.

The invasion of the family by this new concept strikes at the very root of patriarchalism, which is based on the belief that the woman is subsidiary and auxiliary. The biological foundation of this idea, now that science has introduced us not only to the sperm and the ovum, but also to the chromosomes and genes, has blown sky-high. In addition, the freedom and flexibility of modern society in the West has killed the myth that woman is inherently weaker, and more stupid and more sinful than man. Once this happened, the demand for the "fifty-fifty marriage" was inevitable.

This demand has ended the authority/obedience concept of the husband/wife relationship. The result has not proved to be altogether an unmixed blessing. Problems have been created for the wife that she has not yet solved. The old system, at least in its benign manifestations, aided and supported her in her reproductive task, and seemed to meet many of her psychological needs. The modern wife in the West has made tremendous gains in the direction of freedom, and is flushed with victory. But her lot is not easy, and she is deeply confused about her new roles.

4. The reason why freedom is so much desired is that it appears to offer greater possibilities of *fulfillment*. The "pursuit of happiness" is a goal deeply cherished in American society, where it is cultivated with unrivaled intensity.

But if freedom is a heady wine, happiness is an elusive goal. The state of intoxication engendered by the one does not encourage the keen perception required to attain the other. Consequently, the idea that freedom necessarily leads to happiness is one of life's grand illusions.

Once we recognize this, we shall not be surprised to find that the modern quest for fulfillment has contributed a good deal to the wreckage of family life in the West. A narrow preoccupation with one's own desires and wishes is generally destructive of family values, which call for a good deal of self-denial. Consequently the "mess" that Eastern observers see as the distinguishing feature of our Western family life can properly be attributed to an unrestrained orgy of self-seeking which the new freedom of our democratic society has made possible.

This is particularly true of our divorce rates. In an oriented and highly mechanized society where luxury goods are available in abundance, the restless urge to discard material possessions in the hope of replacing them with better models inevitably affects the way in which husbands and wives view one another. This is certainly not the only factor that explains the very high

he United States. But it is one factor, and possibly
it one.

ther way of looking at this. It may seem strange
divorce rate to idealism. Yet that is true. It is
the West have come to expect so much of mar-
, are so hard to please, and are so ready to discard
their spouses and replace them with others. If divorce spelled
disillusionment, the divorced would not seek remarriage. The
fact that the vast majority of Americans do remarry after divorce
indicates that they believe in marriage, but find it hard to attain
through it the fulfillment they are seeking.

Undoubtedly many of them are seeking the unattainable, and
expectations need to be scaled down to the level of reality. Others
are baffled in their quest and need guidance and help, because
the free, fluid, equalitarian type of marriage is much harder to
operate than the stereotyped pattern with its fixed, predeter-
mined roles. If this guidance and help can be adequately given,
the hope is that the high divorce rates will prove to be only a
manifestation of a transitional phase, and will ultimately decline.
There is already evidence enough to encourage cautious hope
that this is beginning to happen.

Certainly the principle of fulfillment in marriage and family life
is not one we wish to discredit. There is in the West today a
determined belief that marriage, parenthood, and family living
can and should be satisfying and rewarding experiences. We
would subscribe to this belief. The task before us is to make this a
reality for increasing numbers of men and women.

*   *   *

The best manifestations of the new democratic family pattern
are impressive. The relationship of husband and wife, based on
mutual love, develops in depth into a rich and fruitful comradeship. The satisfactions they find in the shared task of parenthood
are genuine and lasting. The children growing up in these homes
prove to be able, to a remarkable degree, to develop self-reliance
and social poise at a relatively early age. They grow up to be
mature and wise young people, well equipped to face life in a
society that offers them a terrifying degree of liberty. The family
groups to which these parents and children belong show signs of

being dynamic, healthy, flexible, and well-developed units of human society. They are producing individuals well equipped to handle freedom responsibly and constructively.

No assessment of the present confusion in the family life of the West can afford to ignore the best products of the new democratic pattern. In the high quality of the life lived among these families lies the hope that the "great gamble" could succeed.

Chapter 3

WHAT IS A WOMAN WORTH?

The Empress Jingo is a legendary figure in Japanese history. After the sudden death of her husband, the story goes, she took over the government herself. Following what she believed to be a divine command, she united the warring factions within the nation, invaded Korea at the head of an army, and personally led her troops to victory. At the time of her death she was the ruler of the largest empire Japan ever acquired until World War II.

This half-mythical tale of the third century A.D. portrays a picture of Japanese womanhood that is a far cry indeed from the fragile creature of later ages. Yet it is interesting that all the great cultures seem to have similar stories of bygone days when women were strong and masterful, free and self-assured. The Greeks immortalized the fighting Amazons; the ancient Britons had their warrior Queen Boadicea. The Semitic peoples have their traditions of an ancient era of matriarchy. There are similar traditions in the Indian, Chinese, and Korean cultures.

Why this persistent belief that prehistoric women enjoyed power and influence such as patriarchal society has never accorded them? The heroic females of the past may be fantasy figures, created and preserved to console their less fortunate descendants. But it seems equally possible that the tradition grows out of a racial memory that recalls the true facts.

It seems that the cringing wife of the caveman, prostrated in her leopard skin before her tyrannical, club-swinging mate, is a fiction. The evidence of anthropology is that on the whole woman's status is good among primitive peoples. They enjoy considerable freedom, and work closely with their men on a basis that often approximates equality. In the rough-and-tumble struggle for existence they are well able to hold their own.

It is when civilization develops that the woman's status is depressed. Over and over again in human history, that has been the story. The comrade wife of the nomad hunter becomes the subservient slave or the pampered plaything of the civilized man of property. Only when patriarchalism decays can the women revolt and regain their ancient freedom.

So the history of woman's status is not a long steady ascent from the leopard skin to the mink coat. It is first a descent into thralldom (not always intolerable, and not without its satisfactions), a long period of relative helplessness, and finally a triumphal emergence. For most of human history, women have had to accept the conditions imposed upon them in a world created and dominated by men. Even the woman herself, according to a Japanese saying, is man-made; but it adds whimsically that in this case the creation excelled its creator![1]

* * *

"How sad it is to be a woman! Nothing on earth is held so cheap." So wrote the poet Fu Hsuan, in the third century B.C. By that time, Confucian influence had had time to make its mark on Chinese culture. Everyone seems to agree that in the degradation of woman's status Confucius played a leading role.

About the year 552 B.C., when the Golden Age of ancient Greece had not yet dawned, a young mother of scarcely eighteen presented her seventy-one-year-old husband with a man child. The father was overjoyed, because his former wife had borne him a long succession of daughters and only one sickly, crippled son.

The boy was called K'ung. Later in life he was accorded the title Fu-tse—"the Master." Although he is known to have written only one book, he edited the principal Chinese classics already in existence, and many of his sayings were recorded by the multitudes of disciples he gathered round him. His fame spread, and he became the founder of a philosophical system that was to dominate Chinese culture for nearly twenty-five centuries. His name, K'ung Fu-tse, later became known to the West in its Latinized form, Confucius.

Confucius had little enough to say about women. But what he did say was decisive and far-reaching in its effects. He based his whole teaching about human society upon the patriarchal family,

ancestor worship, and the duty of filial piety. The function of the
woman within this system was simple and clear. It could be
summed up in one four-letter word—"obey." Woman is a creature
born to obedience. Throughout her life her duty is to follow three
simple rules. In childhood and early youth she obeys her father;
when she is married she obeys her husband; in widowhood she
obeys her son. The quality of her obedience is to be unquestioning and absolute.

Once planted, this seed produced abundant fruit. Hundreds of
writers and commentators, in China first, later in Korea and Japan
also, elaborated upon the theme, and drew up detailed rules for
woman's behavior. All were based on the inferior status she was
required to accept and maintain.

The patriarchal view of woman's inferiority was reinforced by
Chinese cosmology. The creation of the world was brought about
by the interaction of the two fundamental elements—*yang,* the
male principle, and *yin,* the female. The male elements were the
positive and superior ones—heaven, sun, height, light, strength,
activity. The female elements were the negative and inferior
counterparts of the male—earth, moon, depth, darkness, weakness,
passivity. It can easily be seen that these ideas powerfully reinforced the Confucian teaching about the status of woman.

Biology, as then understood, helped to round out the picture.
Man was the giver of new life, woman merely the receptacle that
received and nurtured it. The man was by nature active, aggres-
sive; the woman was the one acted upon, the one who received
and responded. The man was concerned with the exterior world.
The woman's concern was with the interior—the womb, the home.

While these ideas were deciding the destiny of the Chinese
woman, new religious influences began to penetrate from India.
About a decade before the birth of Confucius, a son was born into
the home of a wealthy prince, who ruled a stretch of territory
close to Nepal. The boy, Siddhartha Gautama, grew up at first in
leisured ease. Later he began to ponder deeply the meaning of
life, and at twenty-nine left his home, wife and infant son to become a wandering teacher. Meditating under a tree, he received
spiritual illumination and became Buddha, the "Enlightened
One." He also was destined to become one of the great teachers
of mankind.

Buddhism is a religion of abstract ideas, not a philosophy of daily living like Confucianism. Yet in their influence on the status of woman they joined forces. The former taught that woman was basically inferior to man, and the latter that she was "the personification of all evil."[2] "Woman," the Buddhists said, "is a creature with the look of an angel on its countenance, but with a diabolical spirit in its inmost heart." And again, "Woman is full of sin; nothing is to be dreaded so much as a woman."[3]

So the stage was set for the degradation of the woman's status in Chinese culture. The united influence of these ideas succeeded in depriving her of every basic human right.

*   *   *

The sacred writings of the Hindu religion are estimated to run to at least fifteen thousand pages. All the books are not of equal importance. In deciding what is right and wrong in human behavior, the Laws of Manu occupy the position of supreme authority.

Nobody knows who Manu was. Described as the Lawgiver, he has not been portrayed with the same vivid characterization as Moses, the Lawgiver of Israel. Yet the Law of Manu, for the Hindus, was just as important as was the Law of Moses for the Jews.

Like Moses, Manu claimed that he received the laws directly from the Creator. His book begins, "Manu sat reclined, his attention fixed on one object—the Supreme God. When the divine Sages approached him, after mutual salutations in due form, he delivered the following address." Later, it is explained that "in this book appears the system of law in its full extent, with the good and bad properties of human nature."

Manu has a good deal to say about women. His fundamental concept seems to be very similar to that of Confucius, by whose ideas he is obviously influenced, for he quotes the three obediences. However, he spells out his meaning in much greater detail than Confucius did. Here, gathered together in one continuous statement, are most of the teachings about the status of women that are scattered throughout the code:

It is the nature of women in this world to cause the seduction of men; for which reason the wise are never unguarded in the company of females. A female, indeed, is able to draw from the right path in this life not a fool only, but even a sage, and can lead him in subjection to desire or to wrath. Let no man, therefore, sit in a sequestered place even with his nearest female relations.

A girl, or a young woman, or a woman advanced in years, must do nothing, even in her own dwelling place, to advance her mere pleasure.

In childhood a female must be dependent on her father: in youth, on her husband: her lord being dead, on her sons: a woman must never seek independence.

A woman must always live with a cheerful temper. While her husband lives, let her obsequiously honor him: and when he dies, let her never neglect him. A virtuous wife must constantly revere her husband as a god—though he fail to observe the approved usages, or be enamoured of another woman, or be devoid of good qualities.

No sacrifice is allowed to women apart from their husbands, no religious rite: as far as a wife honors her lord, so far is she exalted in heaven. A faithful wife who wishes to attain in heaven the mansion of her husband, must do nothing unkind to him, be he living or dead.

A married woman who violates the duty which she owes to her lord, brings infamy on herself in this life, and in the next she will be afflicted with elephantiasis and other diseases, as a punishment for her crimes. But she who keeps her mind, speech and body devoted to her husband attains his heavenly mansion, and by good men is called virtuous. Yes, a woman whose mind, speech and body are kept in subjection, acquires high renown in this world, and, in the next, the same abode with her husband.

No man of sense will take an oath in vain. To women, however, at a time of dalliance, or on a proposal of marriage, it is no deadly sin to take a light oath.

A wife may be corrected, when she commits faults, with a rope or the small shoot of a cane; but on the back part of her body, and not on a noble part by any means.

Day and night must women be held by their protectors in a state of dependence. Their fathers protect them in childhood; their husbands protect them in youth; their sons protect them in age: a woman is never fit for independence.

No man, indeed, can wholly restrain women by violent measures; but by these expedients, they may be restrained. Let the husband keep his wife employed in the collection and expenditure of wealth, in purification and female duty, in the preparation of daily food, and the superintendence of household utensils. By confinement at home, even under affectionate and observant guardians, they are not secure: but those women are truly secure, who are guarded by their own good inclinations.

Drinking spirituous liquor, associating with evil persons, absence from her husband, rambling abroad, unseasonable sleep, and dwelling in the house of another, are six faults which bring infamy on a married woman. Such women examine not whether their lover be handsome or ugly. They think it enough that he is a man, and pursue their pleasures. Through their passion for men, their mutable temper, their want of settled affection, and their perverse nature, they soon become alienated from their husbands. Yet should their husbands be diligently careful in guarding them, though they well know the disposition, with which the Lord of Creation formed them.

Such women have a love of their bed, of their seat, and of impure appetites, wrath, weak flexibility, desire of mischief, and bad conduct.

Women have no business with the texts of the Veda; having therefore no evidence of law, and no knowledge of expiatory texts, sinful women must be as foul as falsehood itself; and this is a fixed rule.

The picture is clear. Woman is a creature inherently weak, sinful, stupid, and irresponsible. Only by abject obedience to the will of man, her lord and protector, can she save herself from disaster, in this world and in the next.

In fairness to Manu a further statement must be added. "Where females are honored," he says, "the gods are pleased. Where they are dishonored, there all religious acts become fruitless. On whatever houses the women of a family, not being duly honored, pronounce a curse, those houses, and all that belong to them, utterly perish."

This may appear to express a different view. What Manu is saying, however, is simply that women, because they are so weak and stupid, are easily exploited by men; and that men must not on this account take advantage of them.

The Laws of Manu, like the teachings of Confucius, became the inspiration for later writers and interpreters. The proper behavior of a Hindu woman was elaborated in the literature that accumulated with the years.

It is a sad picture of a pitiable creature—abject and sinful. A picture fashioned in the minds of men. A picture accepted, too, by women themselves. For Gangadevi was an Indian poetess. And this is what Gangadevi says of her own sex: "Shady places where all evil blossoms; snares that trap, as a deer is trapped, minds blinded with passion; weapons wielded by the deceiving emissaries of Desire;—how can the wise have confidence in women?"[4]

*   *   *

In the trousseau of a traditional Japanese bride, if she came from a good home, there would probably have been a copy of the marriage manual of Kaibara. This Confucian scholar of the fifteenth century took it upon himself to write a little book for the guidance of the new wife, so that she might understand clearly what was expected of her. The book proved very popular with parents, since it summarized clearly what they were expected to teach their daughters. The following extracts are typical.

It is a girl's destiny, on reaching womanhood, to go to a new home, and to live in submission. . . . Should her parents allow her to grow up self-willed, she will infallibly show herself capricious in her husband's house, and thus alienate his affection. The end of these domestic dissensions will be her dismissal from her husband's house and the covering of herself with ignominy.

The only qualities that befit a woman are gentle obedience, chastity, mercy and quietness.

From her earliest youth a girl should observe the line of demarcation separating women from men, and never, even for an instant, should she be allowed to see or hear the least impropriety. The customs of antiquity did not allow men and women to sit in the same apartment, to keep their wearing apparel in the same place, to bathe in the same place, or to transmit to each other anything directly from hand to hand. . . . A woman must observe a certain distance in her relations even with her husband and her brothers . . . she must form no friendship and no intimacy, except when ordered to do so by her parents. . . .

A woman must consider her husband's home her own. . . . However low and needy her husband's position may be, she must find no fault with him, but consider the poverty of the household which it has pleased heaven to give her as the ordering of fate. Once married, she must never leave her husband's house.

Never should a woman fail, night and morning, to pay her respects to her father-in-law and mother-in-law. Never should she be remiss in performing any tasks they may require of her. She should abandon herself to their direction. Even if they be pleased to vilify her, she should not be angry with them.

A woman must look to her husband as her lord, and must serve him with all worship and reverence. The great lifelong duty of a woman is obedience. In her dealings with her husband, she should be courteous, humble, and conciliatory. . . . When the husband issues his instructions, the wife must never disobey them. . . . She should look on her husband as if he were Heaven itself.

A wife should never dream of jealousy. It will render her countenance frightful and her accent repulsive, and it can only result in completely alienating her husband from her, and making her intolerable in his eyes. Should her husband act ill and unreasonable, she must compose her countenance and soften her voice to remonstrate with him.

A woman must keep a strict watch over her own conduct. . . . She should be intent on the duties of her household, and must not weary of weaving, sewing and spinning. Of tea and wine she must not drink overmuch, nor must she feed her eyes with theatrical performances, ditties and ballads. To temples and other like places where there is a great concourse of people, she should go but sparingly till she has reached the age of forty.

A woman should not be constantly occupied in praying. If only she performs satisfactorily her duties as a human being, she may let prayer alone without ceasing to enjoy the divine protection.

While young, a girl must strictly adhere to the rule of separation between the sexes; and on no account should she enter into correspondence with a young man.

The five worst infirmities that afflict the female are indocility, discontent, slander, jealousy, and silliness. It is from these that arises the inferiority of women to men. Woman's nature is passive. As viewed from the standard of man's nature, the foolishness of woman fails to understand the duties that lie before her very eyes, perceives not the actions that will bring down blame upon her own head. When she blames and accuses she does not see that she is her own enemy, estranging others and incurring their hatred. . . . Such is the stupidity of her character, that it is incumbent upon her, in every particular, to distrust herself and to obey her husband.

A woman should yield to her husband the first, and be herself content with the second place. It is necessary for her to avoid pride, even if there be in her actions aught deserving praise . . . to endure without anger and indignation the jeers of others, suffering such things with patience and humility.

We may well wonder what the proud and gallant Empress Jingo, surveying her descendants from her place among the ancestors, thought of all this!

The picture is by now all too clear. In China, in India, in Japan, it is the same story. The thought of the great Eastern cultures about the nature of woman shows little variation. And if that was what the East believed about her, we can only expect these ideas to be reflected in the way she was treated.

* * *

"It is the law of nature," Confucius said, "that woman should be held under the dominance of man." Let us consider how in the East men set about implementing this principle.

It was clear that a woman could never be trusted to take care of herself. For her own protection, she must always be under the complete control of her male guardian. The best way he could preserve her from evil was to lock her up.

Under the purdah system of India, this was done quite literally. "Women were shut away in crowded, airless and isolated rooms at the back of the house, or screened in by shuttered devices through which only faint glimpses could be obtained of the life outside. These rooms were usually overcrowded, poorly lit and ventilated —the barest and ugliest in the whole house. Under such crowded conditions, shut away from all cultural life, with no stimulation from outside, how could women preserve a sense of beauty? It grew to be an envied boast for a Hindu woman to be able to assert that not even the eye of the sun had ever beheld her face."[5]

The number of Indian women who, as a result of this system, never saw the outside world, from their marriage day throughout the rest of their lives, was estimated as recently as thirty years ago to be somewhere between eleven and seventeen million. In these dismal places of seclusion, disease and death were frequent visitors. In Calcutta, where purdah was extensively practiced, the death rate from tuberculosis in 1926 was five times as great for females as for males.

In the Chinese home, while women were often confined to their own quarters, their conditions were much better than in India. But the same principle was in operation, and the Chinese found an ingenious device to implement it. The women's quarters of the Chinese home were not locked and barred. Instead, the Chinese woman herself was hobbled.

The origins of the foot-binding custom are obscure. It is thought to have begun about the tenth century A.D. One tradition traces it to an empress of an ancient dynasty, who bound her feet to conceal a deformity and thus set a new fashion for the court ladies to follow. Whatever the truth of this story, small feet came to be the supreme mark of quality in a woman. It was more important even than being clever or beautiful. In many communities, a girl whose feet were not bound had little chance of becoming a bride.

Mrs. Mary Bryson gives us, from her personal observation, this description of the procedure:

"The deformity is produced by narrow cotton bandages about three yards long. They are applied when the little girl is six years old. One end of the strip of cotton is placed beneath the instep and then carried over the four small toes, drawing them down beneath the foot. Another twist draws the heel and great toe nearer together. When all the cloth has been used, the end is firmly sewed down, and the feet are left for a week or two in that condition. Clean bandages are now and then put on, but the change has to be very rapidly effected, or the blood begins again to circulate in the poor benumbed feet, and the agony becomes almost unbearable. Not infrequently in the process a girl loses one or two of her toes, but she feels repaid for the pain she endures by being the possessor of still smaller feet. Mothers and nurses frequently perform this duty for their daughters, and in passing a Chinese home one sometimes hears the bitter crying of a child whose feet are being bound.

"At last, after indescribable torture, the girl's foot becomes a mass of distorted and broken bones. She is now the proud possessor of 'golden lilies,' and can wear the fashionable shoes, just three inches long, in which the elegant Chinese lady totters painfully from room to room of the home she hardly ever leaves."[6]

There is a similarity in principle between the bound feet of the Chinese and the high-heeled shoes of the Western woman. Both are supposed to emphasize beauty and sexual attractiveness. Lin Yutang, describing an attractive woman in one of his books, says, "A pair of unbound feet would have completely ruined this perfect harmony of line."[7]

The real reason for foot-binding, however, is clearly not to make the woman beautiful, but to make her immobile. Mrs. Bryson underlines the Chinese belief that if young girls went out of doors they would be sure to get into mischief; and she quotes a story of an eminent lady of olden times who set a splendid example to womanhood by never even looking out of the door of her house for a period of twelve years!

No particular attempt was, in fact, made to conceal the motive for foot-binding. In the famous *Classic for Girls* we read:

> Have you ever learned the reason
>   For the binding of your feet?
> 'Tis from fear that 'twill be easy
>   To go out upon the street.[8]

In Japan foot-binding was not practiced. But the women were shut up within their own quarters. The polite Japanese word for a wife is *okusama*, "the lady of the back parlor." The arrangement of the house was that the servants lived in the front room, while the wife was safely shut away in the rear, cut off from the life of the street and of the outside world.

From an early age, girls in the East were accustomed to the idea that they could not be trusted to guard their own virtue. "Experience has taught," wrote the Abbé Dubois nearly a century ago, "that young Hindu women do not possess sufficient firmness, and sufficient regard for their own honor, to resist the ardent solicitations of a seducer."[9] As a comment on this, the story is told of a woman's club in Bombay whose members demanded the right to take their eleven- and twelve-year-old daughters with them to the afternoon meetings. They admitted they were afraid to leave the girls at home and accessible to the men of the family.

Nora Waln describes a similar attitude in the Chinese home in which she lived. "In the olden days maidens took part in the spring rites. But Kuei-tzu, First Lady in Authority now in the homestead, trusts neither ancient manuscript nor Western custom. Maids under her protection do not join in any festival procession which includes men—except that procession which goes direct to the bridegroom's door.

"On the holiday morning, the wives and girl children went out with the boys and men to join in the Welcome to Spring Procession. We maids of marriageable age were left inside the homestead. Kuei-tzu locked the To-and-from-the-World Gate with the special key she uses on such occasions."[10]

* * *

"Educate a woman and you put a knife into the hands of a monkey," said the Brahmins.[11] However fantastic this may sound in the modern world, it was hard to disprove it in a society where women were shut up in complete seclusion. The Eastern custom of keeping all women in protective custody inevitably denied them social and civic privileges. What use were such privileges to them, since they were not free to exercise them? And if they *were* free, who could tell whether they could be trusted to exercise them responsibly?

Here indeed is a vicious circle. The woman was denied what we now regard as elementary human rights because she was held to be by nature inferior. Then the fact that she did not have such rights was taken as a proof that she was unworthy of them. A shrewd Japanese writer sums up the situation neatly. "The education of our women," he says, "was neglected, and her intelligence became more and more narrow owing to there being little or no chance for her to see things in the outer world. The next thing which was bound to happen was man's contempt and disdain for her narrow-mindedness and stupidity."[12]

Look at the result of this process. "The classical Japanese wife," says Cressy, "almost eludes characterization. It is hard to say what she herself is really like, except that she is self-less. She is the real mainspring of the household, but this is almost totally obscured by her obedience, self-sacrifice, humility and incredible patience. She is more of a pervasive presence than a person. She can best be described as the almost invisible genius of the Japanese home, always there, always busy, always smiling."[13]

Is this a description of what a woman is by nature? Not at all. It is a description of what a woman has become, in a certain culture, under the pressure of close and continuous conditioning. She has become depersonalized because this was the role that her society—more correctly, the men of her society—cast for her.

An Indian businessman, with whom we had a lively discussion one evening in Bombay, put it thus, "The strength of the Indian home is based on sound foundations—the training of the Indian girl to make sacrifices. We men are inconstant creatures, and sacrifice doesn't come easily to us. We need women we can depend on—wives who will tolerate us, be patient with us, forgive us when we let them down. We train our girls to be wives like that. In this way we keep our family life sound."

We asked whether, without "training," women might not also find it difficult to sacrifice, tolerate, and forgive; and whether, if men were given similar training, such capacities might not become possible for them also! But clearly such questions were presumptuous in a patriarchal context.

So the Eastern woman had to be bent to fit the role selected for her. Deprived of personal freedom, of the opportunity to be educated, and of civic rights, she was enslaved within a system dedicated to uphold the rights of men at any cost. "Through a fiat of Nature, it is impossible to get along racially without the aid of women as a means; but the male is considered as the main object. Traditionally, woman has been regarded as a parasite and a social debtor."[14] This was said concerning Japan; but it could apply equally to the East in general. Olga Lang lists the most important of woman's rights as the right to own property, to choose a mate, to sexual equality, to divorce, and to be protected against arbitrary repudiation. In old China, she adds, the woman did not enjoy a single one of these rights.[15]

Indeed, the woman was herself sometimes treated as negotiable property. Throughout the East, young girls have often been sold as slaves, prostitutes, and concubines—sometimes for gain, sometimes under the stress of extreme hardship. Even wives have been sold, though this has usually been done illegally. In Korea, however, in the period 1000–1400 A.D., it was legal for a man to settle his debts by handing over his wife, children, and servants.[16] In Thailand, the sale of a wife without her own consent, and of daughters above the age of fifteen, was not made illegal till the reign of King Mongkut (1850–68).[17]

When a Chinese man marries, one term used to describe what happens is that he "takes the woman by the ear." From this advantageous position, the Eastern husband was apparently at liberty to put his wife to any kind of labor he chose. A recent American visitor to Japan was told of country girls who, after marriage, were put in harness with the family ox.[18] A similar account comes from China, where a Jesuit missionary "assures us that he has seen a woman and an ass yoked together to the same plough, while the inhuman husband was guiding it and driving his team."[19]

These are far from typical situations. They represent, however, the extremes to which the doctrine of woman's inferiority can lead.

* * *

Lest this recital should engender any sense of false pride or superiority, let us now consider the status of women in our own Western tradition.

For every derogatory statement concerning women in the East, the West can produce its counterpart. For a start, listen to Socrates, the fountain of wisdom of ancient Greece: "Woman is the source of all evil; her love is to be dreaded more than the hatred of men; the poor young men who seek women in matrimony are like fish who go out to meet the hook."

The Jewish tradition gives us the Creation story that identifies Eve, the first woman, as the cause of man's fall from grace. In that tradition we also find the blessing in the Morning Prayer— "Blessed art Thou, O Lord. . . . Who hast not made me a gentile . . . a slave . . . a woman."[20]

Let no one suppose, either, that our Christian heritage is free of such slighting judgments. It would be hard to find anywhere a collection of more degrading references to the female sex than the early Church Fathers provide. Lecky, the famous historian, speaks of "these fierce invectives which form so conspicuous and so grotesque a portion of the writings of the Fathers . . . woman was represented as the door of hell, as the mother of all human ills. She should be ashamed at the very thought that she is a woman. She should live in continual penance on account of the curses she has brought upon the world. She should be ashamed of her dress, for it is the memorial of her fall. She should be especially ashamed of her beauty, for it is the most potent instrument of the devil."[21]

One of the most scathing of these attacks on women is that of Tertullian: "Do you know that you are each an Eve? The sentence of God on this sex of yours lives in this age: the guilt must of necessity live too. You are the devil's gateway; you are the unsealer of that (forbidden) tree; you are the first deserter of the divine law; you are she who persuades him whom the devil was not valiant enough to attack. You destroyed so easily God's image, man. On account of your desert—that is death—even the Son of God had to die."[22]

Not only did the Church affirm the inferior status of woman, it deprived her of legal rights she had previously enjoyed. Lecky comments, "The pagan laws during the (Roman) Empire had been continually repealing the old disabilities of women."[23] When the Christian Church gained control, however, this trend was changed. "Out of the Catholic doctrine concerning the subordination of the weaker sex, we find numerous and stringent enactments, which render it impossible for women to succeed to any considerable amount of property. . . . The complete inferiority of the sex was continually maintained by the law; and that generous public opinion which in Rome had frequently revolted against the injustice done to girls, in depriving them of the greater part of the inheritance of their fathers, totally disappeared. Wherever the Canon Law has been the basis of legislation, we find laws of succession sacrificing the interests of daughters and of wives."[24] Sir Henry Maine, the great nineteenth-century authority on ancient law, expressed his pessimism thus, "No society which preserves any tincture of Christian institutions is likely to restore to married women the personal liberty conferred on them by the Middle Roman Law."[25]

Our Jewish-Christian culture has done much for women of

which we may be proud. But it has resolutely and stubbornly maintained, until very recently, the conviction that as a person woman is inferior to man, and that her proper relationship to him is that of dependence and obedience. The laws and customs of Western society have been shaped to support that conviction. They went virtually unchallenged until the end of the eighteenth century.

*   *   *

The trumpet call to arms, in defense of women's rights, was sounded in 1792 by Mary Wollstonecraft, who later died giving birth to a daughter who was to become the wife of the poet Shelley. Her "Vindication of the Rights of Woman" lit a candle in England that later started a world-wide conflagration.

A woman championing her own sex may well be suspect. So let a man speak of the conditions under which women lived, less than a century ago, in the most enlightened country in the Western world. The time is 1869. The man is no less a person than John Stuart Mill, the great philosopher and economist.

It required some courage, in those days, for a man to champion the cause of woman's freedom. John Stuart Mill did it with courage and conviction. In his essay *The Subjection of Women* he draws a picture of the woman's lot. Here are some extracts:

Women are wholly under the rule of men, having no share at all in public concerns, and each in private being under the legal obligation of obedience to the man with whom she has associated her destiny. They are brought up from the earliest years in the belief that their ideal of character is not government by self-control, but submission, and yielding to the control of others. All the moralities tell them that it is the duty of women to make complete abnegation of themselves.

We are continually told that civilization and Christianity have restored to the woman her just rights. Meanwhile the wife is the actual bond-servant of her husband; no less so, as far as legal obligation goes, than slaves commonly so called. She vows a lifelong obedience to him at the altar, and is held to it all through her life by law. She can do no act whatever but by his permission, at least tacit. She can acquire no property but for him; the instant it becomes hers, even if by inheritance, it becomes *ipso facto* his. In this respect the wife's position under the common law of England is worse than that of slaves in the laws of many countries.

What is her position in regard to the children in whom she and her master have a joint interest? They are by law *his* children. He alone has any legal rights over them. Not one act can she do toward or in relation to them, except by delegation from him. Even after he is dead she is not their legal guardian, unless he by will has made her so. He could even send them away from her, and deprive her of the means of seeing them or corresponding with them, until this power was in some degree restricted.

This is her legal state. If she leaves her husband, she can take nothing with her, neither her children nor anything which is rightfully her own. If he chooses, he can compel her to return, by law, or by physical force; or he may content himself with seizing for his own use anything which she may earn, or which may be given to her by her relatives.

I have described the wife's legal position. Men in general do not inflict, nor women suffer, all the misery which could be inflicted and suffered if the full power of tyranny with which the man is legally invested were acted upon. Who doubts that there may be great goodness, and great happiness, and great affection, under the absolute government of a good man? But there are all grades of goodness and wickedness in men. The vilest malefactor has some wretched woman tied to him, against whom he can commit any atrocity except killing her, and, if tolerably cautious, can do that without much danger of the legal penalty.

The sufferings, immoralities, evils of all sorts, produced in innumerable cases by the subjection of individual women to individual men, are far too terrible to be overlooked. The law of servitude in marriage is a monstrous contradiction of all the principles of the modern world. It is the sole case, now that Negro slavery has been abolished, in which a human being in the plenitude of every faculty is delivered up to the tender mercies of another human being. Marriage is the only actual bondage known to our law. There remain no legal slaves, except the mistress of every house.

The moral regeneration of mankind will only really commence, when the most fundamental of the social relations is placed under the rule of equal justice.

John Stuart Mill was not a man to speak lightly or carelessly, or to speak of that which he knew not. The accuracy of the picture he portrays cannot be doubted. He described England in the latter half of the last century. What substantial progress, we may well ask, had been made during the nearly twenty-five centuries since Confucius framed his rule of obedience, or the twenty since Manu drew up his code of law?

* * *

But the trumpet was still sounding. And the summons now began to be answered. The passing in England, in 1882, of the Married Women's Property Act, allowing wives to have exclusive ownership of their own personal estate, swept away the first gross injustice.

On two small islands in the remote South Pacific the greatest blow of all was struck. It proved to be the final death blow of the age-old concept of woman's inferiority. The echo of it rang around the globe. It was a turning point in human history. In 1893, New Zealand gave women the right to vote.

After this initial break-through, the citadels began to topple. But not until grimly fought battles had been won. Australia in 1902, Finland in 1907, Norway in 1913, Iceland in 1914, Denmark in 1915, the U.S.S.R. in 1917.

Still the leading countries of the West held out. In England the struggle was long and bitter, with Mrs. Sylvia Pankhurst the acknowledged leader. The final victory was thus recorded in the diary of a clergyman's wife: "Tuesday, June 19th, 1917. Managed to get into Ladies' Gallery at House of Commons. Suffrage Clause in Reform Bill passed by majority of 330. Only 55 against. *Sursum corda.*"[26]

In the United States, it was Susan B. Anthony who had led the attack. She did not live to see the victory won. She died in 1906. But her soul went marching on, and in 1920 the Nineteenth (Woman Suffrage) Amendment was passed. Long before, in 1869, the very year when John Stuart Mill was writing his essay, the Territory of Wyoming had given women the vote, twenty-four years before any nation in the world did so.

In 1868 Wyoming had been established as a Territory with a temporary government. In 1869 the first Territorial Legislature granted women the right of suffrage in its first session. During the second session, an attempt was made to repeal this law, but without success. The Hon. John W. Kingman, of the Wyoming Supreme Court, declared: "At our first election, before women voted, we had a perfect pandemonium. At the next election, women voted, and perfect order prevailed, and has prevailed ever since. In caucus discussions, the presence of a few ladies is worth more than a whole squad of police."

Today, most countries have recognized the political equality of men and women. One of the exceptions is in Europe. Switzerland, whose enlightened Constitution served as a model for the United States, still denies the right of suffrage to its women.

Lack of voting power was by no means the only obstacle in the way of woman's freedom. Possession of the franchise certainly did not solve all her problems. Yet it was the symbol of what lay at the heart of the whole struggle. The right to vote could have only one meaning—the recognition that a woman and a man, as persons living in society, were entitled to equal power and responsibility. It did not mean that men and women were equal in all respects. That is an absurd notion, which ignores their functional differences. But it meant that the concept of man as a superior being, and woman as an inferior, had at last been given up. This was a highly significant event, a new departure in human history. In all known societies, says Olga Lang, even the matrilineal, woman has been considered inferior to man.[27]

This achievement has not delivered woman from problems. Her freedom to participate along with men in the active life of the world has thrown her on the horns of a dilemma. How can she satisfy her needs as a woman, in marriage and motherhood, and her needs as a person, in achieving social status outside her home, at one and the same time? The Western woman is in the process of finding an answer to that question.

One thing is certain. The security of her old dependent days has gone with the restrictions that made it possible. As a cultivated young Indian woman expressed it, "Women in the West have to fend for themselves. Many of them earn their own living, which again means competition, job-hunting, and eternal rush. When I first traveled in England and France I was amazed to see the restless and unhappy expression of women I met in the street."[28]

The Western woman has achieved freedom. She has yet to gain serenity and peace.

* * *

"On August 1st, 1930, Mrs. Hansa Mehta led her defiant band, five hundred strong, with songs and banners through the streets of Bombay. Women of all ages, castes, and conditions made up that throng. It was the heavy monsoon season.

"For two whole hours the women paraded before the police received orders to stop the procession. Suddenly a wall of blue-clad, yellow-turbaned men blocked a street. Impossible to press forward and pass on. The women would not turn back. The police could not make way.

"Mrs. Mehta quietly and serenely sat down in the squashy yellow mud of the road; down sat her followers; down came the rain. The police ordered and expostulated in vain. Even many of the mothers among Mrs. Mehta's followers did not go home; their babies were brought to them and fed in the street.

"An hour passed, two, three—and still the women sat on. They sang, *sang* at the tops of their voices, hymns, patriotic chants, and songs in memory of the patriot Tilak, far on into the sudden twilight and the deep long night.

"Thousands and thousands of spectators gathered. But no pleading, either from their own supporters or from the police, could induce the women to budge. Mrs. Mehta and her band were fully determined to force the issue. When day dawned, it found them still on the same spot, hollow-eyed but undaunted.

"Meanwhile the police had received orders to disperse them by force. There were numerous wounded and hundreds of arrests."[29]

This was only one of a series of incidents in which the women of India shared in the campaign to free their country. Mahatma Gandhi, in his civil disobedience campaign, treated his women supporters as equals of the men. "Tenderly nurtured women, physically under-developed because of the rigours of former seclusion, women used to soft, silky garments, bejewelled, sheltered, economically dependent, women a short while ago too shy even to speak freely to a stranger and too proud to grant a glimpse of their face even to the most august outsider—these women, dressed in plain rough garments, are now suddenly to be found in the streets of slums even, where they face staring crowds before liquor shops, plead with total strangers, brave the police and are ready to undergo unflinchingly the worst of hardships."[30]

Before this spectacle the men of India stood stupefied and bewildered. It was an incredible sight.

To us it recalls a familiar story. With Mrs. Mehta, surely the spirits of Sylvia Pankhurst and Susan B. Anthony marched again.

In the East, as in the West, women have been vigorously challenging the myth of their inferiority. In political crisis, in war, in social change, they have emerged from their seclusion and demonstrated hitherto unexpected qualities of leadership, of endurance, of devotion to a cause. They have proved their ability to benefit from higher education. They have qualified themselves for professional service. They have shown themselves capable of occupying with distinction high offices of state. We have met personally, worked with, and count among our friends, such outstanding Asian women as Lady Rama Rau and the Rajkumari Amrit Kaur, of India; the widow of Aung San, the Bogyoke, in Burma; and lesser known but equally competent women leaders in half a dozen other Asian lands. There can be no doubt that the emancipated women of the East are in every way comparable with their sisters in the West.

*   *   *

Ever since Eve, the women of our race have, with brief and intermittent intervals, been treated as inferior. Yet we know today that this judgment is quite inaccurate. One contemporary writer[31] (a man!) has even gone so far as to publish a book entitled *The Natural Superiority of Women*.

Why has most of human history been shadowed by such a monstrous misconception?

Clearly it has its roots in the biological differences between men and women. At two points the woman is inherently at a disadvantage.

Sexually her encounter with the male issues in a conquest in which she is the prize. He can, as it were, lay siege to her citadel, conquer her, and literally invade her. The irony of the situation is that for the woman this symbolic defeat is what her womanhood needs and desires for its fruition. If she does not submit, capitulate, yield to the attack of her would-be invader, she abandons her major purpose in life.

The sexual drama of attack and surrender relates, of course, only to one limited area of interaction between man and woman. But it is easy to understand how the biological pattern could have become the blueprint for the sociological structuring of their relative status; and this has evidently taken place.

Again, the woman's function as mother makes her vulnerable and puts her in need of protection. History has its records of fighting women. But no woman in an advanced stage of pregnancy is in a condition to fight. Even a woman general in such circumstances would be obliged to take time out. So the woman, in the very process of fulfilling her womanhood, is forced into a position of inability to compete with the man, and indeed of dependence on him. Where women are fairly frequently pregnant, this state of affairs tends to become habitual, and to settle into a pattern. It has even been suggested that, in the modern world, what has emancipated the woman is not the franchise that enables her to vote, but birth control, which delivers her from a recurring series of disabling and exhausting pregnancies.

Added to these fundamental functional differences between the sexes is the biological misconception we have already referred to —that the male alone produces the life-giving seed that grows into the child, the female merely providing the receptacle for its early growth. This concept is found over and over again in patriarchal society. It appears in ancient Greece, among the Semitic peoples, in Africa, in the theology of St. Thomas Aquinas, and elsewhere, as well as in Asian culture. It implies that in the natural scheme of things the woman plays a part in procreation that is subsidiary rather than complementary to that of the man.

All these ideas assume great importance in a society where the bringing together of men and women is largely confined to the purposes of procreation, and where the cultivation of comradeship and co-operation between husband and wife is given little importance. This explains why women tend to have more freedom and more equal status with men in primitive cultures than they do in highly organized patriarchal communities where the activities of the sexes are sharply separated. It also explains why in patriarchal societies the women of the poorer classes often enjoy privileges denied to the rich. The peasant women of South China, for example, did not bind their feet and stay at home, for the simple reason that they were needed to work alongside their husbands in the fields.

Since all the world's great religions have developed in patriarchal societies, it is not surprising that religion has often been used to support the principle of feminine inferiority. Since ancestor worship was a central feature in early religious thinking, it is easy to understand why the performing of religious rites has been kept exclusively in the hands of males. It is understandable, too, that the Moslem heaven should be, among other things, a kind of super-harem, with alluring women continually available to minister to the beatified male's inexhaustible sexual potency.

A frequently recurring concept is that woman, particularly as a sexual being, is associated with sin and evil. In Buddhism and Christianity particularly, this has been a central idea; and it has been expressed in each case in insistence on a celibate priesthood. Only the man who is undefiled by woman's sexual allurements is fit to perform the highest religious function.

These ideas clearly have complex origins. Among animistic peoples, sex is often associated with demonic forces. The woman's menstrual blood is a particular focus of primitive taboos. Man's sexual desire for woman must also have revealed itself often as a distracting force, generating rivalries and even causing wars, undermining integrity and deflecting from the path of duty, encouraging softness and love of ease. To a religion with ascetic ideals, woman's sexuality certainly presents a constant challenge.

The result has been that men, particularly in Western culture, have constantly struggled to reconcile two opposite views of womanhood—the Madonna and the prostitute. Virgin, sexless woman, typifying the pure, ideal, mother-figure, has been elevated to the highest honor as the Queen of Heaven. Sexual woman, typifying the partner with whom the man slakes his earthy, sexual appetites, has been denounced as the Gate of Hell.

Between the two extremes, poised in uneasy tension, stands woman as wife. Hard indeed has been her lot. Complex indeed, now that she is free to work out her own destiny, is the task that lies before her.

Chapter 4

SEX IN THE ORIENT

An American lady, on a visit to India, was taken for a drive along a country road. She and her host chatted gaily about Indian life. She was intrigued, as all Westerners are, by the strange ways of the East.

The driver swung the car round a bend and brought it suddenly to a halt. The way ahead was blocked by a pair of monkeys in the act of mating. The driver relaxed and settled down to wait till they were finished.

"They are entitled," he explained over his shoulder, "to be undisturbed at such a time."

Embarrassed, the American lady tried to change the subject. The Indian gentleman who was her host, however, was not to be thus diverted. To him, sex was not a topic for prudery or evasion. It was a part of life, to be accepted as such. It was indeed closely allied with religion.

"Why shouldn't the phallus be worshiped?" he asked, "as well as the sun or any other life-giving inhabitant of Heaven or Earth?"[1]

Every Westerner who has lived in the East has undergone some counterpart of this experience. It comes as something of a shock to realize that the sexual function, so furtively hidden away from open recognition in our society, could in another culture be accepted without embarrassment. In this kind of atmosphere, you begin to realize the inadequacy, and the absurdity, of our Western idea that the powerful creative urge that governs life's renewal is inherently disreputable.

In the East the need for such evasion is simply not felt. "Sex and its uses the Indian regards as natural facts calling for no particular reticence. An Indian lady will decline a social invitation, and give for her refusal a physiological reason which would strike a London drawing room dumb with horror; simply because ignorance, real or pretended, of sexual facts to the Indian mind suggests silliness rather than 'innocence.'"[2]

On one of our visits to India we were shown a subfertility clinic in a large city. It contained the usual waiting room, interview rooms, examination rooms, and laboratory. In addition, a small room was provided that to our knowledge has no counterpart in the most elaborate of our Western clinics. Its purpose, the lady doctor in charge explained, was to enable the childless couple to retire and have intercourse, in order that a postcoital examination could be made immediately afterwards. The clinical advantages of this arrangement are obvious, and it would not have occurred to anyone concerned that there was anything indelicate about it.

These modern attitudes are in keeping with tradition. The Abbé Dubois, who recorded his observations of Indian customs nearly a century and a half ago, describes a religious festival in southern Mysore. "The goddess, placed in a beautifully ornamented palanquin, is carried in a procession through the streets. In front of her there is another divinity, a male. These two idols, which are entirely nude, are placed in immodest postures, and by the help of a piece of mechanism, a disgusting movement is imparted to them as long as the procession continues. This spectacle excites transports of mirth, manifested by shouts and bursts of laughter."[3]

The pious French Catholic priest, in relating this incident, is clearly torn between his desire to record what he saw with scientific accuracy, and his horror that the act of sexual union could, in the name of religion, be publicly dramatized. What to the Eastern onlookers was accepted with good-humored amusement could only be interpreted by the Western witness as "immodest" and "disgusting."

In Hindu temples, at Konarak and elsewhere, carved figures are displayed showing men and women in the most frankly sexual embraces. No attempt is made to conceal these particular carvings, or to separate them from figures engaged in other activities that belong to the business of human life. Sex is not set apart. It belongs to the wholeness of living, and as such is incorporated into its proper place in religion, in art, in social and personal life. The child is not surrounded, as in the West, with forbidding taboos, or put off with evasions or falsehoods. "In the Hindu household boys and girls soon become aware, in a natural way, of the facts of life. Marriage and childbirth are freely discussed in family gatherings. No one tells children stories of babies brought in little baskets by doctors or storks. When the children ask questions about physiological facts, they are given the answers."[4]

*   *   *

Dream of the Red Chamber is considered the greatest Chinese novel ever written. In an eighteenth-century setting, it describes the adolescence of a boy growing up in an aristocratic family. Red is the wedding color in China, so the red chamber is a symbol for sexual initiation.

Pao-Yu was twelve years of age when he had the dream. It seemed to him that he heard someone singing on the far side of a hill.

The echo of the song was still in Pao-Yu's ears when a maiden appeared whose beauty and grace were not like anything in the mortal world. Pao-Yu greeted her and said: "Sister Immortal, where have you come from and where are you going? I have lost my way. Would you be my guide?"

The Goddess led him to the Great Void Illusion Land, and explained that she had brought him in order to enlighten him. The fairies sang to him the "Dream of the Red Chamber." Then she said, "Now I am going to marry you to my younger sister Ku-Ching so that you may learn the secrets of the chamber."

Briefly the Goddess taught him the secret of cloud-and-rain and pushed him into the room where her younger sister was sitting. She pulled the door to from the outside. In a trance Pao-Yu followed the instructions of the Goddess. . . .

The next day Pao-Yu found himself deeply in love with his fair companion. Hand in hand they went out for a walk. Suddenly he came to a road beset with prickling thorns and howling wolves and roaring tigers. In front of him was a black chasm filled with darkly ominous water unbridged by anything that might save him from the pursuing wild beasts.

Pao-Yu woke in terror. His maid, Pervading Fragrance, was bending over him, trying to calm him after his evil dream. She asked him what the dream was about.

Pao-Yu had been fond of his hand-maiden and confided to her his dream after having extracted from her the promise of not repeating it to others. The maid laughed and hid her face with her hands when Pao-Yu came to the mysteries that the Goddess of Disillusionment taught him. Pao-Yu offered to demonstrate to her what he had learned. The maid was willing and was not restrained by any scrupulous considerations as she was given to Pao-Yu by the Matriarch. Thenceforward, Pao-Yu treated the maid with more than ordinary thoughtfulness, and the maid in turn redoubled her faithful attentions to Pao-Yu's well-being.[5]

Notice that what caused Pao-Yu to awake in terror was not the sexual part of his dream, but the threat of the wild beasts. And he felt free to confide to his maid the discovery of his sexuality, and to experiment with her as he tried out his new-found powers. Nor did either of them regard this as an improper relationship.

Here again we have the natural, uncomplicated acceptance of sex. This attitude is characteristic of Chinese romantic stories. "The Chinese," says Olga Lang, "have a more realistic attitude toward the human body than Westerners. They do not conceal the physical aspects of love . . . nor do they need a romantic sublimation in order to accept it."[6]

One of the stories in the Liao-chai collection describes how Chu meets Ying Ning under the blossoming pear trees. He decides to declare his love, and does so in the most forthright manner.

"I should like to be with you at night on the same pillow and mat," he says simply.

"I am not accustomed to sleeping with a stranger," is her equally forthright reply.

In most of the stories the boys and girls, when they meet, proceed almost at once to have sex relations. We see this well illustrated in the *Dream of the Red Chamber*, when Phoenix, making a business call at the Water Moon Convent, takes Pao-Yu and his schoolboy friend Chin Chung along with her. During the discussion between Phoenix and the Abbess, Chin Chung, who has found himself attracted to a young nun, slips away to her room. Soon afterwards Pao-Yu, looking for his friend, surprises them in bed together.

The idea here is that sex is something simple and straightfor-

ward, an imperious urge that, when given the ⟨
press itself, is almost impossible to resist. Down
about sexual desire is good Chinese philosophy.

Chinese religion, heavily influenced by Buddhism
as frankly uninhibited about sex as Hinduism. No Eas
however, has surrounded the sexual function with the
ers of prudery with which it has been swathed in ou. Western
culture.

In Japan, one manifestation of the naturalistic attitude is the
lack of self-consciousness about nudity. The Western visitor is invariably taken aback at the unself-conscious way in which men
and women publicly take baths together and recognize no need
for separate toilet facilities. There is a good deal of unembarrassed
freedom, too, in the exchange of sexual jokes, in sensuous dances,
and in the sex play of children.[7]

There are many good reasons why sex in the East is more freely
and openly accepted than in the West. Peasant life means continuous preoccupation with nature's reproductive processes.
Crowded living conditions make personal privacy almost impossible. Austerity and drudgery mean that for many, sexual pleasure
is one of the few available forms of pleasurable excitement. The
subjection of women makes them readily available to meet the
needs of men, for on no other terms can they gain security. These
and other factors have made the approach to sex simple, direct,
and uncomplicated.

*   *   *

From the earliest times, religion and sex have belonged together.

Both are concerned with creation. A Japanese legend describes
how a god and goddess, after some experimentation, discovered
that they were able to have sexual intercourse. The result of their
union was the creation of mountains and seas, of forests and fields,
of animals and men, in a great orgy of reproduction.

Both sex and religion are concerned with the mystery of life.
At the heart of all being there is the continuous interaction of *yin*
and *yang*, the masculine and feminine principles. In the womb
of the earth and in the womb of the woman the ongoing process
of creation is continually renewed, with the planting of the seed
and its growth and fruition. The springtime in which the earth

..ews its vitality is the symbol of the reawakening of sexual desire. Conversely, sexual activity undertaken in the name of the gods of fertility was believed to promote the growth of the crops upon which man's life depended.

Both sex and religion are concerned with parenthood. The supreme service to the ancestors was the procreation of sons. Thus was a man's supreme religious duty fulfilled. But not always did the seed take root in the womb. What more natural explanation than that sexual union alone did not give conception? "The female alone cannot procreate," said Ku-liang, the Confucian commentator, "the male alone cannot propagate. Heaven alone cannot produce a man. The three collaborating, man is born."

It is not at all surprising that religion has been preoccupied with the male sex organ. To the ancient Hebrews, the penis was the most sacred part of a man's body. By its use he was able to attain his full dignity as a co-worker of God, continuing the noble task of creation. In sexual activity he became the procreator, acting for and on behalf of the Supreme Creator. Therefore it was this part of his body that, in circumcision, was dedicated to God. The sacrifice of the foreskin symbolized the solemn offering of the whole penis to which it belonged; and the offering of the penis symbolized the offering of the whole man to which it belonged.

Phallic worship, far from being obscene, is the adoration of creativity, the manifestation of divine activity and purpose in the world. "At the heart of every Shiva temple stands the *lingam*—the phallic symbol which represents Shiva. To the Westerner who seems shocked by such symbolism many Indians pretend ignorance of the meaning of the *lingam*. Among themselves, however, it seems the most obvious, natural, and appropriate symbol of the god whose greatest aspect is that of the Creator."[8]

At a higher level, religion discerns the analogy between the adoration of the lover for the beloved and that of the soul for God. It is this idea that the creators of erotic art in Hindu temples are trying to express. They deliberately chose sexual love for their purpose, because its great intensity made it the most fitting analogy they could find. "Such love," says Chandra Sen, "is the nearest approach in human life to the mystic longings of the devotee's soul for the realization of God; and in fact, in the purity

of its sentiment and in its capacity for devotion and self-sacrifice
it approaches spirituality."9

*   *   *

What the erotic sculptors strove to achieve in wood and stone,
the poets like Vidhyapati did through the medium of words.
Here is a typical poem from the Radha and Krishna cycle:

> The wrath of the wrathful fled afar
> Kanu sank in a sea of nectar:
> But when he asked for her embrace,
> Albeit heavy with love, her lovely body might not bend.
>
> Honeyed was the swain's speech,
> Tremulous the beauty's sighs;
> Her Lord enfolded her upon his lap,
> But yet the flow of nectar was but little.
>
> Gently he kissed her face—her eyes were full of tears,
> And though her heart was full of love, yet love was lacking;
> Bravely he touched her bosom with his hands,
> But even then desire would not awake.
>
> And when at last he loosed her girdle,
> Then even, in Hari's bliss, desire was cold,
> And even then she felt no gladness.
> *Is it pleasure or pain, says Vidhyapati?*10

What is described here is, by analogy, pure religion. Radha represents the human soul. Her modesty suggests the fear of the unknown that holds back the spirit in its response to God. Her desire
(lacking in this poem, but present in others) represents religious
fervor. Her coldness is the unwillingness to surrender the self to
the divine will.

Krishna represents God. He is strong, bold, self-assured. Yet he
is a tender, gentle, understanding lover, and in surrender to him
Radha finds fulfillment and peace. This is described in a verse
from another of the poems:

> When I lay in His arms every hair of my body was glad,
> In the dew of his lips my grieving melted away:
> Fate has fulfilled the hope of all the days of my life,—
> From bending my eyes upon Him I know no rest.11

That this is a dangerous medium for the expression of spiritual truth few will deny. "In the case of persons less well equipped with moral armour," says Lord Ronaldshay dryly, "such cults inevitably lead to results the reverse of spiritual."[12] But one Indian would reply, "The Western fear of voluptuousness is hardly known in the East. The Indian culture is nowhere corrupted by sentimentality. Where life is transparent, the enjoyment of life is never a spiritual bondage."[13] Another would add, "Fools do not understand, and they never will, for they look at it only from the physical side."[14]

What concerns us here is that submission to the husband and submission to God are identified in Hindu religion. So, for a woman, religion offers the natural expression of her full feminine responsiveness. This makes the Indian woman an ideal feminine type. To marriage she can bring all her natural religious fervor; for there is no conflict, as there is for the pious Western woman, between her spirituality and her sexuality. Love, sex, and religious devotion are for the Hindu woman fully integrated into one experience that is central to the whole of life.

*   *   *

Alongside the acceptance of sex there is the fear of sex.

In Thailand we heard of a group of Christian young people who went on a picnic outing to the hills. They decided to climb up to a famous cave. Two of the girls joined the boys. At one point they had to step from one rocky ledge to another. Directly beneath this spot was a Buddhist shrine.

An attendant saw what had happened. He ran in consternation to inform the priests. Pandemonium followed. All this would have made no sense to the Western mind. But what had happened was serious. The sacred precincts had been defiled by the physical presence of a woman!

We inquired further into this concept of the contaminating influence of the female. It is found in Buddhism, in Hinduism, in Shintoism. It appears in innumerable forms. Men's and women's clothes, for instance, must not be washed in the same water, carried in the same basket, hung up to dry on the same line. Even when there are separate lines, they must be at different altitudes, so that no portion of any man's garment is lower than any portion of a woman's garment.

At the root of all these seemingly senseless taboos lies the fear of the woman's sexual uncleanness—particularly of her menstrual functions.

This idea is not strange to us. We find it in the Old Testament. The menstruating woman is ritually unclean. So it was in the Law of Manu. She must keep apart, take no share in domestic activities. She should not show herself to any man, or speak to a man, or prepare food for others to eat. Her husband must not sleep with her in the same bed; or, even "though mad with desire," he must not have intercourse with her.

When her flow ceased the woman must bathe. That sounds simple enough. But the ceremonial seems to have become increasingly elaborate with the passing years. Here is how Dubois describes it in detail:

When a woman is in a state of periodical uncleanness, she is isolated in some place apart, and may have no communication with anyone during the three days that her defilement is supposed to last. The first day she must look upon herself as a Pariah. The second day she must consider herself as unclean as if she had killed a Brahmin. The third day she is supposed to be in an intermediate state between the two preceding ones. The fourth day she purifies herself by ablutions, observing all the ceremonies required on these occasions. Until then she must neither bathe nor wash any part of her body, nor shed tears. She must be very careful not to kill any insect, or any other living creature. She must not ride on a horse, an elephant or a bullock, nor travel in a palanquin, a dooly or a carriage. She must not anoint her head with oil, or play at dice or other games or use sandalwood, musk, or perfumes of any kind. She must not lie on a bed or sleep during the day. She must not brush her teeth or rinse out her mouth. The mere wish to cohabit with her husband would be a serious sin. She must not think of the gods or of the sun, or of the sacrifices and worship due to them. She is forbidden to salute persons of high rank. If several women in this unclean state should find themselves together in one place they must not speak to or touch each other. A woman in this condition must not go near her children, touch them or play with them. After living thus in retirement for three days, on the fourth day she must take off the garments that she has been wearing, and these must be immediately given to the washerman. She must then put on a clean cloth and another over it, and go to the river to purify herself by bathing. On her way there she must walk with her head bent, and must take the greatest care to glance at nobody, for her looks would defile any person on whom they rested. When she has reached the river she must first enter the water and fill the copper vessel, or chamber, which she has brought with her from the house. Then, returning to the bank, she must thoroughly cleanse her teeth, rinse out her mouth twelve times and wash her hands and feet. She must then enter the water and plunge twelve times into it, immersing the whole of her body. She must take the greatest care while doing this not to look at any living soul, and to this end each time her head rises above the water she must turn her eyes towards the sun. On coming out of the water she must take a little fresh cow-dung, some *tulasi* and some earth. These she must mix together in a little water, until they make a thin paste, and with this she must thoroughly rub her hands and feet and then her whole body. After this she must re-enter the water, and completely immerse herself twenty-four times. When she again leaves the water she must rub herself over with saffron, and again dip three times in the water. Then mixing saffron in a little water, she must drink some and pour the rest on her head, after which she must put on a pure cloth freshly washed and the little bodice called *ravikai*. She may then paint the little round red mark on her forehead called *kunkuma* and return home. On entering the house she must take special care that her eyes do not rest on her children, for they would thereby be exposed to the greatest danger. She must immediately send for a Brahmin *purohita* so that he may complete her purification. On his arrival this venerable person first plaits together thirty-two stalks of *darbha* grass, to make the ring called *pavitram*, which he dips in consecrated water that he has brought with him. The woman then takes another bath, drinks a little of the consecrated water, places the *pavitram* on the ring finger of the right hand, and drinks some *pancha-gavia* or some cow's milk. After these ceremonies her purification is complete.[15]

It seems unbelievable that the women of a household should have to go through this hocus-pocus every month. Fortunately for them this was not the case. The Hindu woman was seldom in this condition, because she was invariably pregnant!

If female sexuality threatened defilement, the exercise of the male sexual powers threatened debilitation. Throughout the entire East we found the view tenaciously held that loss of seminal fluid meant the loss of the man's strength and vitality.

"In youth," said Confucius, "when the physical powers are not yet settled, a man must guard against lust." One of the ancient commentators, Hing Ping, offers this interpretation: "Youth embraces all the period below 29. Then, the physical powers are still weak, and sinews and bones have not yet reached their vigor, and indulgence and lust will injure the body."

Manu likewise warns the young man against "wasting his manhood." This applies even to nocturnal emissions. "If he has involuntarily wasted his manly strength during sleep, he must repeat with reverence, having bathed and paid homage to the sun, 'Again let my strength return to me.'"

This idea was elaborated in the later writings. A modern Indian writer sums them up: "The Shastras truly say that those who commit sexual excesses give birth to infirm and defective children, lose their health very early in life, are rendered incapable of all physical and intellectual work, and in the end collapse like a tree that has been eaten up by canker inside."[16]

Even Gandhi, so wise and balanced in other matters, became obsessed with this idea. Sexual intercourse for any other purpose than procreation he regarded as "criminal waste of precious energy." He speaks of the "vital fluid" and adds, "A substance that is capable of producing such a wonderful being as man cannot but, when properly conserved, be transmuted into matchless energy and strength." From his own past experience he says that "sexual union in marriage was invariably followed by exhaustion." The man who can achieve complete continence "will be healthy and will easily live long. He will not even suffer from so much as a headache. Mental and physical work will not cause fatigue. He is ever bright, never slothful."[17]

That excessive preoccupation with sex can lead to moral and spiritual degeneration we do not question. But Gandhi was mistaken in interpreting this in physical terms. Modern sexologists have exploded the age-old fallacy that the sexual function can in any way be damaged by use. It has its own built-in safeguards against overstrain.

These false fears have flourished in the West too. William Acton, a distinguished English physician, wrote in 1875 concerning one of his patients, "His mind had become enfeebled, and there was great pain in his back. . . . I found that he had been in the habit of indulging in connection three times a week, without any idea

that he was committing an excess, or that his present weakness
could depend on this cause."

Sex is natural, asserts the East.

But sex is dangerous, too, it adds.

*   *   *

Katherine Mayo was an obscure American journalist when she
decided to go to India and gather material for a book. For six
months she traveled widely and worked hard. When the book
appeared in May 1927 it caused a sensation. It went through
six reprintings in its first six months.

The *Mother India* controversy shook the civilized world. For
several years it continued at fever heat. A spate of books and
articles appeared as "replies" to Katherine Mayo, who in turn replied to them in further books of her own. Much bitterness resulted.

Even when re-read after thirty years, *Mother India* is a shocking book. The thesis that caused so much indignation was that
India was a decadent country, rotten with sexual excess. This is
certainly the impression that the book conveys. Gandhi aptly described it as "A drain inspector's report." Everything in it might
be true, he said, but what was described was certainly not the
truth about India.

In fact, Hinduism has always emphasized sexual restraint.
Casual observers have been arrested by the Hindu emphasis on
sex as natural, and have missed the accompanying emphasis on
sex as dangerous. The Hindu philosophy of sex is based on an
attempt to hold these two ideas in balance.

The East has mistakenly stressed the physical dangers of sex.
But its real concern has been with the spiritual dangers. To the
world-denying religions of the East, sex was an enemy to be continually kept at bay. The road to salvation lay in the direction of
detachment from the material world by the renunciation of desire. This went against the pull of human nature; and often it was
the clinging tentacles of sexual desire that pulled hardest of all.

Buddhism solved this problem by insisting on celibacy in those
who devoted their lives to religion—as the Roman Catholic Church
has done in the West. Hinduism, however, took the harder way
of trying to achieve a life balanced between involvement and re-

nunciation. Thus, a Hindu temple can, without inconsistency, present the odd spectacle of erotic carvings on its walls, while celibate ascetics are prostrated in meditation below.

An Indian professor has thus expressed the Hindu dilemma: "At its lowest level of manifestation, *kama* is understood in the sense of pure sex drive, and is said to be one of the six enemies of a human being (lust, anger, greed, temptation, conceit and jealousy). But it is equally true that a human being cannot conduct his life without *kama*, which helps the propagation of the species."[18] The good of man therefore consists in the harmonious co-ordination of these two facts of sex. Hinduism has tried to achieve this in the following manner.

A man's life, once childhood is past, is divided into three separate stages. First, he becomes a *brahmachari*—a celibate student of the Vedas, the sacred books on which Hindu philosophy is based. This is a period of rigid discipline. Youth, it was argued, was the time to learn self-control, to gain mastery over the body and its urges.

The years of studenthood normally cover adolescence. In India early marriage is recommended for the girl, but not for the boy. During his teen years, and often his early twenties also, the boy is expected to observe strict continence. By restraining his sexual urges it was believed that he would increase his mental and spiritual powers. Some authorities enjoin him at this time not to look at a woman. According to Manu, even if he masturbates, he breaks the vow he has taken at his initiation as a *brahmachari*.

The student, Manu goes on, must learn to control the senses, as a charioteer controls his restive steeds. Desire is like a consuming fire. The more it is fed, the more powerful it grows. All religious rites, sacrifices and austerities are valueless if a man's heart is stained by sensuality. When a student loses control of any one of his bodily organs, all his wisdom will trickle away, as the water carrier will lose his water if there is a hole in his leather bag.

All Hindu boys, except those of the lowest caste, were expected to undergo these years of rigid discipline. Sexual abstinence was so basic that the years of studenthood came to be known as the period of celibacy.

Once the student has qualified, he is free to marry and become a householder. For many years he devotes himself to the task of establishing a family and begetting sons. Sex in this phase of life is entirely legitimate and good. It may be freely enjoyed, because this is the time and place for its proper exercise.

Yet even here the emphasis is on moderation. "Let a man not, from a selfish appetite, be strongly addicted to any sensual gratification," says Manu. And again, "In caressing women there is no turpitude; for to such enjoyments men are naturally prone; but a virtuous abstinence from them produces a signal compensation."

There are special times, too, for restraint. On no account may a man have intercourse with his wife while she is menstruating. The other occasions are related to the moon's phases. "On the dark night of the moon, and on the eighth, on the night of the full moon, and on the fourteenth, let a householder be continually chaste as a student in theology, even in the season of nuptial embraces."

Clearly there is no room for unbridled license here. A husband who wants to make full use of his sexual opportunities has to be well informed about his wife's menstrual cycle and to keep his eye on the calendar! If, however, he wishes to attain special merit, he may do so by accepting further restraints. "He who avoids conjugal embraces on the reprehended nights and on eight others, is equal in chastity to a *brahmachari*."

Gandhi favored an even stricter abstinence than this. In his autobiography he describes how he arrived at the decision to accept complete celibacy in marriage:

After full discussion and mature deliberation, I took the vow of *Brahmacharya* in 1906. I had not shared my thoughts with my wife until then, but only consulted her at the time of taking the vow. She had no objection. But I was hard put to it in making the final resolve. I had not the necessary strength. How was I to control my passions? The elimination of carnal relationships with one's wife seemed then a strange thing. But I launched forth with faith in the sustaining power of God.

As I look back upon the twenty years of the vow, I am filled with pleasure and wonderment. Before the vow I had been open to being overcome by temptation at any moment. Now the vow was a sure shield against temptation.

But if it was a matter of ever increasing joy, let no one believe it was an easy thing for me. Even while I am past fifty-six years, I realize how hard a thing it is. Every day I see more and more that it is like walking on the sword's edge, and I see every moment the necessity for eternal vigilance.[19]

It should be made clear that Gandhi, in accepting and advocating married celibacy, was going beyond anything that his Hindu faith enjoined. Yet his choice of the ascetic extreme is by no means out of keeping with the spirit of Hinduism.

When the householder reaches fullness of years, sees grandsons born to him and his hair turning gray, it is time for him to prepare himself for life's final phase. He returns now to the discipline of renunciation he learned in youth. Laying aside the desire for physical comfort and material security, he gives himself up to a life of prayer and meditation, accompanied by whatever rigors may be needed to school his spirit as it sets forth upon its ultimate task, the renunciation of all desire.

Who can say, in the light of these facts, that India is a land where sexual excess is either encouraged or condoned? In every culture there are individuals who go against the established codes, and periods when the codes fall into neglect. A drain inspector's report from any land on earth can be made to sound revolting.

* * *

In India, the vow of celibacy required of the young men, together with the practice of marrying off the girls soon after puberty, went a long way toward preserving sex morality.

In China and Japan the problem was more difficult. The boys, as the story of Chin Chung's escapade in the Water Moon Convent suggests, were regarded as hungry dogs straining at the leash, ready to seize any sexual opportunity that came their way. The girls, strictly trained to obedience, were poorly equipped, and often feebly inclined, to protect their chastity.

In these circumstances, society had to build up the strongest possible deterrents. The most elaborate efforts had to be made to keep boys and girls apart. The girls had to be induced not to give the boys the slightest encouragement. The boys had to be convinced that illicit sexual indulgences might bring on the most catastrophic consequences.

All these methods were employed. The separation of the sexes is basic to the Confucian concept of a well-ordered society. "The ceremonial usages," says the Li Ki, or Book of Ceremonies, "serve as dykes for the people against evil excesses. They exemplify the separation between the sexes which should be maintained, that there may be no ground for suspicion and human relations may be clearly defined. So it was intended to guard the people." This general principle is then spelled out in some detail. "Men and women, in giving and receiving, allow not their hands to touch. When a young aunt, a sister, or a daughter is wed, and returns to her father's house, no male relative should sit with her upon the mat." Again, the wise man should at all costs avoid the least possibility of suspicion. "One does not pay a visit to the son of a widow. Also, in calling upon a friend, if the master of the house be not at home, unless there be some great cause for it, the guest does not cross the threshold." The principle of separation is carried even to the point that a man was not permitted to die in the hands of women, or a woman in the hands of men!

Brothers and sisters, in some aristocratic Chinese homes, were separated at an early age. Kwei-Lan, in Pearl Buck's *East Wind, West Wind*, writes:

As little children my brother and I were ever together, and he it was who first taught me to brush the ink over the characters outlined in my primer. But he was a boy and I only a girl, and when he was nine and I six years of age, he was taken out of the women's apartments into those where my father lived. We seldom met then, for as he grew older he considered it shameful to visit among the women; and moreover, my mother did not encourage it.

I, of course, was never allowed into the courts where the men lived. When first they separated my brother from the women I crept once in the dusk of the evening to the round moon-gate that opened into the men's apartments; and leaning against the wall opposite it, I peered into the courts beyond, hoping to see my brother perhaps in the garden.

Suddenly I felt my arm sharply pulled. It was Wong Da Ma, my mother's chief servant, and she cried,

"Now will I tell your mother if I see this again! Who has ever seen before such an immodest maid to go peeping at the men?"

"I sought my brother only!"

But she answered firmly,

"Your brother now is also a man."

Therefore I seldom saw him again.[20]

The Confucian rule is that, after the seventh year, boys and girls should no longer sit near each other. In India rather more latitude is permitted. "But after a girl passes her tenth year she is strictly warned against free conduct with boys. The company of the very boys with whom, not long ago, she used to run and romp about, becomes anathema."[21]

This separation of the sexes is still widely practiced in the East. In many Christian churches, it is customary for men to sit on one side of the aisle and women on the other. Even in Japan, where Western ideas have become widely accepted since World War II, Cressy describes a government high school for girls that arranged an annual exhibit of the students' work. The girls were forbidden to invite even their fathers and brothers, and were told that this was "to avoid temptation." At another school, three girls were seen walking in the street with boyfriends. The girls were suspended for a month and later left the school.[22]

Similar stories could be told from all over Asia. The almost unlimited mingling of the sexes that is now the rule in the West is looked at askance by many Asians of otherwise liberal outlook. They regard it as unreasonable, in these conditions, to expect the preservation of premarital chastity. They would agree with Confucius, who said, "He who thinks the old embankments useless and destroys them, is sure to suffer from the desolation caused by overflowing water; and he who should consider the old rules of propriety useless and abolish them, would be sure to suffer from the calamities of disorder."

The Eastern devices set up to prevent young men and women being left alone together seem prudish to us. They are in fact based on realism. The Asian believes that without these safeguards there will, sooner or later, be an increasing incidence of illicit sex relations. This he does not wish to happen. He considers that if we in the West desire to preserve our traditional code of sex morality, we are going about it in a very unrealistic way.

As the fifteenth-century Indian poet Chandidas expressed it, "Who is able to make a frog dance in the mouth of a snake?" Or, in the words of a mother in modern Thailand, "When the sugar is near the ant, the temptation is too great."

*　　*　　*

In the wild there is a young lady
With thoughts natural to the spring,
And a fine gentleman would lead her astray.
She says, Slowly; gently, gently;
Do not move my girdle;
Do not make my dogs bark.

This poem, from the Book of Odes,[23] was written before 600 B.C. The girl is resisting the man's advances. She warns him that, if he persists, she will have to be offensive in voicing her objections. Her dogs will bark and drive him away.

The second line of defense, in the preservation of sex morality, was to train the girls so that, if they found themselves in moral peril, their dogs would be sure to bark.

This was not at all easy. When you have devised a system to train girls to be submissive and obedient in all other respects, how can you make them defensive in one particular situation?

This difficulty was well understood. In the great Indian epic, the Mahabharata, Bhishma observes that women possess a sensitive temperament which quickly responds to any offer of love or affection. In the same epic Chira-karin says, "Women can commit no sin. It is the man who becomes sullied with sin. Indeed, on account of the natural weakness of the sex as shown in every act, and their liability to solicitation, women cannot be considered as offenders."

A modern Indian agrees, but suggests that the woman behaves thus because she has been conditioned to do so. "Women's minds," says Professor Phadke, "are saturated with the idea that nature designed woman for the enjoyment of man, and that she has no other function than to serve him."[24]

The principal of an Indian girls' college had ample opportunity to observe the effects of this process of conditioning. She says:

The inbred submissiveness to masculine domination and the instinct to evade responsibility and leave it all with the man who gives the command which she obeys while knowing it is wrong, renders a girl helpless. . . . Her temptation does not lie in her own unruly passions, for practically every Indian woman would personally prefer what is customary and right; but she may be unable to resist the imperiousness of a man's call, even if she has no wish to follow it and shrinks from obedience almost as much as she shrinks from disobedience. And, if she does wrong, she will suffer from the consequences, but she will not have the added pain of remorse. The guilt and the sin lie with him who ordered her to do wrong; she is the victim of a cruel necessity.

She then gives this interesting illustration of her point:

The American teacher of philosophy was passing through the outer office late one evening, and paused near the foot of the stairs to read the extracts on the History Notice Board. While she studied these the telephone bell rang and aroused a student sitting absorbed in her books at the telephone table. It was Amala's turn just then to watch over the telephone at hours when the office clerks were not available. Amala was one of the best of the students of her time, and indeed it was only the best who were entrusted with this office. . . . Amala dutifully took up the receiver, and Miss Cleveland listened with approval to her slow distinct answers. "Yes." "Women's Christian College, yes."
"Please give your name." "No, the students do not use the telephone." "No, the students are not brought to the telephone." "No, it is forbidden." "It is forbidden; please give a message." "If you will give your name and a message, I will tell her this evening." "No, she cannot come to the telephone." This went on for a minute or two. Then Amala carefully laid the receiver on the table and rose from her chair. "Where are you going?" asked Miss Cleveland. "It's a man; he will not give his name; he wants me to fetch Rani Royappa, I suppose she is in the Library; I am going to see."
"Of course not, Amala, it is forbidden."
"But he says that I am to call her."
"But did you not tell him it is forbidden?"
"I told him that; I told him several times. But he insists."
Amala had nothing to gain by her obedience to the voice of the unknown man and nothing to fear if she disobeyed. But she felt she must do as she was told. . . . So deep-rooted is the habit of obedience to the voice of a man that she would not only have broken the rule, but she would also have endangered her own position as one of the telephone attenders, if another authority had not intervened. And when it is not a distant, unknown voice, but the overpowering bodily presence of one of the strong dominant sex, it is indeed too much to expect that a girl should find courage to refuse. . . .
It seems to be the actual voice of the man that is so dominating. It seems to penetrate to a very deep spring of action.[25]

It seems, then, that if the Chinese young lady of pre-Confucian days knew how to safeguard her virtue, Eastern girls born in the later era of feminine submission had lost the power to do so. The advances of the male failed to make their dogs bark.

So there was nothing for it but to preserve them from the advances of the male.

"Girls of marriageable age," said Shun-ko, Nora Waln's adoptive Chinese mother, "are as dangerous to the peace of a family as smuggled salt. Don't ever, while under my chaperonage, look at a man. Direct your gaze modestly to the ground when one is in front of you."[26]

She was merely echoing the age-old etiquette for Chinese girls, passed on generation after generation from mother to daughter:

Never move your knees when sitting, nor when standing shake your
　　dress;
Laugh not loud when pleased; when angry never talk with over-stress;
Let the sexes ne'er commingle, whether they be rich or poor;
Never go beyond the gateway, nor stand gazing from the door.

So it goes on, verse after verse. The girl committed it to memory. She also learned the stories of virtuous women that go with the rules of etiquette. A collection of these was made in 1591 by Lu Hsin-wu. Here is the substance of two of them:

1. A girl of 30 lived with her old mother. Never in her life had she spoken to a man. One day, while washing silk at the river's edge, she was startled to find herself addressed by an army officer of high rank, on horseback. He begged for food and drink, which she gave him.

He explained that he was fleeing from his enemies, and had lost his way. He asked her to direct him, which she did. He thanked her, and continued his journey.

Soon after, he returned. "You must tell no one you have seen me, or where I have gone," he said. "You need have no fears," she replied. "Never before in all my life have I spoken to a man. Now I am dishonored, and have no wish to live."

Taking up a large stone, and clasping it to her bosom, she threw herself into the stream, and was quickly drowned.

2. A maiden of Kao Yu found herself stranded in a swamp. The mosquitoes were ferocious.

An elderly gentleman invited her to share the protection of his mosquito net. But the maiden chose rather to spend the night outdoors among the reeds and rushes, where she was slowly stung to death by the mosquitoes. They sucked her blood so viciously that, in the morning, little was left but her skeleton.

This maiden's purity stands out in sharp contrast with the unworthy behavior of her sister, who basely accepted the gentleman's offer, shared his bed for the night, and survived.[27]

It is clear that a girl of any principle, once placed in a compromising situation, had nothing left to live for. She must be ready, says Lu, to use the white and shining knife without hesitation if the red blush of shame should be brought to her cheeks. Even though she is not to blame, because her weakness has been exploited, she still is not entitled to honorable survival.

> Ah, thou young lady,
> Seek no licentious pleasure with a gentleman.
> When a gentleman indulges in such pleasure,
> Something may still be said for him;
> When a lady does so,
> Nothing can be said for her.[28]

* * *

In 1937 a friend of Gandhi's, in a letter to him, narrated this incident: "About two and a half years ago this city was convulsed by a social tragedy. A Vaishya gentleman had a sixteen-year-old daughter. She had a maternal uncle aged twenty-one years studying in college in the same city. The two fell secretly in love with each other.

"The girl is said to have become pregnant. When the true state of affairs at last became known, the lovers committed suicide by taking poison. The girl died immediately, but the boy died a couple of days later in the hospital.

"Nobody had a kind word to say about the unfortunate lovers."

Was the behavior of this couple, in committing suicide, typical?

Not at all. Human beings do not necessarily act as their traditions seem to require. In China the girl who had lost her chastity was expected to take her life. She often did. But plenty of cases are on record where she went on living, kept her illegitimate child, and even found a man to marry her. The threat of a dire penalty for unchastity was a deterrent. But if it failed to deter, it was not necessarily carried out.

If that was true of the girl, it was much more true of the boy.

The young Indian who committed suicide probably did so out of love for the girl, and not because he feared retribution. The Law of Manu does not deal harshly with illicit sex. "He who vitiates a damsel without her consent shall suffer corporal punishment instantly: but he who enjoys a willing damsel shall not be corporally punished. If he makes love to a maid of equal rank, he shall give the nuptial gift and marry her, if her father pleases."

The fundamental basis of Eastern sex morality, in fact, was to preserve the chastity of girls so that they might be offered as virgins in marriage. Otherwise their chances of finding a husband were slender.

Society therefore concentrated its efforts upon restraining young men from having sex relations with girls whose prospects of marriage would be endangered thereby; or with women already married. If they involved themselves with women who had already lost their virtue, nobody was greatly concerned. The Code of Manu says explicitly that the penalties do not apply to incidents involving women of loose morals. "He who has a private connection with such women, or with servant-girls kept by one master, or with female anchorets of a heretical religion, shall be compelled to pay a small fine."

"A small fine." Clearly such offenses would be difficult to detect, and the likelihood is that the modest penalty prescribed would not often be imposed. In short, the East shrugged its shoulders nonchalantly so far as prostitution was concerned.

In fact, prostitution was probably welcomed, even if nobody said so out loud. In a social system as rigid as that of the East, it is impossible to restrain the sexual desires of individuals. The sexual instinct, it was believed, exercised a tyranny over men that few were able to resist. The story of King Pandu, told in the Mahabharata, is significant in this connection. Although he knew that he was under a curse, and would die the moment he entered into sexual union, he ultimately succumbed to the temptation.

The nature of patriarchal society inevitably created a certain number of sexually frustrated individuals. Where polygamy was practiced, there were often not enough women to go round. Some men had little or no chance of marrying at all. Despite the pleas of their religious leaders, not all of them were disposed to accept a life of celibacy.

At the same time, there were bored husbands whose obsequiously obedient wives offered them little stimulation, sexual or otherwise. These men craved occasional variety, excitement, romance. Wang Lung, in *The Good Earth,* when he had grown prosperous, began to leave his home in the evenings and to go into the town.

"Day after day he went to this tea shop and bought tea and sat alone and drank it, and stared at the pictures of the beautiful women. Up the narrow stairway, in the rooms above him, there were these women in flesh and blood, and men went up to them. And he looked at every painted face closely. And out of the score and more he chose three most beautiful, and out of the three he chose again and he chose one most beautiful. He stared at her and as he stared a heat likewise poured through his veins."[29]

The prostitute not only drained off the excess of male sexuality in the community. By doing so she also safeguarded the virtue of her more morally upright sisters. Her function, in the vivid phrase of Lecky, the historian, was to be "the eternal priestess of humanity, blasted for the sins of the people."[30]

Patriarchal society has always seemed to require, as one of its undesirable corollaries, some system of prostitution. In the West this fact was so unacceptable that it tended to be suppressed, and the business of buying sexual favors was driven underground. The East has been more willing to accept with resignation what seemed to be inevitable. Peter Schmid says, "Sex here is so free of all moral and social discrimination that even the haunts of sin breathe a charm of innocence, almost of respectability, which no one in Europe could possibly imagine. In Thailand those who are interested can buy a guide in the bookshops, published by the Central Trading Company, to these paradises of the young, beautiful nightingales of the night—together with the prices."[31]

*   *   *

One of the outstanding women of the Bible was named Rahab. Both in the Old and New Testaments, she is praised and held up as an example of deep religious faith. She was not a married woman. She was, in fact, a professional prostitute. No attempt is made to conceal this fact. The Bible refers to her as "Rahab the harlot."

To the Western mind, nothing is more degrading than for a woman to sell herself sexually to men. To the Eastern mind, this is not necessarily disgraceful. It may imply a high level of devotion, of cultural attainment, or even of religious consecration.

We must remember that until recent times almost all other doors were closed to the woman who did not wish to marry, or whose marriage for some reason did not succeed. Her opportunities to find gainful employment or social recognition were few and far between. There were normally only four occupations that she could follow—matchmaker, midwife, procuress, and prostitute. Some ability was needed for the first three. For the fourth, it sufficed that nature had made her a woman.

A girl might find herself alone in the world through no fault of her own. Her parents might die, or be too poor to keep her. She might be rejected by her husband—because she was childless, or for some other reason. Her husband might die and his family might turn her out. In any of these situations, her body was her only salable asset—all that stood between her and starvation. Thousands of women in the East have taken up prostitution because it was literally the only means of livelihood available to them. Who will censure them because in that predicament they preferred life to death?

Sometimes it was not for her own sake that a woman sold her body, but to earn food for her aged parents or for her children. In China and Japan, in times of famine, parents would feel justified in selling their daughters. A daughter herself might, in order to fulfill her duty of filial piety, sell herself to redeem her parents from financial ruin. Owners of brothels sometimes visited stricken families and suggested to the daughters that they would be acting nobly to take up the life of a prostitute and have their wages sent home. Dr. Allen Faust relates how a Tokyo social worker brought such a girl to a missionary. The girl was on her way to a brothel which had promised four dollars to her family. Social worker and missionary between them paid the money and found a husband for the girl, and she settled down to a happy married life.[32]

Kamala Markandaya tells the story of a South India family in desperate want. Ira, the daughter, can no longer bear to see her parents and her infant brother slowly dying of starvation. She makes her decision and tells her mother.

Her father came in from the fields at sundown as Ira was setting forth.

"Where do you go at this hour?"

"It is better not to speak."

"I will not have it said—I will not have you parading at night—"

"Tonight and tomorrow and every night, so long as there is need. I will not hunger any more."

"Like a harlot," he said. "A common strumpet."

Ira stood defiant before him, uttering no denial, plucking at the fringe of her sari.

"These are but words," she said at last. "There are others, kinder ones."

Well, we let her go. With her earnings she was able to buy rice and salt, and milk for the child, who was too weak for anything else.[33]

Prostitution may be undertaken for survival. Sometimes it may provide little more than that. The wife of an American doctor inquired in Bombay what common prostitutes were paid. The first floor girls, she was told, could command the equivalent of sixty cents a customer. Those on the top floor could be purchased for two cents.[34]

*   *   *

At the other end of the social scale are the geisha—"the proud and exquisite Geisha, married to their profession, with a Gräfenberg ring confined within the walls of their uteri, which keeps them sterile during their normal productive years."[35] They are the Eastern counterparts of the sophisticated Greek hetairae and the dazzling Roman courtesans of the ancient West, and cousins to the accomplished ganikas of India.

The "red-light district" of a Western city becomes the "gay quarter" in Japan. Prosperity brings to wealthy merchants and professional men the need for places of diversion. To meet this need, the functions of the prostitute were extended, and the brothel became a center of colorful social life, a luxurious place where men with money to spend, weary of their meek, submissive wives, might seek all kinds of entertainment—good food, good company, and good sport.

The prostitute in these plush establishments had to have much more to offer than sex. Indeed, her primary function shifted from sexual to social intercourse. In the upper brackets, she became a charming, cultured, and highly talented entertainer and hostess. Often she was trained in singing and dancing, polished in manners and witty in conversation. The derivation of the name "geisha" is interesting in this connection. It is simply the combination of *gei*, meaning "art," and *sha*, meaning "person."

An outstanding geisha could achieve considerable influence. She would be treated with great courtesy and respect. Her sexual favors were not lightly bestowed. She might even contrive to remain a virgin, for a geisha is not necessarily a prostitute.

The geisha have achieved a remarkable position in Japanese life. Outshining the timid, stay-at-home wives, they often set the fashionable standards for dress and hair styles, become the acknowledged authorities on flower arrangement and social etiquette. They have made themselves almost indispensable to the organization of successful parties. Kunpei Sheba, the Japanese editor, estimates that 90 per cent of geisha parties are paid for today by business firms or government offices. "A Geisha," he says, "is respectable enough to be seen at a garden party given by the prime minister."

Only a minority of Japanese prostitutes, obviously, are in this class. But in both China and Japan, the prestige gained by the great ladies who adorned the profession has cast reflected glory on their humbler colleagues. Even the slave girl at the highway inn, who doubles as waitress and kitchen help by day, and sleeping companion to her master's patrons by night, feels, as no Western prostitute could, that she belongs to the lower ranks of an honorable profession.

*   *   *

"Try to imagine what London would be like if in St. Paul's Cathedral, Westminster Abbey, and other leading churches large establishments of prostitutes had been kept for centuries past for the use of the clergy and worshipers.

"That would be parallel to the state of affairs actually existing in South India where the *Devadasis*, women and little children married to the god and maintained as prostitutes, have for many centuries been kept in the large temples."

In these words the Right Reverend Henry Whitehead, Bishop

of Madras for twenty-three years, commented on one of the baf-
fling problems raised in *Mother India*.

Much has been written about the Indian temple prostitutes that
is sensational and highly colored. Some of Katherine Mayo's
stories are obviously selected for the shock they are calculated to
impart to the reader. An impartial examination of the available
facts suggests that the institution began innocently enough, but
became degraded through the exploitation of the Brahmins.

Parents might, as an act of piety, dedicate a daughter to the
service of the gods. Originally, the girls seemed to have been
trained as temple attendants and carefully guarded. They minis-
tered before the shrine, wove sacred garlands, and performed
ritual dances.

It seems that the priests, realizing that these women offer
tempting possibilities of providing both sexual pleasure and income, began to seduce the devadasis, and the circle of their clients
gradually widened until they became, to all intents and purposes,
public prostitutes.

The Abbé Dubois, a keen observer, if not an entirely accurate
reporter, of Indian customs, gives us this account based on his
personal investigations in the early nineteenth century:

"The courtesans or dancing girls attached to each temple are
called deva-dasis (servants or slaves of the gods), but the public
call them by the more vulgar name of prostitutes. And in fact
they are bound by their profession to grant their favors, if such
they be, to anybody demanding them in return for ready money.
It appears that at first they were reserved exclusively for the enjoyment of the Brahmins. And these lewd women, who make a
public traffic of their charms, are consecrated in a special manner
to the worship of the divinities of India. Every temple of any importance has in its service a band of eight, twelve, or more. Their
official duties consist in dancing and singing within the temple
twice a day, morning and evening, and also at all public ceremonies. The first they execute with sufficient grace, although their
attitudes are lascivious and their gestures indecorous. As regards
their singing, it is almost always confined to obscene verses describing some licentious episode in the history of their gods."[36]

Religious prostitution is now a matter of past history in India.
There was nothing unique, or even unusual, about it, except its

survival there until comparatively modern times. It has frequently been found throughout the world, in many different cultures. It had its place in our own Western heritage. Some of the warnings of St. Paul to his converts, in which he urges them to avoid the sins of the flesh, were based on his awareness of the manifold temptations that daily assailed them. The Temple of Venus in Corinth, for example, is said to have been served in New Testament times by as many as a thousand religious prostitutes who were freely available to the worshipers.

*   *   *

The East has dealt with the problems of human sexuality in its own way, according to the knowledge it had. The picture is confused in detail. But taken as a whole it shows a good deal of restraint, and also a good deal of indulgence.

Our Western pattern could be summarized in much the same way. The Victorian gentleman appeared outwardly a model of austerity. Yet he too had access, through more private sources, to a printed publication similar to that which could till recently be purchased in Bangkok, directing him to the sources in which his sensual desires might be gratified at the price indicated. We do not have the geisha but we do have the call girl, who is a somewhat less refined person. We may have fewer brothels, but we offer our women so many opportunities of earning a livelihood in other ways, and our men so many sexual opportunities without the necessity of cash payment, that this fact does us little credit.

We undoubtedly understand sex better, in scientific terms, in the West. But this certainly does not mean that our emotional attitudes to it are healthier. And there is no convincing evidence that, for all our sophistication, we have learned to derive from sex, when it is legitimately enjoyed in marriage, any greater degree of fulfillment and delight than it brings to the Asian married couple.

Chapter 5

ROMANCE IS TOO DANGEROUS

In *The Allegory of Love*, C. S. Lewis suggests that St. Thomas Aquinas ignored the subject of romantic love in his writings for precisely the same reason that he ignored the steam engine—because he had never heard of either of them!

It is certainly not true, as many people in the West seem to believe, that the East has never heard of romantic love. To remove all possible doubt on this point, we begin our discussion with a brief Eastern anthology on the subject.

First, a love lyric from the Book of Odes, that rich treasury of ancient Chinese poetry. Written about three thousand years ago, it expresses the heartache that lovers feel when they are separated from one another.

> There he is gathering the dolichos!
> A day without seeing him
> Is like three months!
>
> There he is gathering the oxtail-southernwood!
> A day without seeing him
> Is like three seasons!
>
> There he is gathering the mugwort!
> A day without seeing him
> Is like three years!

The lovesick swain is a characteristic figure in romantic literature. Where can the West provide a better illustration than in *Dream of the Red Chamber*, where Pao-Yu declares his desperate attachment to the lovely but frail Black Jade:

"Dearest Mei-mei, later perhaps I will not be able to tell you how I feel, now I am taking courage to do so. If I die, at least

I will have expressed myself. I am sick, sick because of you, and do not dare to tell anybody. I shall recover my health only if you do. I do not forget you even in my dreams."

A Hindu poetess, Mira Bai, portrays for us in one verse the intensity and the completeness of love's self-surrender:

> Kanh have I bought; the price he asked I paid:
> Some cry, "Too great," while others jeer, "'Twas small":
> I paid in full, weighed to the utmost grain,
> My love, my life, my self, my soul, my all.[1]

Another Indian woman, Priyambada Debi, has portrayed vividly the depth of love's devotion, and the inevitable tragedy that shadows the perfection of its experience. Here is a translation from the Bengali in which she wrote:

> Dearest, I know that thy body is but transitory; that the kindled life, thy shining eyes, shall be quenched by the touch of death, I know; that this thy body, the meeting place of all beauty, in seeing which I count my life well-lived, shall become but a heap of bones, I know.
>
> Yet I love thy body. Day by day afresh through it have I satisfied a woman's love and desire by serving thy feet and worshipping thee. On days of good omen I have decked thee with a flower-garland; on days of woe I have wiped away with my *sari* end thy tears of grief.
>
> O my lord, I know that thy soul is with the Everlasting One, yet waking suddenly some nights I have wept in loneliness, thinking how thou didst drive away my fear, clasping me to thy breast. And so I count thy body as the chief goal of my love, as very heaven.[2]

Finally, here is a passage from the Ramayana, one of the two great Hindu epics. Rama is condemned to a fourteen-year exile in the forest. His devoted wife Sita (a model of ideal Indian womanhood) begs earnestly to be allowed to accompany him and share his sufferings. Nowhere in all the world's literature is the constancy and selflessness of love more magnificently expressed:

> Thou art my king, my guide, my only refuge, my divinity.
> It is my fixed resolve to follow thee. If thou must wander forth
> Through thorny trackless forests, I will go before thee, treading down
> The prickly brambles to make smooth thy path. Walking before thee, I
> Shall feel no weariness: the forest thorns will seem like silken robes;
> The bed of leaves, a couch of down. To me the shelter of thy presence
> Is better far than stately palaces, and paradise itself.

Protected by thy arm, gods, demons, men shall have no power to harm
me.
Roaming with thee in desert wastes, a thousand years will be a day:
Dwelling with thee, e'en hell itself would be to me a heaven of bliss.

Let no one dare to say, against the testimony of a vast literature
from which these fragments are taken, that the East does not know
or understand what love means.

*   *   *

Although the East understood and valued love, yet it outlawed
love. Why?

Because it valued marriage more.

This statement, to Western ears, sounds absurd. In the West
love and marriage have almost been equated. How could love be
hostile to marriage?

If by love we mean romantic love, the answer is that it could
be, and it was. That was why it was suppressed in the East.

It was not always suppressed. In China, in ancient times, tradition suggests that life was gay and carefree. The young people
had love affairs to their hearts' content. They arranged trysts, they
danced on the river banks or outside the city gates. Some of their
old songs of love and courtship remain and give us glimpses of
those ancient times.

But changes came. Confucius ushered in a new era. The new
poets were staid gentlemen who considered love an unworthy
sentiment. Love themes still appeared in the novels and short
stories. But they had to reflect the new dominant sentiment by
having unhappy endings. In the literature of China and Japan
romantic love is nearly always linked with tragedy.

"The China shaped by Confucius and his followers was not
propitious to love and courtship," says Olga Lang. "The stultifying
rules of propriety invented by old men now held sway."[3]

This is true, but it is only one side of the picture. The Confucian commentators suggest that, in the gay, earlier era, moral
standards were low and social life was in a state of disorder.
Confucius gave China a stable culture based on a stable family
life. It lasted, surviving many disturbances, at least two thousand
years. That was no mean achievement—even if part of the price
was that romantic love had to be suppressed.

India, likewise, has its tradition of an early age when romantic love flourished. "Indian literature," says Johann Meyer, "is filled with the most splendid love stories and descriptions of the passion of sex—the glowingly sensual and sweetly tender."[4] In the two epics—the Mahabharata and the Ramayana—these stories of love are everywhere to be found.

Vatsyayana, whose *Kama Sutra* is India's classic guide to the arts of love, discusses the gentle art of courtship, and gives the young man directions on how to win a maiden's heart. He should encourage her to join him in gathering flowers, and then make garlands with which to adorn her. He should shower upon her gifts that will be especially pleasing to her. He may invite her to join him in playing pleasant indoor games, and try to impress her by giving demonstrations of his athletic and artistic skills. Sending love letters will also stir her heart. When by these means he has gained her affection, the two, with the connivance of a few well-chosen friends, may make a rendezvous in the forest, and there exchange vows in a *gandharva* marriage. This completed, they would inform their parents and hope for the best!

In the *gandharva* form of marriage the couple chose each other on the basis of mutual love. Many of the heroines of the epic stories married freely the men of their own personal choice— Arjuna, Rukmini, Satyavana, Sakuntola, and others.

However, in India as in China, these pleasant practices were progressively discouraged. Manu denounced the *gandharva* marriage as being based on lust and therefore unworthy. He was voicing the attitude of the legal mind and of the priestly class. To put an edge on his denunciation, he warned that children born of this kind of marriage would be "cruel, and speakers of untruth, who hate the sacred law."

So romantic love was outlawed. When we seek the concrete reasons for which this was done, we find three of them. Romance, it was believed, led to sexual license; it encouraged unwise choices of marriage partners; and it undermined the stability of family life.

*   *   *

"Licentious youths and unchaste maidens all offer the apology that love of beauty is without lewdness and insist on the distinc-

tion between love and passion. What sophistry! Love of beauty
is lewdness; love itself is more so. The meetings at Wu-San and
the delights of cloud-and-rain* all began with the worship of this
abstract Beauty and this chaste Love."[5]

The speaker is the Goddess who officiated at Pao-Yu's initiation.
Her view of romantic love as a cloak for sexual desire would have
commanded widespread assent in China. Ideas of platonic or
purely spiritual love were viewed with scepticism. Romantic feeling was regarded simply as a ferment in the blood, activated by
biological urges. All love feelings between men and women point
to, and if not thwarted lead to, the same ultimate goal—sexual
union.

If then this was what young people were really after, it could
be arranged. Marriage could take care of all that. A man needed a
woman. A woman needed a man. All right, this need would be
met, in an orderly way that need not cause unnecessary dis-
turbance.

When Wang Lung had said to his father, "Am I never to have
a woman?" his father had stirred himself, and gone to the House of
Hwang, and asked if there was a slave to spare.

"Not a slave too young, and above all, not a pretty one," he had said.
Seeing his son's mutinous face he had cried out at him.

"And what will we do with a pretty woman? She will be for ever
thinking about clothes to go with her face. No, not a pretty woman in
our house."

Wang Lung knew that his father spoke well. Nevertheless he said,
"At least, I will not have a woman who is pock-marked, or who has a
split upper lip."

Well, the woman was not pock-marked nor had she a split upper lip.
Beyond this, Wang Lung knew nothing of the woman who was to be
his, except that on this day he could go and get her.[6]

The idea is that sexual desire is of itself almost impersonal. A
normal man will be able to satisfy his desire with almost any
woman. A normal woman will be able to respond to almost any
man—or at least to become pregnant by him, which is what really
matters. These are the fundamental realities.

To allow sexual appetite to go beyond this point, and to become
fastidious about its objects, is to invite trouble. It is to develop

* A figure used to symbolize sexual union.

luxurious tastes that disdain good wholesome bread and cry for cake. That is what romantic inclinations, if fostered, are apt to do. They encourage young people to want what they have no right to, what is against the moral code.

This attitude is rather like an extension of the incest taboo. All human societies have had to inhibit the stirring of sexual desire among men and women closely related to each other. To allow such feelings to develop would be explosively disruptive of family life. Similarly, in the closely knit Eastern pattern of social organization, the unhindered expression of sexual urges was regarded as a serious threat to law and order. And it was taken for granted that wherever romantic love took root, a harvest of sexual license would result. Professor Phadke does not mince matters when he says that the reason why many Indians are against the principle of marrying for love is that it is "bound to lead to the atrocious anarchy of sexual relations which is today observable in European society."[7]

Needless to say, the policy of suppression could not always hope to be successful. And in fact, some latitude was allowed—to men. The fact that prostitution was invariably associated with patriarchal society gave the man an opportunity to develop a glamorous love life outside his marriage, without violating his duty to his wife. In Chinese love stories, the courtesan is a more frequent heroine than the young marriageable girl. The house of prostitution, and the prostitute herself, set out, as we have seen, to create a romantic atmosphere, so catering to this need. It was not sex alone that a man sought along the "willow lanes" and in the exotic teahouse. He could have plain sex at home. What he wanted was sex in a romantic setting. And this was what the well-organized establishments set out to provide. That they did it successfully is indicated by the fact that the man often fell deeply in love with the courtesan and, if he could afford it, took her home to be his pampered concubine.

In Japan particularly, the tradition has persisted that a man have two kinds of relationship with a woman—the dutiful but unexciting obligation he owes to his wife at home, and the less inhibited romantic experience he enjoys, in his free time and on a recreational basis, at the geisha house.

But this was no more than a concession to the all-powerful male. And it was a concession to. weakness. Romantic feelings toward women in general were sternly discouraged. This was particularly true of Japan's warrior caste, the samurai. The Japanese code of chivalry differed markedly in this respect from that of the medieval knight errant in the West. "Though the Bushi was taught to protect the weaker of either sex, yet extreme severity and coolness of demeanor toward the fair sex was regarded as a proof of a man's martial endurance. He never performed his valiant deeds for such a fanciful reward as a woman's smile. Love was understood to be inconsistent with valor; attachment to a woman was feared as a discouragement rather than a stimulant to achievement."[8]

In short, the power a Delilah could exercise over a Samson was all too clearly understood!

Toward the woman there were no concessions. She was recognized to be the expert in this field. "The woman in Old India, as throughout the world, has far greater gifts for love than the man."[9] This made her a dangerous person. She could turn men's heads and divert them from their purposes. Therefore she must be restrained. She must be kept in subjection, lest by her amorous adventures and her romantic intrigues she throw society into chaos and disorder. History can record more than one instance of a glamorous woman who has done precisely that.

The East took all possible precautions to keep that kind of thing strictly under control.

> I pray you, Mr. Chung,
> Do not come leaping into my hamlet;
> Do not break my willow trees.
> Do I care for them?
> But I fear my parents.
> You, O Chung, are to be loved,
> But the words of my parents
> Are also to be feared.

> I pray you, Mr. Chung,
> Do not come leaping into my garden.
> Do not break down my sandal trees.
> Do I care for them?

But I dread the talk of the people.
You, O Chung, are to be loved,
But the talk of the people
Is also to be feared.[10]

*   *   *

Rabindranath Tagore, India's great poet and playwright, wrote:
"The way to marriage which is shown by the torchlight of passion has not for its goal the welfare of society, but the satisfaction of desire. In our *shastras*, therefore, the *Brahma* marriage is considered to be the best. According to this, the bride should be given to a man who has not solicited her. Marriage needs must be rescued from the control of the heart, and brought under the province of the intellect; otherwise insoluble problems will keep on arising, for passion reeks not of consequences, nor brooks interference by outside judges. For the purpose of marriage, spontaneous love is unreliable."[11]

The Chinese attitude is virtually the same. It is well summarized by Legge in his interpretation of the Confucian doctrine:
"Young people, especially young ladies, have nothing to do with the business of being married. Their parents will see to it. They have merely to wait for their orders. If they do not do so, but rush to marriage on the impulse of their own desires or preferences, they transgress the rules of Heaven, and violate the laws of their lot."[12]

Eastern marriage, as we shall see, is hedged about with many regulations concerning what is right and proper, and what is not, in the relative status of the partners. How could inexperienced young people understand all these matters? Love, it is said, laughs at locksmiths. It laughs, similarly, at differences of caste, of religion, of social status, and the like, which to the Eastern mind would make a union wholly unacceptable. It laughs at horoscopes that do not match. In fact, it makes nonsense of all the distinctions that society, rightly or wrongly, views as insurmountable barriers to a successful marriage.

Romantic love tends, also, to blind the partners to the realities about one another as persons. "Nothing except fear makes the heart beat as fast as love; and the faster the heart beats, the more our conscious thinking is obscured."[13] The traditional portrayal of Cupid, his eyes blindfolded, firing his arrows wildly in all di-

rections, reflects long centuries of bitter human expe
cultures where marriages often take place at an early
where opportunities are lacking for young people to g
quaintance close and continuous enough for first and even second impressions to be corrected, allowing youthful emotions to
be a factor in choice would be utter folly. "Early marriage, coupled
with an acceptance of the privilege to choose one's own mate,
spells youth running riot, matrimonially speaking."[14]

The Eastern view, therefore, is that romance is such an untrust-
worthy factor in choosing a marriage partner that it is best to
eliminate it completely. This lies behind the widespread custom
of not permitting the young people to meet until they come together on their wedding day. Once the principle of allowing the
feelings of the couple to enter into the process is granted, the fear
is that, like the camel permitted to insert its nose into the Arab's
tent, it will ultimately take over and become the only deciding
factor.

Does this mean that the East encourages loveless marriages?
Not at all. At no point does the Western mind more seriously fail
to understand the Eastern pattern. Though expectations may be
nothing like as high, most young people in the East look forward
to finding love in marriage, just as young people do in the West.
The difference lies not in the goal, but in the way in which it is
hoped to attain it.

"In the West you fall in love, then marry. In the East we marry,
then fall in love." That is how the Asian describes the difference.
In a discussion in which we participated in Hong Kong, one
speaker used the analogy of the kettle on the fire. "When marriage begins in the West," he said, "the fire is roaring and the
kettle is boiling. From that time on the water gradually gets colder
and colder. When our Eastern marriages begin, the fire is low and
the kettle is cold. But as time goes on, the fire burns brighter, the
water gets hotter, and the couple feel that their marriage is getting
better and better every day!"

An interesting commentary on this idea is found in the story
told in *The Fortunate Union*. Ping Hsin and Tieh Chang-yu were
afraid that they had been disqualified for marriage because they
had unfortunately met and fallen in love beforehand! Only when
their parents overruled them, and insisted that there was no rea-

son why the marriage should not succeed despite the fact that they were already in love, were they reassured!

Tagore explains how the Indian girl, as she grows up, is encouraged to look forward to love in her marriage, but not to allow this desire to be focused in advance on a particular man. "From their earliest years, the husband as an ideal is held up before our girls, in verse and story, through ceremonial and worship. When at length they get this husband, he is to them not a person but a principle. And if the husband is a man of sensitive soul the flame of this ideal love is transmitted to his own life also. Such mutual illumination it has often been our lot to witness."[15]

Raziyya Begam, an Indian poetess of the thirteenth century, expresses this attachment to her future husband from the woman's point of view:

"Without seeing thy face I have given thee a place in my own eye, like the pupil.

"I have only heard thy name and I love thee. I have not seen thee, and yet I love thee as if I had seen and known thee."

We are all aware that young people build up in this way idealized images of the perfect mate. In the West today we allow them to project this image upon a number of actual persons, one after the other, searching for the one who comes nearest to identification with the ideal. But these experiences can be disturbing and confusing. And there is always the question, how many possible candidates should be passed under review before a choice is finally made? Moreover, when the chosen partner is settled upon, there may be painful awareness that he lacks qualities that have been encountered and enjoyed in others who were rejected.

The Indian girl never experiences uncertainty because she does not have to choose. She has only to give the love of her full heart, unhesitatingly and completely, to the one chosen for her. She is brought up to believe that she will inevitably develop love for any man who is kind to her, and that the way to make him kind is to give him unstinted devotion and adoration.

Which of these two approaches to marriage is most likely to lead to a successful union? That is a question not easily answered. The Westerner who considers the answer to be a foregone conclusion still has much to learn.

* * *

A boy and girl who were members of a Christian church in Korea fell in love and met secretly on a number of occasions. When their romance was discovered, they were turned out of the church. They had done nothing morally wrong by our standards. What was wrong by Korean standards was that they were in love. Even when, later, they wished to be married, the pastor refused them a Christian ceremony.

This incident puzzled us until we found the following statement in a study of Korean family life: "A romance between a boy and a girl is regarded as most disgraceful and sinful. Any type of love that would lead to marriage is supposed to be unfilial to the parents."[16] The code of the Yi dynasty, which continued in Korea until 1910, declared a love marriage to be illegitimate and subject to severe punishment.

A Chinese girl, quoted by Nora Waln, speaks scathingly of "the degeneracy to which the West has sunk, in putting its faith in propinquity, and the biological urge, for the continuation of the race. Marriage," she asserts, "is not a relation for personal pleasure, but a contract involving the ancestors, the descendants, and the property."[17]

It is quite clear that the sentiment of romance could easily become the deadly enemy of filial obedience, and that this could set up tensions that would be deeply destructive of family unity. Mencius sternly warns young people not to try to get in touch with one another, even if they know that their parents are in process of arranging a marriage between them. "If the young people, without waiting for the orders of their parents, and the arrangements of the go-between, shall bore holes in the fence to steal a sight of one another, then their parents and other people will despise them."[18]

It is a rigid principle of Eastern life that the stability of the family, and the maintenance of the social order, always come before the happiness of the individual. Romantic love is an unruly emotion, which out of control can do as much damage as uncontrolled anger. It has its rightful place within the marriage relationship. Anywhere else it is a menace.

In the large Eastern family, the growth of wayward impulses between men and women all too often shattered the peace of the household. In *Dream of the Red Chamber*, there are several such intrigues. Chia Jui, for instance, develops an infatuation for Phoenix, whose husband is away from home. Twice she lays traps for him to bring him to his senses. She arranges to meet him in an open passageway after dark, and he finds himself locked out and shivering with cold all night. Undiscouraged, he agrees to meet her again in a lonely room, where two of the men, following her instructions, deal firmly with him.

When he thought of Phoenix's treachery, Chia Jui resolved never to have anything to do with her again; but then he would see Phoenix's image before him, lovelier than ever and all the more desirable now that he knew that she had never cared for him. He told himself that he would gladly die if he could have her in his arms for one brief moment.

This proved only the beginning of his real troubles. His desire stimulated by the constant image of Phoenix, he gave way to evil habits and slept but poorly. The two nights of exposure produced their effects, and he soon took to bed.

One day a lame Taoist priest came asking for alms. He looked at Chia Jui and said, "I have a magic mirror here which will cure you. It is intended for youths such as you. Do not look into the right side. Use only the reverse side of the mirror."

Chia Jui looked into the reverse side as the Taoist had directed. He threw it down in horror, for he saw a gruesome skeleton staring at him through its hollow eyes. Then he thought he would see what was on the right side. When he did so, he saw Phoenix standing there and beckoning to him. Chia Jui felt himself wafted into a mirror world, wherein he fulfilled his desire. He felt exhausted by the experience, but he could not resist the temptation of looking into the right side again. Again he saw Phoenix beckoning to him and again he yielded to the temptation. This happened three or four times. When he was about to leave the mirror on his last visit, he was seized by two men and put in chains.

"Just a moment, officers," Chia Jui pleaded. "Let me take my mirror with me." These were his last words.[19]

This story portrays well the damaging consequences that could result from romantic attachments developing within the large household. Had Phoenix yielded to Chia Jui's entreaties, the situation would have been even more serious. Nora Waln tells how, while she dwelt in the House of Lin, Ko-nen, a young wife whose husband was away from home, became involved in an affair with an unmarried cousin of twenty-two who also lived in the household. As a result she became pregnant. By Chinese law no action could be taken till her child was born.

In the fullness of time she delivered a boy without pain. At breakfast call next day, when her serving woman took her gruel, Ko-nen had swallowed gold and given gold to her child. Beautiful, as all love children seem to be, he rested in the curve of his mother's arm.

Sin in a son can rot the foundation of a homestead and bring a family to corruption. The most insidious of sins is to trespass beyond the Orchid Door.

He who was suspected of knowing the wife of his cousin was brought to audience with his assembled kindred. He was denounced by his nearest of kin—his own mother. He had been a well-loved lad. But his guilt was beyond doubt, and among the Lins there was not one dissenting voice.

Disinherited, he was sent forth from the homestead, doomed forever to use only the name "outcast" with no place to lay his body in the earth among kindred, or to set his spirit tablet—and no rights in the patrimony, either for himself or for his descendants, beyond the cotton gown and straw sandals in which he was dressed, and the packet of rice, food for three days, tied to his shoulder.[20]

Order had to be maintained in the family, and in the community. Experience had taught that the consequence of romantic love, all too often, was the destruction of order. Love was good, and love was valued, in its right place. That place was within marriage. Before marriage, and outside marriage, love must be sternly suppressed.

*   *   *

The attempt to suppress romantic love has not been easy. And it has not been successful.

Some years ago newspapers all over Japan headlined the story of a Christian boy and girl who took part in a suicide pact. The couple had fallen deeply in love. For social reasons, their parents had refused to let them marry and had forbidden them to continue their association.

Secretly they arranged to meet on a lonely mountainside. Here they drank poison together. When their bodies were found, the girl was in bridal attire; they were garlanded with flowers; and beside them was a message that said, "We go to heaven together, to marry in the presence of God."

Love suicides in Japan have been an institution since the end of the seventeenth century. They have figured in scandal sheets and in romantic tales, and have been top news. At one time, they became so frequent that in 1722 plays depicting love suicides were for a time officially prohibited. Those who made unsuccessful suicide attempts were severely punished, and the corpses of the successful ones were publicly exhibited, like those of common criminals.

In plays and stories, the suicide pact has been dramatized with sensational effect—the journey together to the chosen place, the leaving behind forever of familiar scenes, the agonizing mental conflicts, the last tender farewells.

In Japanese thought, suicide is not ignoble. It is the final vindication of what a man believes. When it is glorified by frustrated love, it becomes a sublime tragedy. According to the Buddhist tradition, in the Lotus Sutra, the lovers who died together would be reborn on the same lotus calyx, on the lake before Amida's throne in the Western paradise. So the lovers believe that they are leaving behind the scene of their sorrows and frustrations, to gain perpetual union and bliss in the next life. The love suicide was thus surrounded by a religious aura that almost sanctified it.[21]

In olden times, the lovesick couple would sometimes throw themselves into the well of the parents who had refused to sanction their marriage. In the modern era, they would tie themselves together and throw themselves in front of a train. Jumping off a cliff has always been a popular method, and on some railroad routes any young couple who took one-way tickets might be under suspicion. At one time the taking of rat poison gained great popularity, and the drugstores were warned not to sell it to young people.

The defiance of young lovers did not always take such extreme form as this. In countries where the social system was less rigid— Burma and Thailand, for instance—elopement was quite common. Usually, when presented with a *fait accompli*, the parents relented and accepted the inevitable.

With the increasing infiltration of Western ideas, the struggle to suppress romantic love has steadily lost ground. Hollywood movies have had a profound effect on young people in the East. At first, parents made every effort to keep their sons and daughters away

from such evil influences. When this proved fruitless, efforts were
made to have the films modified to suit Eastern ideas.

One consequence of Asian attempts to suppress romance has
been a violent opposition to all public demonstrations of affection.
It is almost amusing for a Westerner to watch love scenes acted
by classical dancers in India or Thailand. The lovers will go
through a seemingly endless pantomime of writhing movements,
gazing longingly at each other, sighing deeply, stretching out
their arms yearningly to grasp the air—but never touching one
another.

To audiences accustomed to this degree of restraint, the behavior of our forthright and full-blooded movie stars is nearly as
shocking as it would be for us to watch them engaging in sexual
intercourse. Consequently the operator at a showing of a Western
movie had to negotiate a fadeout whenever the lovers kissed each
other. If he omitted to do this, cries of rage and indignation would
arise from the audience, and any women present would bury their
faces in their hands.

So great is the aversion to expressions of affection that a husband who spoke tenderly to his wife, or took her hand lovingly in
his, might be exposed to pitiless ridicule by his relatives and
friends. Dr. Francis Hsu tells the story of a modern young Chinese
couple from Hong Kong who, in the early 1940's, went to a town
in Yunnan for their honeymoon. The young bride and bridegroom
committed the serious indiscretion of walking hand in hand together down a narrow street. The local residents were so incensed
at this shockingly improper behavior that the next time they appeared, the hapless couple had a bucket of excrement poured
over their heads![22]

This kind of violent opposition has now been considerably
modified. In Eastern cities today, Western movies are shown un-
altered. Indeed, the Western trend is influencing Eastern habits.
Traditional Japanese plays and movies with romantic themes
were supposed to end in tragedy. The advertisements would emphasize their emotional intensity by advising patrons to bring an
extra handkerchief! A Tokyo paper a few years ago introduced a
novel variation of the usual promotional approach by announcing
"This picture will make you cry pleasantly."

Happy endings are now in vogue! The day of the love suicide may soon be over.

*   *   *

It is one thing to watch romance on the screen. It is something else again to be personally involved.

On a beautiful evening we were taken for a stroll in the famous Hanging Gardens of Bombay. As the brief Indian twilight faded, the white lamps shone out along the curve of the city's splendid marine drive—the "pearl necklace," as they aptly call it. In the park, thousands of colored lights in the trees created the atmosphere of fairyland. Colored fountains poured glittering columns of cascading water high into the air. Haunting Indian music was wafted on the cool, gentle breeze.

In such a setting, in the West, the park would have been filled with courting couples, hand in hand and arm in arm. As we wandered round for nearly an hour, we observed closely the crowds of people around us. There were groups of men, groups of women, parents with children. But not a single boy-girl pair. Such a spectacle would still offend the sensitivities of most Eastern cities.

So love is still a dream for Eastern youth. A boy and a girl may venture to look affectionately at one another, but they would be too overcome with emotion to put their feelings into words. To avoid embarrassment, they might have recourse to writing love letters. This is a tremendous craze in Eastern schools. Students found writing or receiving such incriminating documents are liable to be severely punished. But the traffic in love letters still goes on.

The following poem was written by a Japanese wit:

> High school girl, beautiful as a flowery bud,
> Before her parents writes a love-letter in English.
> The parents, not knowing it to be a love-letter,
> Praise her for studying so diligently.

Professor Embree dryly comments, "About the only use a young farm girl ever gets out of her education is the ability to write a misspelled love letter."[23]

As more and more young people get education, they are using it not only to write, but to read. Romantic literature patterned on the Western ideas is especially popular. In Rangoon, for example, girls in charge of street stalls may be seen reading when no customers require their attention. The literature that so engrosses their attention is the two-cent novelette. The stories "were largely drug-like and pornographic in nature. There was a great trade in them, about 30,000 being sold annually in Rangoon. Hawker boys went round to houses, selling them at two cents each, returning the next week to buy the used copies for one cent and selling a fresh lot."[24]

English and American magazines, with their "frank, outspoken articles," their sexy advertisements and illustrations, are eagerly devoured by questing Asian youth, who view them as products of an "emancipated" society.

In "progressive" student groups, Western ways begin to be copied—clumsily at first, but with increasing boldness. Here is an account from a college campus in Burma that plainly shows the transitional process:

"Sentimental love flourished. It surged among all the back benches of the lecture rooms and flowed into the corridors where the poor stricken couples blushed and spoke in whispers in spite of the applause of all passers-by. It flowed along the shores of the Inya Lake on whose banks the girls walked in groups of two or three after their evening bath and toilet, and the youths walked in other bands until they met and spoke to the girls."[25]

And here, from Lahore, Pakistan, is another kind of manifestation of the same trend:

The wide-eyed college youths were riding their bicycles, following as usual the carriages of young women. Most kept a respectful distance, but some bold ones were holding on to the carriages with one hand and their cycles with the other. They were singing songs about unrequited love, making the women grow angry or giggle. One came and hung on to our carriage. It was lucky for him that my father or uncle was not with us, for there would not have been much left of him or his silly song—

> Black eyes with veiling lashes, silently questioning:
>   What do you ask of me?
> Black eyes dreaming of love, lingering on my lips,
>   Feeling the shape of them.

Here my friend interrupted him: "Go away, you silly boy." But he continued—

> Black eyes dreaming of love, I am seeking my only one.
> I know not her smile,
> I know not her ways,
> But I shall know her whenever we meet.

"Shameless, isn't he?" said my friend. I agreed, but the youth just grinned.[26]

Where are these trends leading the East? The age-old battle to suppress romanticism is steadily being lost. It is hard to imagine what would happen if the flood gates, long held closed, were now to burst open. Our flexible Western society has been able so far, though not without difficulty, to cope with the consequences of youth's unrestrained freedom. But how would the East, with its rigid conservatism, handle such an avalanche? How would it react to free dating between boys and girls, and to all that would inevitably follow—the necking and petting; the premarital intercourse; the shotgun weddings, illegitimate births, abortions; the rising tide of divorces and broken homes. For these are, directly or indirectly, the consequences of romance rampant. The East has known this, in its heart, for more than two thousand years. To avoid these things, it has tolerated many abuses—harsh discipline, and denial of personal freedom—because they seemed to be the inevitable price of social stability.

Can the East hold the line? Or must it capitulate, and start again on a different and more dangerous way?

Chapter 6

WHO PICKS YOUR PARTNER?

When Madame Wu arrived in Washington, D.C., where her husband had been appointed China's new minister to the U.S.A., a press reporter asked her for her views on love and marriage.[1] The following conversation took place:

"Suppose the man picked out for you doesn't tally with your ideal?"

"My what?"

"Your ideal; all women have ideals, you know."

"I don't know that. I guess not Chinese women."

"Didn't you ever wonder what he would be like?"

"No. Chinese girls no time think about love. Before time comes think about love, Chinese girl has husband."

"Suppose you didn't like the husband picked out for you?"

"But I did. I loved him when I saw him."

"Which wasn't till your wedding day?"

"No."

"Suppose it hadn't been Mr. Wu, but somebody else—would you have loved him?"

"I would love the husband my parents choose; that is my duty. But they not choose anyone else for me. In China we believe in fate. Every couple that ought to marry is tied together with an invisible red string. So when parents make arrangements, fate leads. Matches are made in moon. So it always is right. Fate make one certain man for each woman."

The smiling, imperturbable Madame Wu was speaking for more than two thousand years of Eastern experience. She was not impressed by Western ways.

"Americans love and marry and get divorce," she added. "We

marry and love and get home and happiness and children. Which
way you like?"

Madame Wu spoke, however, for a generation now grown old.
In India, in 1954, we met the new generation.

"Tell us," said Kusima, "about the young people in the West.
We want to know how *they* get married."

Night was falling at the close of a sultry Indian day. A cool,
refreshing breeze playfully caressed the glittering black tresses
of the girls' hair and set their gay saris fluttering. All teen-agers,
they had been invited along by our host because we had expressed a desire to know what Indian young people thought about
love and marriage. The girls, ten of them, were squatting on the
veranda floor in a wide circle. Being awkward Westerners who
couldn't sit comfortably on folded legs, we had been provided
with low stools.

We gave as good an account as we could of how our young
people are free to meet each other and have dates; how a boy
and girl will fall in love; and how, after a period of going steady,
they become engaged and then get married. We knew that young
people in the East live a very restricted life, and have their marriages arranged for them by their parents, so we felt a little relieved that they had chosen to question us about our delightful
romantic traditions. We didn't want to make them *too* envious,
but we naturally were glad to demonstrate our superiority in this
matter of finding a mate.

When we had finished, there was a meditative silence. Con-
cluding that they had been impressed, we decided to start a
discussion.

"Wouldn't you like to be free to choose your own marriage partners, like the young people do in the West?"

"Oh no!" several voices replied in chorus.

Taken aback, we searched their faces.

"Why not?"

"For one thing," said one of them, "doesn't it put the girl in a
very humiliating position?"

"Humiliating? In what way?"

"Well, doesn't it mean that she has to try to look pretty, and
call attention to herself, and attract a boy, to be sure she'll get
married?"

"Well, perhaps so."

"And if she doesn't want to do that, or if she feels it's undignified, wouldn't that mean she mightn't get a husband?"

"Yes, that's possible."

"So a girl who is shy and doesn't push herself forward might not be able to get married. Does that happen?"

"Sometimes it does."

"Well, surely that's humiliating. It makes getting married a sort of competition in which the girls are fighting each other for the boys. And it encourages a girl to pretend she's better than she really is. She can't relax and be herself. She has to make a good impression to get a boy, and then she has to go on making a good impression to get him to marry her."

Before we could think of an answer to this unexpected line of argument, another girl broke in.

"In our system, you see," she explained, "we girls don't have to worry at all. We *know* we'll get married. When we are old enough, our parents will find a suitable boy, and everything will be arranged. We don't have to go into competition with each other."

"Besides," said a third girl, "how would we be able to judge the character of a boy we met and got friendly with? We are young and inexperienced. Our parents are older and wiser, and they aren't as easily deceived as we would be. I'd far rather have my parents choose for me. It's so important that the man I marry should be the right one. I could so easily make a mistake if I had to find him for myself."

Another girl had her hand stretched out eagerly.

"But *does* the girl really have any choice in the West?" she said. "From what I've read, it seems that the boy does all the choosing. All the girl can do is to say yes or no. She can't go up to a boy and say 'I like you. Will you marry me?' can she?"

We admitted that this was not the done thing.

"So," she went on eagerly, "when you talk about men and women being equal in the West, it isn't true. When our parents are looking for a husband for us, they don't have to wait until some boy takes it into his head to ask for us. They just find out what families are looking for wives for their sons, and see whether one of the boys would be suitable. Then, if his family agree that it would be a good match, they arrange it together."

This lively discussion gave us a good deal to think about. It was our first visit to the East. In our innocence, we had simply assumed that, because we in the West are so far advanced in technology and research, in medical and social services, in educational facilities and standards of living, we must naturally also have superior attitudes to love, marriage, and family relationships. We knew that arranged marriages had once been the rule in some of our Western lands, but that they had been given up in favor of free individual choice. It had seemed so obvious that this was a manifestation of human progress that we had simply taken it for granted. We did not for one moment consider that there was anything to be said on the other side.

* * *

"When parents make arrangements, fate leads," said Madame Wu. In other words, mate selection in the East has a religious basis.

Not all Asians are as sure as Madame Wu about the invisible red string—that fate ordained "one certain man for each woman." But most of them profoundly believe that the number of suitable partners is strictly limited, and that the supernatural powers will visit dire penalties on a union concerning which they have not been consulted.

The time-honored way of avoiding this danger has been to call in the astrologer. In *The Illustrated Weekly of India* on February 2, 1958, a Readers' Forum printed a series of letters from readers on this subject. Here is part of one of them:

"It can be safely assumed that every second Indian believes in astrology, and swears by it. Horoscope-agreement must precede matchmaking in most Hindu marriages.

"The marked relationship which exists between the movement of the stars and terrestrial objects has been proved beyond doubt. Since the universe we live in is not chaos, but cosmos, what happens in other parts of the universe must have its repercussions on the inhabitants of the earth also.

"Women, for example, are much affected by the phases of the moon. Their menstrual cycle follows the pattern of the moon.

"A closer study of the phsyical and mental make-up of man and wife, and of agreement between parents and children, would reveal that planets and stars play a decisive role. Even though planets may not decide a man's career, they certainly indicate his fate, as a thermometer does temperature."

Another correspondent relates the following story:

"A girl was in the marriage market; astrologers read her horoscope and said she must not be married for the next two years, else she risked bringing deaths in the new family, and herself faced the prospect of widowhood. Old in limb, and weak in mind, her father, nothing daunted, set about finding a husband for her. One day, while going out, he slipped down the stairs and suffered a fractured arm! None the less, arm in sling, he ventured forth and, at long last, forged an alliance. Four days later, the boy's aunt died, suddenly, and the engagement was called off.

"Unwilling to accept defeat, the father arranged yet another match. The boy lost his mother on the eighth day of his engagement. Disbelieving the astrologers, however, the boy celebrated his marriage next summer. His father lost his eye, having his optic nerve snapped within three months of the event. Six months later, the girl lost her father, suddenly. Eight years later she lost her husband. What the astrologers had indicated from the start thus came to pass."

In the face of such opinions as these, the folly of defying the fates is plain to most Asians. It is obviously wise to take no chances, but to base the choice of marriage partners on the matching of their horoscopes. This has been the traditional practice. "The most determining factor in match-making," says Professor Phadke, "is not the fitness or unfitness of the parties, but the fitness of their horoscopes. An irrevocable ban is put on the union of two persons if the astrologer fails to find any harmony in their horoscopes, no matter how ideally fit and worthy of each other they may really be."[2]

How is this matching process carried out? In the East care is always taken to record the precise hour of a child's birth. When the marriage of a boy and girl is considered, the animals which, in zodiac symbolism, represent their dates of birth are considered together, to determine whether they are compatible. The tiger or serpent, for instance, would be likely to devour the sheep or dog, so that combinations of this kind should be avoided.

The relation of birth dates to the so-called "Five Elements"—

Metal, Wood, Water, Fire, and Earth—may also be determined. Certain combinations of these elements are propitious, others unpropitious. Here, for instance, is a possible couple:

Young Man

YEAR—Far-flowing Water
MONTH—Divine-river Water
DAY—Great Post-station Earth
HOUR—Sand-surrounded Earth

Young Woman

YEAR—Sand-surrounded Metal
MONTH—Brook-lower Water
DAY—Sand-surrounded Earth
HOUR—Divine-river Water.

The verdict on this particular couple is, alas, that they are unsuited to each other, and should not marry!

It can be seen that the astrologer's task is a complex one—so complex that mistakes can be made, and authorities can disagree. This offers some advantages. While in general parents in the East abandon a proposed match if the horoscopes of the couple seem to clash, it is sometimes possible, by calling in further expert opinion, to get a favorable verdict on a marriage that is otherwise very much desired.

This system has another practical advantage. If the marriage doesn't turn out satisfactorily, the family need not lose face. Obviously the astrologer must have been careless or inefficient in his matching of the horoscopes!

*   *   *

Next to fate, in deciding who shall marry whom, comes the approval of the families concerned—and that may include the ancestors!

"Marriage," Shun-ko explained, "is a contract between two families and must be made with the free consent of both. A maid is wed in accord with the wisdom of her clan. We are careful to have our descendants mate well. The name of Mai-da's proposed husband will lie with her name for three days on our family altar. Mai-da's name will lie with his name for three days on his homestead family altar. Only if there is peace in both households during this time will the considered alliance go further. If criticism of their union be spoken in either homestead, the matter will be dropped. But as the cards are on the altar no person will speak without real concern."[3]

What sort of qualities are families looking for? Pick up almost any Indian newspaper, and turn to the "Matrimonial" section. Here are a few typical extracts, taken at random from *The Times of India* and *The Hindu* in January 1957:

Wanted an educated, fair and beautiful girl aged 18/20, for a fair, good-looking, educated, rich Brahmin youth aged 23.

Wanted educated, well-established youth to marry a healthy, smart Saiva Vellala (Mudaliar) vegetarian girl of respectable family, aged 17. Reply with details and horoscope.

Very fair, charming bride, preferably music-knowing, no dowry. Brahmin or any high caste, for handsome bachelor, over 1,000 rupees per month, strict teetotaller, non-smoker, vegetarian.

Correspondence invited from Brahmin family regarding medical or engineering graduate between 23 and 28 for accomplished very good-looking girl from very respectable family; and an accomplished very good-looking educated girl for her brother 26, chartered accountant, well started and with substantial property.

Wanted fair Dakhni girl below 20 to marry respectable, fair and tall Dakhni Muslim graduate, aged 25, holding responsible position in leading firm with income 850 rupees per month, with car and still brighter prospects.

Social status clearly takes precedence. In India and Ceylon this means caste. The ironclad tradition permitted a man to marry only a woman of his own caste, or of a lower caste in certain circumstances.

As caste barriers begin to disappear, other factors define status. "Respectable family" is the phrase that constantly recurs. It includes such assets as wealth, standing in the community, cultural and educational attainments, rank, business and professional prestige, and the like.

Another factor is that the couple should not be related within the forbidden degrees of *kinship*. "Within the caste, but outside the clan" is the general rule for finding a marriage partner in India. The rule does not hold absolutely, however. Its possible modifications and variations open up a very complex subject.

In China, no exceptions have been permitted. "A man in taking a wife," said Confucius, "does not choose one of the same surname as himself." This has been strictly followed in Chinese practice. According to tradition, there are only a hundred surnames. Actually, there are nearer five hundred.[4] In Korea, where the same principle applies, the situation is confused because the same clan name may be shared by unrelated kinship groups. The notorious case is the Kims, of whom there are about eighty distinct clans. A visitor to Korea may easily form the impression that every other person in the country is called Kim!

While Confucius strictly forbade a boy to marry any girl of his father's clan, relatives of his mother, unless they were very close, were not prohibited. In India, on the other hand, a boy should not be married to any relative of his mother up to the sixth degree.

Age is another important question. All over the East there is a strong feeling against a man marrying a woman older than himself. If the male has to play the dominant role, seniority is an obvious advantage! In India the bridegroom should be at least three years older than his bride. This rule has been carried to excessive lengths. As we shall see when we later discuss child marriage, it has not been unusual to find in India a man who was five times his wife's age or even more!

Indian boys, in contrast to girls, have tended to marry fairly late, because they were expected first to fulfill the requirements of the *brahmacharya*. Vatsyayana says expressly that only the youth who has completed his studentship (which Manu says should normally occupy the first quarter of a man's lifetime) is entitled to take a wife. Gandhi emphasizes the same point: "According to the Hindu Shastras the lowest age at which boys may marry is 25."[5] In China and Japan this restriction did not apply. But a prejudice in these countries against the too early marriage of girls, and the strong tradition that the bridegroom should be a few years older than his bride, tended to have the same effect. The marriage of young boys has therefore not been common, except where an elderly father was impatient to see a grandson born to him before his death.

* * *

Only when fate and tradition had been propitiated was it proper to consider the personal qualities of the prospective marriage partner.

"The desirable woman to marry," said Manu, "walks like an elephant."

The Western mind, which considers the elephant large and ungainly, finds this reasoning hard to follow. To the Easterner, however, it is unseemly for a woman to be in a hurry. In his eyes, therefore, the elephant's leisurely gait manifests the height of feminine grace and delicacy!

Manu goes on to say that the desirable woman should also have small teeth and soft limbs. Physical qualities to be avoided are thick hair on the body, a history of certain diseases (hemorrhoids, phthisis, dyspepsia, epilepsy, leprosy, and elephantiasis), red hair, a deformed limb, no hair or too much hair.

Vatsyayana gives his own account of physical features to be avoided in a prospective bride. They include red hair, spots on the face, masculine characteristics, a big head, bandy legs, a broad forehead, and a moist hand.[6]

What of the bridegroom? Narada says that a boy will make a good prospective husband "if his collar-bone, his knee and leg bones are strongly made, if his shoulders and his hair are also strongly made; if the nape of his neck is stout and his thigh and skin strong, and if his gait and voice are full of vigor." He is also expected to undergo a test of his virility; unfortunately no details of this are disclosed.[7]

Warnings are given of undesirable qualities other than physical ones. Avoid, says Manu, a girl from a family neglectful of religion, or one to which no male children have been born. Avoid also an immoderate talker. Vatsyayana warns against a girl with an uncouth name, one who has been kept hidden by her family, one who has been betrothed to another man, one born of an improper marriage, and one who has a younger sister more beautiful than herself. The chosen girl should have both parents alive, come from a well-to-do family of good character, and be herself beautiful and well behaved.

The Elder Thai lists some Chinese criteria in the Record of Rites. He confines himself to five types of girl who should not be taken in marriage—one from a rebellious family, one from a disorderly family, one from a family that has produced more than one generation of criminals, one from a leprous family, and one who has lost her mother and grown old.

Many of these instructions to parents make obvious good sense. Others of them are based on ancient superstitions. They illustrate, however, that the search for really suitable mates for their children was taken seriously by Eastern parents.

Indeed, it must be obvious that a good deal of involved negotiation, hard bargaining and even sharp practice were involved in mate selection. Each family was out to enhance its own status by an alliance with another family of good standing, as well as to find a good match for son or daughter.

In India and Ceylon, the dowry was, and still is, an important bargaining counter in this process. A girl with desirable personal qualities, such as light skin color, beauty of face and figure, and accomplishments, can be well married with a relatively small dowry. On the other hand, an ugly girl of dark color will require a large dowry to compensate for her personal deficiencies.

All these processes—investigating the prospective partners available, weighing their respective merits, striking a good bargain, and making the arrangements for the marriage—require a great deal more time, effort, knowledge, skill and tact than the average family possesses. To meet the need thus created, there appeared on the stage of Eastern life a highly colorful figure—the marriage broker or professional go-between.

*   *   *

> How do we proceed in splitting firewood?
> Without an ax it cannot be done.
> How do we proceed in taking a wife?
> Without a go-between it cannot be done.[8]

This opinion, from an ancient Chinese poet of the pre-Confucian era, shows that the marriage broker's profession was considered a necessary and honorable one from the earliest times. It seems to have been one of the few professions open to women. Indeed, in China it was, according to Professor Headland,[9] customary for the marriage broker to be a woman.

Dr. Bryce Ryan gives a good description of the professional

marriage broker in a rural community in contemporary Ceylon. "He is a rustic traveling salesman working the ground in perhaps twenty or more neighboring villages. He is necessarily a distinctive and popular character. Jovial, garrulous, and extroverted, he makes his calling known by habits of dress that have become proverbial. A gaudy sarong topped off with a shirt and black coat, given added distinction by a black umbrella, is his traditional garb. His visits, filled with good humor and color, relieve the sameness of life and provide the gossipy substance for good tea-shop conversation."[10]

When professionally employed, the go-between naturally expected to be paid for his services. Evidently this could lead to abuses, because in the 1931 Family Code of Nationalist China, the marriage broker was forbidden to take a fee.[11] However, this had little effect, because in the East it is almost impossible in practice to distinguish between paying a fee for services rendered, and making a gift of recognized value as a token of appreciation.

Let us consider a family in which there is a daughter of marriageable age. In due course, the father will send for the go-between. Food and drink will be served, accompanied by leisurely conversation. Then the talk will turn to the business at hand. The girl will be brought in, and the broker will ask many questions. He will want to know the social status of the family, the amount that will be settled on the daughter, her education and accomplishments, the state of her health, and so forth. He will, of course, require her horoscope.

At this time or later, the broker may tentatively refer to a few families in the neighborhood who have sons for whom they are seeking wives. By the reactions of the girl's family he will form an opinion of the kind of alliance they are likely to favor. If they seem interested in a particular boy as a prospective son-in-law, the broker may suggest an exchange of horoscopes by way of a first exploratory step.

If the family astrologers on both sides report favorably, the broker may feel ready to plan a conference between the family elders. Usually only male representatives of the family are involved in this kind of discussion. Exchanges between the families at this stage are likely to be very formal and polite, and no commitments are made. If, however, both sides seem satisfied with the facts placed before them, further conferences will follow, and there may be hard bargaining about the dowry that is considered to be appropriate.

The successful conclusion of these negotiations will be marked by the fixing of an auspicious day on which the betrothal ceremony will take place, usually at the home of the bride. At each point in the process, which often is complex and prolonged, the go-between will be exercising all the tact and skill necessary to bring about this happy issue.

—Negotiations may be complicated by the fact that each family employs its own go-between. This is often done as a safeguard against fraud. A marriage broker will naturally tend to be biased in favor of his own client. He will be willing, if well rewarded, to stretch the facts in order to convey the most favorable impression. He may even invent virtues that his candidate does not possess, or suppress unfavorable facts. For instance, in India a go-between can be bribed to mistake a very dark color, concealed under a yellow haldi paste coating, for a lovely moon-gold tint, or to interpret dullness of mind as sweetness of temper. Only after the marriage do the true facts become known, and by that time the head of the household has no wish to admit to outsiders that he is displeased with his new daughter-in-law.[12]

We ourselves encountered in India a very unhappy situation in which a college student had been married to a girl who was then discovered to be in an advanced stage of pulmonary tuberculosis. It was clear after investigation that the go-between had conspired with the girl's family to conceal the facts about her state of health. The result was that the unhappy young man had to send the girl back to her home, and provide the means for her treatment, after spending less than a week with her. And being now married to her, he was unable to seek another wife. Although he scarcely knew her, he hesitated to add to her distress the humiliation of initiating divorce proceedings.

When both families employ marriage brokers, a great deal of crosschecking of the facts goes on. Sometimes the go-between or his agent, disguised as a peddler, will secure entrance into the household of the other party and gather information from the servants. Often the friends of the prospective bride or bridegroom will be closely questioned to find out about the character and personal habits of the young woman or man concerned. We have been deeply impressed by the thoroughness with which responsible parents will carry out these investigations, in order to make really good matches for their children.

The functions of the go-between may extend far beyond the task of finding the prospective marriage partner. He may, for example, conduct the marriage ceremony. In Japan he acts as a kind of godfather to the young couple, and is called in if any dispute arises between them or their families. If there is trouble in the marriage, he acts as marriage counselor in the attempt to bring about a reconciliation. If this attempt is not successful, it is his responsibility to negotiate a separation or divorce. When this occurs, it is considered a humiliation for the go-between, and is likely to be damaging to his reputation.

Altogether the marriage broker's task is not an easy one. Today, as a result of Western influences, his functions are tending to be taken over by an agency approach to mate selection. In Tokyo a municipal marriage bureau, offering free services, was established in 1934. By 1955 it was reported to have 14 branch offices and to list 4,000 girls and 2,600 boys in quest of mates.[13] We have encountered similar organizations, on a smaller scale, in several Eastern cities. Such matrimonial agencies have for many years been a feature of our own Western culture.

*　　*　　*

Throughout the East it is a primary duty of parents to arrange suitable marriages for their children. Under the law of the Chinese Empire, as codified about 1700 A.D., any family elder who fails to find a husband for a daughter, a sister, a niece, a female slave, or any girl belonging to his household, is condemning her to an unfulfilled life, and is liable to receive publicly eighty blows with the bamboo.[14]

No excuse was acceptable for failing in this duty. A daughter might not, as in the West, be put under obligation to renounce marriage in order to care for her aged parents. She could not be retained in the household because her labor was needed. She had an absolute right to marriage—to a proper ceremony, appropriate gifts, a suitable dowry.

In India, if a girl's parents had failed to find a husband for her three years after she reached puberty, she was entitled to arrange a marriage for herself. If she had to do this, it would obviously bring great disgrace upon her family. To fail to marry off a daughter was considered a grave sin. Even to delay getting her married might mean that she deteriorated in marriageable value.

In marrying off their children, however, parents had to observe the proper rules. They should be married in order of their age. In Japan a very bad impression may be created if a younger daughter is married before her elder sister. In India the same principle applies to the boys of the family. Manu says, "A man who marries before his elder brother, together with the damsel thus wedded, the one who gives her in wedlock, and the performer of the nuptial sacrifice—all shall sink into a region of torment."

This creates problems if the older child is unattractive. A fair-skinned Indian girl may be much sought after yet have to wait years before marrying, because a husband cannot be found for her dark-skinned sister. The Law of Manu suggests that a distracted father would on occasion show one daughter to the go-between, then try to substitute another less desirable girl in the actual wedding ceremony. This kind of trickery, made possible by the fact that the bride was veiled, is found in the Bible story of Jacob's marriage. Jacob does not discover until the next morning that the bride with whom he has spent the night is not Rachel, as he supposed, but her elder sister Leah.[15] Pao-Yu, in *Dream of the Red Chamber*, is deceived by a similar stratagem. He thinks he is marrying his beloved Black Jade only to find, on removing the veil, that he has instead been given Precious Virtue as wife.

Normally the parents together chose their son's or daughter's marriage partner. Professor Headland reports, however, that in China it was usual for the final verdict on a prospective husband to be made by the girl's father, on the principle that a man best knows how to judge another man; and for the wife likewise to select her son's prospective wife.[16] A Chinese peasant quoted by Olga Lang puts it thus, "My wife will have to deal with the new daughter-in-law, so she had better choose her!"[17]

Other family members were often consulted, however, before the final choice was made. In traditional Sinhalese law the choice was supposed to be approved by all adult relatives of both families up to the third degree![18] Matchmaking the world over has always been a fascinating enterprise, and sometimes everyone in the family had a share in it—except the boy and girl who were to be married!

Eastern tradition was opposed to giving the boy and girl concerned any say in the arrangement of their marriage. The contract was between two families, not two individuals. To avoid trouble it was considered advisable that the young couple should not meet beforehand.

In China, when the ceremony had been concluded, the heads of the two families signed the marriage certificate. The signatures of the bride and bridegroom were not required!

There is evidence that this highhanded procedure had not always been the rule in China. In the Book of Odes, there is a poem about a young lady of Shin who was promised in marriage to a man of Fung. However, the ceremonial offerings from his family proved inadequate, and the bride, supported by her friends, refused to go on with the marriage.

> Who can say that you did not get me betrothed?
> How else could you have urged me to this trial?
> But though you have forced me to trial,
> I will still not follow you.[19]

This was a daring stand for a bride to take. No doubt she was able to act because her family, and not herself, had been insulted, and only then because her friends supported her. Traditionally, the proper procedure for a daughter dissatisfied with her parents' choice was to take a substantial dose of raw opium.

A more modern Chinese girl who ventured to challenge her parents' choice wrote to a friend, "I have committed the unpardonable sin in a Chinese daughter. I can imagine how word has gone to him [the betrothed man] in Canton that 'our lovely daughter has died of a loathsome disease,' and that the middleman fingers a fuller purse the while."[20]

An Indian girl in the same situation describes what happened.

" 'We hear you refuse to marry,' continued the Second One.

" 'That's my wish,' I answered.

" 'And who asked you about your wish? You must do what is demanded of you.' "[21]

This was the Eastern way of mate selection. The choice was

made by the parents. The parties concerned were not consulted. Their consent was not required.

*   *   *

It was Japan that first broke away from the traditional Eastern pattern, by introducing "seeing sessions" in which the boy and girl were brought together before the marriage was finally agreed upon.

This meeting was organized at the go-between's house. Often the parents and uncles and aunts on both sides were present. The atmosphere was very formal, and there was much bowing. Politeness forbade any mention being made of the object of the meeting, and the boy and girl had little chance to talk with each other. Even when attempts were made to get them to talk, these were not generally successful. "Some young couples are so shy that they keep silent from beginning to end. The matchmaker tries to make them talk but usually fails. Then when a daughter who has kept her eyes cast down on the *tatami* throughout the interview is later asked by her family how she likes the man, she says she cannot say because she didn't see him!"[22]

However, what is important here is the emergence of the principle that the judgment of the young people themselves deserves consideration. Throughout Asia this view is rapidly gaining ground today. We have been told stories of families which arranged that the young man under consideration should pass along the street outside, while the girl peeped through the shutter; or of cases where the two were taken separately to some social gathering (often a wedding) and were discreetly pointed out to each other. This latter practice has given rise to the saying, in India, "One wedding leads to another."

"Seeing sessions" of the formal or informal type establish the principle. But do they really imply choice? That depends on how much real freedom there is to say no. Moslem marriage requires the consent of the parties. But this has often been taken for granted, or obtained under pressure—even weeping or silence being interpreted as agreement!

So, logically, if the young couple are to have a say in the matter, they must be really free to reject their parents' choice. But this can create all sorts of difficulties. "I decided to give my son the right to choose his wife," a Japanese mother said to us. "One after the other I picked out half a dozen girls, all from good families and of good character. My son turned them all down. When I asked him why, he said, 'Not beautiful enough.' What do I do next?"

It was clear, from further conversation, that this mother's criteria were the old-fashioned ones, whereas her son's head was full of what she scornfully called "American ideas."

Effective choice means, also, the opportunity to get to know the other person. How much can be learned in the furtive glances that are exchanged in a formal "seeing session?" Yet in the East, allowing the couple to spend time together would involve many problems. They would have to be chaperoned, because it would be contrary to all custom to leave them alone.

One way has been tried in the Punjab. "The parents choose a few boys or girls for their sons or daughters; then the young ones are allowed to make a choice between these. This is to prevent the giving of love, the richest of all blessings, to an unworthy one."[23]

But even this amount of limited choice involves the possibility of rejection. In old China, it seems, there was a time when the girl had to be spoken for by a young man before a marriage could be arranged. The anguish of the waiting girl is vividly portrayed in this sad little poem:

> Dropping are the fruits from the plum-tree;
> There are but seven tenths of them left!
> For the gentlemen who seek me,
> This is the fortunate time!
>
> Dropping are the fruits from the plum-tree;
> There are but three tenths of them left!
> For the gentlemen who seek me,
> Now is the time!
>
> Dropt are the fruits of the plum-tree;
> In my shallow basket I have collected them.
> Would the gentlemen who seek me
> Only speak about it![24]

Greater still, perhaps, is the anguish of being sought out and then, after a period of acquaintance, put aside in favor of another.

The Eastern mind is so sensitive about this kind of experience that in India a breakup during courtship would be severely censured. Once a couple, following the new pattern, start going steady, they virtually have to marry. This was the explanation given to us of the curious condition required of those who registered as clients in a Bombay matrimonial agency. They had to sign a declaration that, if they found a suitable partner through the agency, they would undertake to marry within two months of being introduced. To extend an association over a period of weeks and then break up would be too painful and would bring discredit on the agency.

But most Asians, as a result of their conditioning, would be quite unable to function comfortably in a courtship situation. Kazuko, a Japanese girl, tried to do so. "On a few occasions she was introduced to young men and liked some of them. She remembers one particularly. She was eager to talk to him naturally, but found herself unable to do so. She was too stiff. Their eyes spoke to one another, but she felt cruelly inhibited in giving expression to her romantic longings."[25]

*   *   *

Transition from the traditional arranged marriage to the Western concept of free choice bristles with difficulties. Eastern parents are therefore skeptical of the new ideas.

"Peng-wen said that the younger Republicans disapproved of family-arranged marriages. His mother retorted—'Ah! Ah! Then when this Republic gets itself established, girls will have to go out and hunt for their mates! If their families cannot help them get married, then they will have to become bold and deceitful, preying on any man they can get, yet pretending that they're not wanting one. Only the most artful will mate! Shy, plain, good maids will wither into a fruitless age!' "[26]

It is not only the parents who are skeptical. Young people, too, are made aware of the difficulties. "A marriage not arranged by families carries considerable hardship and danger. If the family does not make the marriage, there is no responsibility for dowry and no assurance of cooperative assistance in crisis. The rightness of parental decision is so deeply rooted that children who evade it will sooner or later feel the opprobrium."[27]

Frieda Hauswirth tells the story of a cultured young Indian, educated in the West, who decided to find his own wife on his return.

"Mohan looked around for a wife. However, he had flatly stipulated that he would not marry a girl unless he was given the opportunity to 'have a look.' The circle that would permit even the merest peep at an intended bride was still very restricted in those days. But at last news came of a girl who belonged to the same caste (the mother's stipulation) and was 'grown up and accomplished.' So Mohan had set out on his trip of bride-inspection. This first attempt to inaugurate such a modern and revolutionary marriage arrangement within his orthodox group proved also his last. Mohan was received in an outer room by the grandfather. Some time later the girl herself was summoned to appear. Mohan was dumb-founded to see a shy little thing of at most 13 years come up timidly and lean against her grandfather in painful embarrassment.

" 'Show what you can do,' she was ordered, and she read in a halting childish voice a fable out of a third reader. The grandfather's face beamed with pride. He then went on to mention all the other advantages of the prospective bride, distinctly stressing her physical attractions. To lend his argument convincing weight, he slipped his hand over the body of the shrinking girl and gloatingly raised the folds of her garment to show Mohan how enticing and shapely were the slender limbs above the knee.

"Mohan was speechless with embarrassment and revolt. He ached with indignation at seeing a child's feelings so violated, a girl shown off physically like a young bullock for sale in the market place, at the shame she must feel, especially if, after all, she were refused. Yet with his Western ideas, he simply could not bring himself to marry this particular, or indeed any, child. He left as soon as he could possibly get away without giving too much offence. On his way home he swore that never again would he be a party, however passive, to the humiliation by exposure and rejection of any other helpless Indian girl. Even orthodox Hindu marriage, he told his mother, seemed better than such a bastard innovation, and he asked her to go ahead with the choice and arrangement of both bride and wedding in the good old style all by herself.

"Thus it came about that Mohan married a girl who had never before beheld the face of any man other than her father, brother, and nearest relative."[28]

This is typical. Even if young people wish to exercise free choice, the difficulties confronting them, in a society not adapted to such a pattern, are formidable. The principal of an Indian women's college writes of a gifted girl, the Senior Student of her class, who firmly insisted that she wished to have no communication with the boy chosen as her future husband, either by letter or by interview, before the wedding ceremony. "Love should come after marriage, not before," she declared. In her case, according to the principal, it did.[29]

Other girls will adopt the same attitude for a different reason. They do not wish to be involved in any way in the choice, because, if the marriage turns out unhappily, they will not have to accept the blame for making a mistake!

We met in Bombay a talented girl who put the case for the arranged marriage eloquently.

"I am twenty-two," she said, "and have just finished college. My plan is to go into business with my brother. We will work hard together for two years, and build up the business. Then we will both marry. His wife will take my place in the firm. I will have had the experience, which will be useful to me later."

"How will you go about getting married?"

She smiled.

"Fortunately I'm not a Western girl, or it might be complicated. But here in India there will be no difficulty. When I am ready, I shall begin to make inquiries about eligible young men. By going to weddings and other social functions I shall have a chance to look them over carefully. When I have picked out one or two who seem promising, in consultation with my family, I shall ask my parents to negotiate a match with one of them."

"It all sounds very simple."

"Yes, it is—quite simple and straightforward. Much better, don't you think, than your complicated Western ways?"

Chapter 7

GETTING MARRIED, EASTERN STYLE

"Marriage is the most important act in life. It is the seed of all future existence."

This old Chinese saying embodies the Eastern conviction. It finds an echo in an Indian census report:

"Everybody marries, fit or unfit. For a Hindu, marriage is a sacrament which must be performed regardless of the fitness of the parties to bear the responsibilities of a mated existence. A Hindu male must marry and beget children—sons, if you please—to perform the funeral rites lest his spirit wander uneasily. A Hindu maiden unmarried at puberty is a source of social obloquy to her family and of damnation to her ancestors."[1]

For the Indian woman, it has been said, marriage was as inevitable as adolescence. There were only two recognized stages in her life—childhood and matrimony. Her wedding was the rite of initiation that corresponded to the youth's initiation into studentship. As she served her husband, said Manu, it was as if she lived in the house of her teacher. Her household duties were for her the equivalent of the daily worship of the sacred fire. By her marriage she delivered her father from the danger of suffering in hell, and she herself found salvation through the worship of her husband as lord.

"From childhood," says Dalip Singh Saund, "the woman has been trained to be the ideal of the husband whom marriage will give her. Dropping longingly into his embrace with almost divine confidence in his protection and love, she begins to look at the whole universe in a different light.

"I have seen my own sister given in marriage, a girl of 18—a slender, playful, fond child with barely a sign of womanhood in her habits and carriage; and after a month, when I went for a visit to her home, I found it difficult to recognize her! In the place of a slender, sprightly girl was now a woman, seemingly surcharged with radiant energy; in the place of a straight childish look in the eyes there was a look of happiness, wisdom, understanding that was inspiring and ennobling.

"The explanation is very simple. In the mind of my sister, as in the mind of every other Indian girl, the idea of a husband had been uppermost since her very childhood. And when the ideal of her childhood was realized, no wonder she found in his company that height of emotional exaltation which springs from the proper union of the sexes and is the noblest gift of God to man. The American girl thinks my sister married a stranger; but she had married an ideal, a creation of her imagination, and a part of her own being."[2]

The Mahabharata tells the story of a lady who declined to marry because she claimed she could not find her equal. She devoted her life to ascetic practices. Despite her religious devotion, the sage Narada rebuked her, saying that she could not obtain ultimate bliss unless she was sanctified by the marriage rites.

The Marathi poetess, Lakshmi Bai Tilak, uses an appropriate simile to show the dependence of man and woman on each other in marriage:

"Husband and wife are like two wheels in the cart of life; and vainly will one try to draw it without the help of the other.

"Apart from his wife, a husband is lame; and so is she apart from him."

Confucius used another simile, but with the same essential meaning, when he said "The happy union of a man with his wife and children is like the music of lutes and harps."

Manu sees marriage as the gateway to true prosperity: "In whatever family the husband is contented with his wife, and the wife with her husband, in that house will fortune be assuredly permanent."

The Book of Decorum of the Han Dynasty (206 B.C.–221 A.D.) accorded to marriage the central place in human relationships: "There are Five Relationships: Citizen and state, parent and child, husband and wife, brother and brother, friend and friend; but that of husband and wife is first."

So fundamental is marriage to life that it is natural for the Eastern worshiper to think of his gods and goddesses as married couples. The amours of the Hindu deities occupy a substantial place in the old epic stories. And the Chinese and Japanese peasants, despite Buddhist influence, cling to the age-old traditions of the household gods, who from their own married bliss know how to fulfill the deepest longings of their worshipers.

"Wandering the Chinese country roads outside our city, we came upon a peasant standing in quiet reverence before a wayside shrine. Inside the shrine two gods sat, male and female, a married pair, for so the peasants conceived their gods to be. They cannot imagine a solitary god, a male without a female. That, they believe, would be against the law of life. So before the divine pair the peasant stood to light a stick of incense and speak in his heart a wish."[3]

*   *   *

Marriage in the East begins with betrothal. This means much more than does our modern Western engagement. As we understand it today, engagement is tentative, a trial period in which there are not yet any finally binding obligations. This is demonstrated by the estimate that about one third of American engagements are broken. By contrast, the Eastern betrothal has a binding power almost equal to the marriage contract itself.

Dr. Bryce Ryan describes a betrothal ceremony in Ceylon. "The prospective bridegroom, accompanied by his male relatives, all dressed up in the best clothes they possess or can borrow, walks in procession to the house of the girl, where her relatives, also decked in finery, receive them formally. Tea, rice and curries are served. Then the agreement, in involved legal language, is read out, and the astrologer announces in detail the propitious times for the various stages of preparation, and for the wedding itself. Now the prospective bride and groom solemnly exchange rings, flowery speeches are made by the representatives of both families, and half of the promised dowry is handed over. The party breaks up, and the preparations for the wedding begin soon after."[4]

The serious nature of betrothal is well illustrated in two stories in *Dream of the Red Chamber*. In the first, Phoenix is asked to help the Chang family, whose daughter Kin-Kuo, engaged to the son of a commander in the army, receives another proposal of marriage from a family which did not know she was already betrothed. The commander, hearing a garbled account of this, accuses the Changs of trying to negotiate a better match for their daughter, and files suit against them. The Changs, outraged by such action, decide to break the engagement as a protest. Hearing of this, poor Kin-Kuo is so humiliated at appearing to be unfaithful to her betrothed that she commits suicide. The commander's son, not to be outdone by the devotion of his fiancée, responds by drowning himself.

In the other story, Liu Hsiang-lien, before going on a journey, becomes engaged to the beautiful San-chieh. He leaves his sword, a family heirloom, as his betrothal gift to her. On his return some years later, however, he has changed his mind, and begs that the sword be returned to him. While he is discussing this with Chia Lien, San-chieh herself enters the room.

"In her left hand was the sheath, and in her right, which was behind her back, was the sword. She handed the sheath to Hsiang-lien. As Hsiang-lien extended his hand to receive it, she pressed the keen edge of the sword to her throat.

"Too late did those in the room rush forward to prevent it. They were paralyzed by the flash of the sword. They saw her swing it towards her throat. When they recovered from the shock, San-chieh had already fallen dead."[5]

Later the ghost of San-chieh visited her former fiancé and said "I have waited five years for you, but your heart is as cold as your face. So I have died to atone for my love for you." In deep remorse, the young man cut off his hair and followed a Taoist priest to an unknown destination.

Normally the betrothal took place between a boy and a girl who were of marriageable age. Child betrothal, however, was not unusual. In China and Korea, a family too destitute to bring up a daughter might, rather than sell her into slavery or prostitution, betroth her to a boy and hand her over to his parents to be brought up as his future wife. Sometimes this was done not because they could not afford to support her, but for fear that she might lose her chastity before the appropriate time had come for her to be married.

Infant betrothal has also been practiced in India.

She called her betrothed. "Raj! Come and meet my eldest cousin."

Turning to me, she continued, "This is my betrothed. I am six and he is nine. We suit each other, Raj and I, don't we?"

The boy said, "I shall deck my Satya more richly than that bride [the occasion was the wedding of another relative]. She shall have bracelets of gold studded with diamonds, reaching from the wrist to the elbows, and from the elbows to the shoulders."

Like my parents, these two had been betrothed soon after the birth of the girl. Nothing could part them but death.[6]

Indian betrothal was indeed so final that, in the event of the boy's death, the girl was regarded as a widow and was forbidden to remarry for the rest of her life.

*   *   *

Betrothal was somewhat like the clinching of a deal by the making of a down payment. Indeed, agreement concerning financial transactions was usually involved, and often there was an exchange of money or gifts.

In many parts of the world, the bridegroom's family makes a payment to the parents of the bride, by way of compensating them for the loss of their daughter. The bride-price is well-nigh universal in Africa and among Semitic peoples.

It is found also, to some extent, in the East. In Thailand the suitor of the girl was expected not only to build and furnish a house for his bride, but to compensate her parents by paying them "the price of the mother's milk."[7] Among low-caste Hindus, the custom of *palla* requires an agreed payment to be made to the father of the bride.[8] Among the poorer peasant families in China also, a cash payment was customary to the bride's family.[9]

However, the idea of the bride-price was disliked in Eastern culture. Manu attacks the custom, declaring that any Brahmin who accepts even the smallest gift from the bridegroom's family must be reckoned as having sold his daughter. However, he makes a clear distinction between this and the commendable practice of handing over all gifts to the bride herself. "When money or goods are given to damsels, whose kinsmen receive them not for their own use, it is no sale: it is merely a token of courtesy and affection to the bride."

In China and Korea we find the same attitude. It is excusable in the desperately poor that they keep the money given by the bridegroom's family. But for all families in a position to do so, it is a point of honor that such money be used in providing the bride with clothes, jewelry, and furniture. Indeed, among aristocratic families it was bad taste to offer any money at all, and gifts were made in kind. Several Chinese emperors tried to do away with all money transactions connected with marriage; but the practices were too deeply engrained among the poor, and their efforts were unsuccessful.

The accepted custom of the East, therefore, was not for the bridegroom's people to pay a bride-price, but for the bride's family to give her a dowry. Between the two systems there is an interesting difference of outlook. The bride-price system implies that a daughter has been an unprofitable expense for which her family should be compensated. The dowry system sees her as a participating member of the family who is entitled to take her share from the common pool when she finally ceases to belong to the household. By the first system, the bridegroom's family stand to lose on the occasion of his marriage. By the second they stand to gain.

The bride's dowry, therefore, "represents a daughter's share in her family inheritance, and settles all claims. Henceforth, her husband's family must accept all responsibility for her economic needs."[10]

Normally the dowry is settled upon the girl herself, although her husband often receives part of it for his own use. The Chinese principle was that a bride brought with her all the clothes she would need for the four seasons, and provided the household furniture. The Japanese bride who could afford it brought seven wedding dresses, "one of soft white linen, emblem of her death to her own family; one of scarlet silk, emblem of birth into her husband's family; and five other beautiful gowns embroidered with pine for strength, bamboo for obedience, and plum for the gentle perseverance of loyal womanhood."[11]

In India part of the dowry is in the form of personal jewelry that is the exclusive property of the bride. This provides her, in case of emergency, with a source of ready money to which she can turn. When a family is in serious financial straits, the wife's personal jewelry is usually the last source of income to be realized.

Thus an adequate dowry has come to be identified with the self-respect and psychological security of the new wife. "It is important for her to be able to say 'I did not come to you as a beggar.' The well dowered and fully paid up bride can enter her home with a firm step and face her new relatives with a high head."[12]

The dowry has come to be the means, not only of settling a daughter well, but also of bringing prestige to her own family. Bestowing a large sum on a marriageable girl can move her up the social scale. A smallholder who has managed his money well may be in a position to pay enough to marry his daughter to a schoolteacher or government official. If he is an ambitious man, he may consider it worth while to make this financial outlay in order to improve his family status.

At this point, however, a custom that has served several useful purposes can begin to fall into serious abuse. The opinion is widespread in India today that the dowry system has become an evil and should be abolished. Mrs. Hate, who in 1948 made a study of marriage in Bombay, says, "The dowry system has played considerable havoc among the Hindus. As education progresses, it was expected that the evil would be rooted out. But unfortunately, experience has been quite the contrary. Instances are not lacking where educated men have demanded large dowry on the ground that they had to expend a lot on their education. Men from those castes in which dowry was not customary have nowadays on the strength of their education started demanding it."[13]

Professor Phadke is of the same opinion. The dowry system "has reduced many a father to penury and driven many a desperate girl to suicide as a relief from ignominious virginity. Instances could be given of scores of strong, intelligent and remarkable boys chained to ugly and totally unfit girls, because the latter brought with them fat dowries and the boys' parents had their eyes on nothing else. And equally common are cases of lovely and clever girls mated with the very dregs of society because their parents were poor."[14]

In any Indian community this can be confirmed. Frieda Hauswirth tells of a professor and well-known historian who had the misfortune to have many daughters and a small income. "His daughters, fully grown, were really accomplished and educated, but one young man on whom he had had his eye as a desirable son-in-law had been married off suddenly to the ignorant 15-year-old daughter of a village land-owner, because a greater dowry was offered than the 3,000 rupees which the professor could manage to scrape together."[15]

One impecunious father with three daughters worked out an ingenious solution to the problem of getting them well settled. "He wanted to marry them off on the same date, so as to save on wedding expenses. Not being rich enough for three substantial dowries, he found another way to increase their value in prospective in-laws' eyes. For about half a year the poor girls had to cram for the Senior Cambridge exam, though they had no foundation to build upon and were bound to fail. Their father had thought things out very carefully. The moment they had sat for the exam, he sent out go-betweens to arrange for their marriage. 'She has sat for Senior Cambridge,' he let it be understood. The results of the exam were made public only many months later. When the girls learned they had failed, all three of them were safely married off."[16]

A group of Indian students, comparing notes about what they had been offered by fathers of eligible daughters, came up with the following list (roughly, one American dollar is today equivalent to five rupees):

1. 5,000 rupees, together with 300 tolas* of silver, 500 tolas of gold ornaments, and a gold wrist watch as a special gift for the bridegroom.
2. 8,000 rupees, a phonograph, and a platinum watch.
3. An offer to pay all costs for four years of study in England.
4. 10,000 rupees and a radio.[17]

The bartering that goes on in connection with a girl's dowry may lead a family, at the time of betrothal, to make promises that cannot be fulfilled. The wedding day comes, and the bride's people fail to produce the cash. The bridegroom's family are in an awkward situation. They must either halt the ceremony and bring pressure to bear, or let the wedding proceed and accept humiliation.

We were told in Bombay a dramatic story of a young man who,

* A "tola" is a measure of weight roughly equal to two fifths of an ounce.

on his wedding day, decided to put up his price. The guests were assembled and the ritual was about to begin. Taking the bride's father aside, he declared that he was unwilling to go ahead unless they could produce, in addition to what had been agreed, a radio and a diamond ring. The father, in desperation, assembled his relatives. They agreed to the radio but said the diamond ring was impossible. The young man refused to moderate his demands.

At this point the bride, becoming aware that there was some trouble, demanded an explanation. She was a girl of some spirit. When she learned what had happened, she formed the opinion that this man would prove to be a poor husband.

She informed the assembled company that she had decided not to marry the bridegroom. Instead, she was ready to marry any eligible man present who would take her as she was, without dowry. After some hesitation a young man stepped forward, and she placed the garland intended for the bridegroom round his neck! The marriage, we were told, has turned out very happily.

*   *   *

The betrothal and the wedding ceremonies are two successive steps that lead to the establishment of a marriage. The relationship between them varies greatly among Eastern cultures. Sometimes the second ceremony immediately follows the first. Sometimes, if the betrothed girl is considered to be too young to assume wifely responsibilities, a period of years may elapse before the wedding.

Generally the betrothal is focused on the contract, while the wedding leads up to the consummation. The first ceremony takes place, as a rule, in the bride's home, the second in that of the bridegroom.

Betrothal has, as we have seen, the legal binding force of marriage—especially among the Hindus. Dalip Singh Saund says this was a result of the Moghul invasions of India. To protect the virtue of betrothed Hindu girls, it was explained to the marauding Moslems that they already had marital status.[18]

As soon as the betrothal was concluded, and the financial settlements agreed on, the next step was to call in the astrologist and name an auspicious day for the wedding. The finding of a lucky day means, as it did in ancient Rome, securing the favor of the gods.

In Chinese society a marriage should never take place during a period of mourning. The death of a parent after betrothal would delay a marriage by twenty-seven months. Confucius prescribed this period of mourning, on the ground that a child did not leave the arms of its parents until he was three years old—counting from conception, in Chinese fashion. Therefore, during a similar period a child must mourn his parents.

The planning of a traditional Hindu wedding was complicated by the fact that there were eight different recognized forms of marriage. The distinctions between them, as Manu describes them, are not always clear.

The first four forms are all, for one reason or another, discouraged by Manu, on the ground that they will produce cruel and wicked sons. They are:

1. *Rakshasa,* or marriage by capture—the forcible abduction of a maiden after her kinsmen have been slain. This is exclusively reserved for Ksatryas—members of the warrior caste. The abductions carried out in comparatively recent times may reflect this ancient tradition.

2. *Paisacha,* or marriage by seduction—the girl is sexually violated while she is asleep, intoxicated, or mentally disordered. Though this is simply rape, it interestingly enough constitutes a valid marriage. Manu remarks that it is appropriate only to the lower castes, and is base and sinful.

3. *Asura,* or marriage by payment of bride-price. This is beneath the dignity of any Brahmin. There is another good reason against it—a man who sells his daughter thus will suffer continuously in hell.

4. *Gandharva,* the love marriage, in which the boy and girl come together by mutual desire. As we have seen, this motive is frowned upon. Such a marriage is contracted "for the purpose of amorous embraces, and proceeding from sensual inclination." It is therefore discreditable.

The remaining forms of marriage are entirely respectable and are prescribed for Brahmins. They all have the characteristic that the father makes a gift of his daughter to a man who has not sought her. They are:

5. *Brahma*—the girl is given, with a single robe, to a man learned in the Vedas, or sacred writings.

6. *Daiva*—the girl is given, decked in gay garments, to a priest while he is officiating at a sacrifice.

7. *Prajapatya*—the girl is given "with due honor." What this means is not made clear.

8. *Arsha*—in return for his daughter, the father receives from the groom one or two head of cattle, "for uses prescribed by the law." Presumably this means that nothing remotely resembling a bride-price is involved.

No doubt these latter four forms once had distinctive characteristics, which are not clear to us today. All of them, says Manu, will secure for the couple wealth and fame, beauty and virtue, long life and happiness.

* * *

These prosaic details no doubt have their importance to the Eastern mind. To the Westerner they sound boring and irrelevant. What he needs, in order to understand an Eastern marriage, is to capture its atmosphere, to feel the emotions that are stirred in those who participate.

In an attempt to achieve this, we reproduce the most vivid description we have been able to find. Kumut Chandruang, remembering his boyhood in rural Thailand, draws this moving word picture of a Buddhist wedding in the village of Chang Noi:

On the wedding day the village was engaging in a jubilant celebration. The new wedding house was being decorated with white-elephant flags, trimmed banana and coco-palm leaves. The roof, thatched with dry grass, was neatly bound at its edge with red paper. From the bamboo rafters, Kamnan hung the various fruits of the season, and on every door and window he draped strings of the fragrant yellow *jampa* flowers. On the long ladder leading down to the ground, Kamnan put six white dots arranged in the shape of a triangle, to keep evil away from the house.

The mother and many neighbor women prepared the food for the guests, laughing and chatting, many of them boasting of their own wedding days. One woman danced with a chicken leg in her hand. In a corner of the room, a couple of women started a song to tease the bride:

Don't make him wait,
For he may run away. . . .

The bride was in her room dressing. This "nymph of the jungle," as the young men in the village sometimes called her, was like a blooming flower; her dark eyes were as innocent as those of a mountain deer. Today was her wedding day; her heart was beating like a drum, toom-toom-tom-tom. She put on a sarong of sky-blue, the color of sincerity, and from one shoulder and around her bosom she draped a shawl of pink, the color of love and loyalty. Her soft hair she allowed to hang loose, to cover her shoulders.

Meanwhile Muang Song, the bridegroom, and a score of his friends were forming a parade at one end of the village, many fields away from the wedding house. Dressed in his brightest and best, a red *panung* and a green silk jacket, the bridegroom was seated on a gaily decorated elephant, borrowed from the monastery, while his friends were riding on horses.

When the lucky hour arrived as the sun rose above the tall palm tree, the procession started to move. Children playing along the roadside followed along. The village dogs began barking and howling as they heard the drums and gongs. The villagers joined the parade when it passed by their houses, all noisily adding to the excitement.

The spirited cavalcade reached the gate of the wedding house. The mother stood behind the bride's little brothers, instructing them.

"Do you bring the wedding gold with you?"

"Yes. I do," answered Muang Song.

"Do you have live gifts with you?"

"I have ducks, chickens, three goats, two pigs and a calf."

"Our golden gate is open. And when you walk through it you will find great wealth, great happiness, and Lord Buddha's blessing on you."

Muang Na, the white-haired father of the bridegroom, stepped up the ladder to the verandah, where Kamnan welcomed him. Muang Na's smile burst into words: "Today my heart is blooming with joy. Through our son and daughter, we shall be linked together with a golden chain."

"Your grandson will also be my grandson," Kamnan heartily replied.

Muang Na's thoughts marched ahead as he saw his family line carried far into the future.

The temple bells were now heard ringing out across the village and fields, in signal that the priests had left the monastery for the nuptial ceremony. Soon the line of priests in their yellow robes was observed coming out of the bamboo underbrush.

When all had been courteously welcomed, and the bride and bridegroom had come forth, Kamnan invited the priests to pronounce the five commandments. Then the old priest tied a yellow string around the silver vessel in front of the statue of Buddha, and all the priests took hold of it and formed a holy circle; then they closed their eyes and prayed in unison. The bride and bridegroom were next encircled with a garland of flowers. One by one the priests and guests sprinkled sacred water over them, pronouncing blessings and good wishes.

The father and mother wished the same thing, "May your first child be a boy!"

After this ceremony the food prepared for the priests was served. When they had finished eating and had left the house, more food and drinks were brought in for the guests. Everybody ate and drank with all his might, shouting and cheering, singing and dancing. Soon the house was occupied by empty dishes and bones. Before the evening sun went down, most of the men were lying about, embracing the empty rum jars.

At night an old couple, known to have lived together happily, came to make the bed for the bride and bridegroom. As they spread the mattress and arranged the pillows and the mosquito net, they hummed a traditional song, calling upon the angels, the house spirits, the sun, moon, and rain to be kind to the young couple.

As soon as the bed was made ready, the old man struck a gong as a signal to the guests below. Kamnan and his wife then led their daughter into the room, where the bridegroom was waiting. Friends came up to congratulate them. Some jested with them, some offered the bridegroom drinks to give him courage. The couple tried their best to remain quiet and calm, concealing as they could the great excitement within.

The father and mother kissed their daughter's cheek with their noses. The mother's eyes were filled with tears of joy as she said, "Away from your mother's breast into your husband's arms. Muang Song, my son, keep her and love her. And you, my daughter, serve him as his loyal wife." In response the couple bowed respectfully at the feet of their parents.

The drums and gongs from below now began their final pounding and beating. The sound covered the entire valley; it echoed among the mountains and in the caves; it shook the heart of the jungle; it vibrated along the waves of the moving river. It symbolized the voice of Rama Sura, the Mighty Thunder, roaring his sanction throughout the three worlds, Heaven, Earth, and Hell, that Muang Song and Nang Onn were now man and wife—man and wife.

The father and mother turned out the lights in every corner of the room. The guests bade the couple good night and departed. The drums and gongs ceased. Under the shade of the coconut palms and bamboo trees, with the yellow light of the new moon above, stood the wedding house, solemn but blessed.[19]

*   *   *

In one important respect Kumut Chandruang's picture is not representative. Almost everywhere in the East, except in Thailand, the bridegroom fetches his bride and takes her to his own home for the main marriage ceremony.

When her wedding day comes the bride is dressed for the occasion. In China and Japan she begins the day attired in white, the color of mourning. Today she will take leave of her parental home, with all its associations. If she returns, it will be only as a visitor. Her true home henceforth will be that of her husband's people, her true family will be his family. Her marriage is therefore symbolically an act of dying to the family of her birth. In Korea, the bride was traditionally expected, in order to respect the solemnity of the occasion, neither to smile nor to speak throughout her wedding day—although often her friends and relatives teased her to do so. If she smiled, it was believed that all her children would be girls.[20]

The Indian bride is dressed to display her beauty—although she is veiled for the ceremony. "Dayal was one of those girls who, the week before her wedding day, looked plain and unattractive. But now she looked really beautiful. For several days she had stayed in out of the sun, and every day her mother had put a fresh mask of flour-cream mixed with ochre on her face, so now it was a beautiful pale golden brown.

"I asked my mother how it was that Dayal had suddenly become beautiful. She answered, 'That is the way with all the girls when they are about to become brides.'"[21]

The bridegroom, arriving with his party at the bride's home, is also attired in suitable finery—usually borrowed or hired for the occasion! In Rajputana, for instance, the groom wears a red turban, crowned with silver brocade; a scarlet wedding coat with narrow pink trousers; and he carries a sword to commemorate the old days when Rajputs had to fight for their brides.[22]

Hindu customs vary greatly from one locality to another. The first part of the wedding ceremony, however—the giving away of the bride—is traditionally performed in her parental home.[23]

The father pours out water, symbolizing the surrender of his daughter. He offers it to the bridegroom, who accepts the gift, swearing that he will not fail to be a good husband. The bridegroom now makes offerings before the sacred fire. Taking his bride's hand and facing west, the bridegroom then says:

> I take thy hand in mine,
> Yearning for happiness;
> I ask thee
> To live with me
> As thy husband,
> Till both of us
> With age, grow old.

Now the bride offers a sacrifice of fried grain, and a prayer is recited. The priest ties their garments together, and the bridegroom leads her three times round the sacred fire, while he says:

> Let us join together
> And beget our little ones.
> Loving each other,
> With genial minds and hearts,
> May we live
> Through a hundred autumns.

The most important of all the rites follows—the seven steps. The bridegroom leads the bride. At each step they pause, while the bridegroom recites the appropriate prayer:

Let us pray together,
For life-sap, as we tread one step;
For life-power, as we tread two steps;
For abundant wealth, as we tread three steps;
For happiness, as we tread four steps;
For offspring, as we tread five steps;
For long life together, as we tread six steps;
Be thou now my life-mate as we tread seven steps together.
Thus may we go together for ever and ever
Let us acquire many, many sons; and long may they live, we pray.

Once the seventh step has been taken the marriage is considered to be complete. Thereafter, it cannot be revoked or annulled.

Now the wedded pair start off on their journey to the bridegroom's home, carrying with them the nuptial fire. As they leave the bride's father gives her his parting blessing:

I give thee up uninjured with thy consort
I set thee free. O bounteous Indra
May she live blest with fortune and with sons.

In China there was little ceremony in the bride's home. The grand bridal chair of brilliant scarlet arrived to carry her to her wedding. Traditionally the bridegroom came to fetch her, but the custom more recently was for him to await the procession at his own door.

The bride dons a large scarlet robe and takes leave of her relatives, who remain in their home and bewail their loss. Her chair is adorned with a massive headdress of gilt ornaments, and her head is covered with a veil of scarlet silk or cloth, which completely conceals her features.[24] Slowly and sadly, she "passes out of the door" and enters the waiting sedan chair.

*   *   *

"When the religious ceremonies had been completed, we left, my husband and I. How well I remember the day, and the sudden sickness that overcame me when the moment of departure came! My mother in the doorway, no tears in her eyes but her face bloated with their weight. My father standing a little in front of her, waiting to see us safely on our way. My husband, seated already on the bullock cart with the tin trunk full of cooking vessels and my saris next to him. Somehow I found myself also sitting in the cart, in finery, with downcast eyes. Then the cart began to move, lurching as the bullocks got awkwardly into rhythm, and I was sick. Such a disgrace for me. . . . How shall I ever live it down? I remember thinking."[25]

The disciplined Chinese bride from an aristocratic home would be more controlled than this little Indian peasant girl. But as she sits enclosed in the scarlet chair, heading the long procession of uniformed porters who carry her possessions through the streets to her bridegroom's home, she probably harbors in her heart the same fears and apprehensions.

At last the procession halts. The bridegroom bows to the attendants, taps with his fan on the scarlet chair. This is the signal for the door to be opened. The bride steps out and enters her new home.

Bride and bridegroom are greeted by the family elders. They kneel together before the ancestral tablets and the household gods. The marriage ceremonies in China, Korea and Japan vary according to religious affiliation and local custom. According to the old Chinese tradition, the couple were made man and wife by being tied together with the red string referred to by Madame Wu. The Family Elder acted as the officiating minister. The significant act in the Japanese tradition is the sipping of rice wine (*sake*) from the same three cups, three times over, by the groom and bride, in the presence of the officiating go-between.

Greetings and congratulations are exchanged. Appropriate Chinese forms of address are: To the Family Elder, "May you soon have another descendant on your knee!" To the bridegroom's parents, "May you embrace grandchildren and great-grandchildren!" To the couple, "May you live together five generations!"[26]

The wedding feast follows. Only the bride and bridegroom sit down. The bride eats nothing. She sits, silent and impassive, her face still concealed behind her veil.

The Indian couple are already man and wife when they arrive at the groom's home. Here the family have been eagerly expecting them.

"The day on which Uncle Ray brought his bride home, our house was all decorated and full of rejoicing. It was a great day for my mother and Aunt Tara, his sisters. They were gorgeously dressed.

"In the afternoon of that day a messenger arrived to announce that the procession was nearing the North Gate; so we came down the broad steps in front of our house to greet them. All my great aunts were there, standing behind my grandmother—even the eldest one. Then we saw my Uncle Ray coming toward us, riding on a decorated white horse, followed by a palanquin in which was his bride."[27]

The bridegroom's father greets the couple. He welcomes his son's bride, and addresses them both:

> Closely unite thy body with this man thy lord.
> So shall ye, full of years, address your company,
> Dwell ye here; be ye not parted:
> Reach the full time of human life.

With sons and grandsons, sport and play;
Rejoicing in your own house.

The sacred fire, which they have brought with them, is now kindled in their future home, and sacrifices are offered, the bridegroom praying:

> O bounteous Indra, make this bride
> Blest in her sons and fortunate;
> Vouchsafe to her ten sons
> So may the Waters join our hands,
> The Universal Gods together bind us close.

*   *   *

The drama of the marriage now moves towards its climax—the consummation.

This begins with the unveiling of the bride. In India, this is done at the close of the wedding ceremony. The Chinese bridegroom, at the appropriate time, leads his bride into the decorated bridal chamber. Removing the veil, he looks for the first time at the face of the girl who has become his wife. They are seated together on the bed, and the Chinese saying is that the one who sits down first will be dominated throughout life by the other!

Chinese custom now requires the bridegroom to return to his guests, and what is called "the tumult of the bridal room" follows. The guests file in and tease the bride with ribald jests, to test her self-control. This ordeal may last for as long as two hours, during which the poor girl is expected to remain composed and impassive.[28]

Finally the couple are left in peace, and the supreme test draws near. The bride's virginity is an essential condition of an acceptable marriage, and proof of it must be furnished. Here is a description of the procedure in Ceylon:

"Anxiety reigns in the household, and indeed back in the bride's own home. Before retiring, a new aunt of the bride offers advice and best wishes for a happy night, and then there is spread the white cloth (*hela*), given her during the *poruva* ceremony, upon which the couple is to sleep. It is by the examination of this cloth, on the following morning, that the relatives determine whether or not the new daughter-in-law was indeed a virgin.

"Early in the morning the family's *dhobi* woman enters the

bridal chamber and examines the *hela*. If the cloth is stained, by the flow from a ruptured hymen, haste is made to announce the tidings to the waiting household. When the girl is thus shown to be a virgin, the house becomes alive with renewed celebration. Fire-crackers will be set off, the drum (*raban*) played, and so the entire village is aware that a good girl was married into their midst. If the girl's parents live nearby or in an adjacent village, a messenger is dispatched bearing betel and red flowers indicative of the happy climax."[29]

One Chinese tradition was to present the bride's bloodstained nether garment to the bridegroom's mother, so that she might know that all was well. The Cantonese custom was to send a pig to the bride's mother after the consummation. If the animal was intact, she had nothing to fear. If it was mutilated, the bride's virginity was in question.[30]

Another approach was to send the bride's mother an invitation to the "After the Rites of the Marriage Bed Breakfast." The invitation set the seal on the marriage by indicating that the groom's family were satisfied.

It is difficult to decide how effective these virginity tests were, or how strictly they were observed. In the old days they were probably taken seriously. The Japanese bride was expected, in the event of her chastity being questioned, to use her *obi*, or sash, to strangle herself. More recently, there is evidence that the bridegroom's word has frequently been taken as sufficient evidence; and there would obviously be no satisfaction for him in exposing himself to ridicule. It seems likely, therefore, that some discreet "covering up" has been done in situations where the test did not prove to be satisfactory.[31]

The newly married Hindu couple were not expected to consummate the marriage on their first night together. In the Sankhyayana Sutra of the Rig-Veda, they are enjoined if possible to observe continence for three nights, sleeping together on the ground. Vatsyayana explains that this does not mean there must be no advances, no expressions of love; only that intercourse should not take place. This voluntary period of self-restraint is considered an act of merit.

On the fourth night, after appropriate sacrifices, the marriage is consummated. As he approaches his wife, the husband says:

> United are our minds,
> United our hearts,
> United our bodies,
> I will bind thee with the bond of love:
> And the bond shall be indissoluble.

Kissing her, and with fervent prayers to the gods for the gift of a son, he then unites with her sexually, saying:

> I do with thee this sacred work:
> May an embryo enter thy womb:
> May a child be born without blemish.

Virginity in the bride was essential to a valid Hindu marriage. "The holy nuptial texts," said Manu, "are applied solely to virgins, and nowhere on earth to girls who have lost their virginity." A man who gives a girl in marriage, falsely representing her to be a virgin, is subject to a fine. However, an even greater fine is imposed upon a man who declares that a damsel is no virgin and cannot prove his statement.

*   *   *

A wedding is a time of festivity the world over. The full traditional Hindu ceremony extends throughout five days. Nowadays, however, it is generally considerably abbreviated.

Besides plenty of food, entertainment is provided. There usually is music and dancing. "In some parts of the Punjab, the girls of the two families perform graceful dances in which they move slowly in a circle, swaying their bodies, clapping their hands or snapping their fingers. The dances are sometimes accompanied by songs which may be very sentimental, telling perhaps a love-story of old time; or they may be full of harmless jests at the expense of friends."[32]

In Japan such entertainment may be much less restrained in its symbolism. The women dancers "indulge in all kinds of imitations and exaggerations of copulation to the accompaniment of a vigorous female chorus which inevitably ends up in roars of laughter."[33] As Professor Embree puts it, "The wedding is the extreme example of the pattern whereby a social gathering begins with stiff formality and ends in orgiastic abandon."[34]

Other kinds of entertainers, such as conjurers and actors, may be engaged to amuse the wedding guests. An unusual but apt performance staged in India is the wedding of the monkeys. "First the gentleman monkey, dressed in a white coat and trousers and a red fez over his head, came forward and sat himself down on a low stool on the right hand of the magician. Soon after him followed his lady. She was dressed in gay bridal robes and looked very bashful. After giving the gentleman a few sidelong glances, and looking what seemed to me rather doubtful, she nodded her head to show she was willing. Then controlled by the voice of the magician and the beating of the drum they went through a proper marriage ceremony. Finally the gentleman got up and the bride followed him, wiping many a tear with her scarf as if sad to part from her home. At the end of the performance the monkeys were given a marriage feast of nuts and sweets.

"I thought the gentleman monkey a poor performer, until it came to the wedding feast, for throughout the ceremony he had done nothing but gaze restlessly at his audience or scratch himself furiously. On the other hand, the bride had acted beautifully; the only thing was that she had a baby monkey clasped to her breast, from which she refused to be parted, and it kept popping its head out from underneath her blouse to see what was going on."[35]

These lavish festivities cost money—often more money than the family can afford. An Indian observer in Orissa estimates that a father would have to spend on his son's wedding about as much as the youth himself could earn in an entire year.[36] A study made in Peiping in 1933,[37] involving 283 families, indicated that the expenses involved in a wedding varied from 1.5 to nine times the family's monthly income. Since the Eastern family usually has little financial reserve, a wedding in the family may prove as crippling an economic disaster as a serious illness can be to a modern American family. When this money had to be borrowed, the Peiping study showed that interest rates ran as high as 20 per cent or more.

Fortunately the wedding guests customarily help. It is heartening, at an Eastern wedding, to watch the guests file in, bringing their money gifts in envelopes. As they are received, the names and amounts are carefully listed, to provide a basis for estimating what should be given to the families concerned when their turn comes to have weddings of their own. In effect it is almost a group co-operative movement to help meet the costs of marriages! The Peiping study indicated that families were able to cover from one quarter to one half of their total costs out of these gifts.

Wedding expenditures include new clothes for family members; the special garments needed for bride or bridegroom; dowry or home equipment for the bride; appurtenances of the wedding procession—hire of sedan chair, carriage or automobile, attendants, and often a band; and the cost of the feast. Often the ceremony and feast cannot be held in the home, where space is inadequate. At a really big Eastern wedding, a meal might be served to several thousand guests. We have attended Indian weddings on vacant city lots upon which pavilions have been erected and which have been made gay with gaudy decorations and colored lights. The Chinese and Japanese trend in recent years has been to engage the services of restaurants that specialize in catering for wedding parties.

*   *   *

To the Hindus, marriage has a deeply religious significance. The vows, the prayers, the sacred fire, the offerings to the gods, make the wedding a solemn occasion. The Brahmin or priest officiates. Marriage is regarded not merely as a contract. The Hindus speak of it as a sacrament.

Among Buddhists, Taoists, and Shintoists there are also religious aspects included in the wedding ceremony. However, the ceremony does not make the union between husband and wife binding as the Hindu ritual does. In China, the bride traditionally prepared a meal for her parents-in-law on the third day after her wedding, and offered a sacrifice to the ancestors. This marked her final acceptance into the clan. It was then customary for her to return to her parents for a time. George Riley Scott, the sexologist, considers that this was to enable her ruptured hymen to heal. A similar custom is found in Japan.

The Japanese marriage was in fact not made legal by the ceremony. The marriage had to be registered by the head of the bridegroom's family, who reported the event to the authorities and had the bride's name erased from her parental household records and entered in the records of her new household.

Sometimes this procedure was delayed to give husband and

wife a trial period together, during which they could decide not to continue the union if they were dissatisfied with each other. The family head might extend this period for weeks and months— sometimes merely as a result of procrastination, but sometimes for other reasons. It became quite common practice in some regions, for instance, to put off the registration of the marriage till the new wife had become pregnant, or even until she had borne a child.

To indicate that the marriage was duly registered, the Japanese had an ancient custom of "showing the bride." A servant would go round to the homes of the immediate neighbors, knocking at the doors. The sister-in-law of the new wife would then present the girl herself—attired in her bridal garments, her face thickly plastered with white powder. With an expression as impassive as a mask of wax, the bride would salute the neighbors with a low bow, then move on to the next house. Once this round of the neighborhood was completed, her status in the new family was secure.

Chapter 8

CHILD WIVES OF INDIA

When Santha Rama Rau was a rapidly growing teen-ager her grandmother once said to her, "My dear child, where in India will we find a husband tall enough for you?"

"I don't think you need worry about that for some time," was the reply. "After all, I'm only sixteen!"

"Only sixteen!" exclaimed the grandmother. "Why, that's nearly twice as old as I was on my wedding day."[1]

The Indian custom of giving young girls in marriage became in 1927 the focus of the far-reaching *Mother India* controversy. Katherine Mayo painstakingly collected all the facts she could find. There was plenty of material available.

What were the dimensions of the problem? The answer may be found in the Census Reports. While accurate statistics are hard to come by in the East, the figures published by the British Government must have been fairly trustworthy.

The Census Report of 1921 gives us the number of girls of various ages who were married. If we take a period of three decades before the *Mother India* controversy broke out, here are the figures.[2]

Between the ages of five and ten, thirteen girls in one hundred were already married in 1891, and nine in 1921. Roughly this means that every tenth Indian girl between five and ten was a wife.

Between the ages of ten and fifteen, fifty-one girls in one hundred were already married in 1891, and forty in 1921. Thus nearly half of the girls in this age group were married.

Combine these totals, and we find that during this period, one Indian girl in four between the ages of five and fifteen was already a wife. Every one of these girls was below the age at which most Western countries today legally permit marriage.

Clearly Miss Mayo had an arresting story to tell her Western readers.

However, figures have little emotional impact. What *Mother India* did was to get behind the scenes and find out what was happening to these girls as human beings. Moreover, Katherine Mayo was not primarily interested in the ones whose lives were happy and uneventful. Her purpose was to find out the worst that *could* happen in these circumstances. In the pursuit of this objective she did a devastatingly thorough job, as the following illustrations will show.

First she concentrated a good deal of attention upon the sexual exploitation of the child wife. She found a collection of cases, compiled in 1891 by Western women doctors, describing girls who were their patients. She quotes the following illustrations:

A. Aged 9. Day after marriage. Left femur dislocated, pelvis crushed out of shape. Flesh hanging in shreds.

B. Aged 10. Unable to stand, bleeding profusely, flesh much lacerated.

C. Aged 9. So completely ravished as to be almost beyond surgical repair. Her husband had two other living wives and spoke very fine English.

I. Aged about 7. Living with husband. Died in great agony after three days.

M. Aged about 10. Crawled to hospital on her hands and knees. Has never been able to stand erect since her marriage.[3]

Miss Mayo also pictured the sufferings of pregnant young wives under the primitive conditions in which children were then born in India.

"Such labor may last three, four, five, even six days. During all this period the woman is given no nourishment whatever—such is the code—and the *dhai* (midwife) resorts to all her traditions. She kneads the patient with her fists; stands her against the wall and butts her with her head; props her upright on the bare ground, seizes her hands and shoves against her thighs with gruesome bare feet, until, so the doctors state, the patient's flesh is often torn to ribbons by the *dhai's* long, ragged toe-nails. Or, she lays the woman flat and walks up and down her body, like one treading grapes.

. . . As a result of their infant marriage and premature sexual use and infection, a heavy percentage of the women of India are either too small-boned or too internally misshapen and diseased to give normal birth to a child, but require surgical aid. It may safely be said that all these cases die by slow torture, unless they receive the care of a British or American woman doctor, or of an Indian woman, British trained."[4]

Further, Miss Mayo focused attention on the hard lot of the girl who found herself widowed while yet a child.

"The Hindu widow is accursed. That so hideous a fate as widowhood should befall a woman can be but for one cause—the enormity of her sins in a former incarnation. From the moment of her husband's decease till the last hour of her own life, she must expiate those sins in shame and suffering and self-immolation, chained in every thought to the service of his soul. Be she a child of three, who knows nothing of the marriage that bound her, or be she a wife in fact, having lived with her husband, her case is the same. By his death she is revealed as a creature of innate guilt and evil portent."[5]

These are only illustrations. There was plenty more in the same vein. It added up to a pretty ugly picture.

The publication of *Mother India* quite justifiably aroused a storm of protest, both in the East and in the West. Miss Mayo wrote several later books defending her position—*Slaves of the Gods* (1929), *Soldiers, What Next?* (1934), and *The Face of Mother India* (1935). Replies and counterreplies followed each other in rapid succession, until a considerable literature had accumulated. The following, in the order of their appearance, are some of the more significant volumes in the series:

Dalip Singh Saund, *My Mother India;* Edith Craske, *Sister India;* C. Ranga Iyer, *Father India;* Savel Zimand, *Living India;* Gertrude Williams, *Understanding India;* Dahn Gopal Mukerji, *A Son of Mother India Answers;* Agnes Burr, *Neighbour India;* Lajpat Rai, *Unhappy India;* Sir Claude Hill, *India, Step-Mother;* J. A. Chapman, *India: Its Character, A Reply to Mother India;* R. J. Minney, *Shiva, or the Future of India.*

Besides books, there were innumerable articles and letters to the press. All kinds of people plunged in and joined the battle—

physicians, legislators, missionaries, government officials, feminists, and many others.

Miss Mayo was accused of distortion, misrepresentation, misquotation, downright deception. Her critics said she had used cheap sensational methods to gain publicity for herself and for her writing. The book even had political repercussions. It was interpreted in some quarters as a color-biased attack on the rights of Indians to self-government, and therefore in support of British colonial policy. The echoes of the controversy went right around the world, and lingered loud and long.

The dust finally settled. It was conceded that Katherine Mayo's facts, as facts, were substantially accurate. It was recognized that she had taken up a serious issue and drawn attention to it, which had helped in some measure to hasten much-needed reforms. But at the same time her book had done a grave injustice to India, in presenting a one-sided and distorted picture of an aspect of Indian life that could only be properly understood within the context of the entire culture.

*　　*　　*

"He who gives a girl of eight in marriage attains heaven; the giver of a girl of nine attains a higher heaven; the giver of a girl who has attained the tenth year, but not puberty, is given a place in the highest heaven; and the giver of a mature woman is condemned to hell."[6]

This often-quoted saying of Marichi indicates the pressure that tradition brought to bear in favor of child marriage. The sage Parashara elaborates the dire penalties of nonconformity thus: "If a man fails to marry his daughter even after she has reached her twelfth year, his ancestors are cursed to drink of her menstrual flow from month to month."[7]

Whence came this stern insistence on child marriage?

It seems, in its origins, to go a long way back. "The idea that a Hindu father is in duty bound to marry his daughter at a very early age dates back to before the Christian era, and is so deeply implanted that it has yielded with great reluctance to the Western idea that girls should be physically and mentally ready for matrimony before the ceremony takes place."[8]

One view is that this was an early Buddhist practice that infil-

trated Hinduism. It is certainly true that one reason for which it
was justified was the feeling that incipient life would be destroyed
if a girl had her first menstrual period without the chance of being
impregnated. Johann Meyer quotes a number of ancient Hindu
legal authorities on this point, and summarizes their views thus:
"Each time a (ripe) unwedded maiden has her courses, her
parents or guardians are guilty of the heinous crime of slaying the
embryo."[9]

Another reason, quoted by Tagore,[10] is that it is advisable to
get the girl safely married before the age at which sex attraction
may become destructively powerful. This is interpreted in two
ways. There is the fear that the girl, because of her charms, may
become the innocent victim of male sexual assaults in the community where she lives, or even within the joint family. And there
is the view that she herself should not be exposed to the powerful
urges of her own unsatisfied sexual desires. Once the girl, by some
such misfortune, had lost her virginity, her chances of being accepted in marriage were remote. Better, then, for the family to
take no chances, and get her safely into her husband's care as
early as possible.

Sometimes the Moghul invasions of India have been blamed for
the custom of child marriage. According to Sir William Hunter,[11]
Moslem atrocities perpetrated on Hindu women drove the population to adopt child marriage as a measure of safety, because the
Moslems were reluctant to violate any woman who was already
married. In support of this theory it has been pointed out that in
some remote jungle areas into which the Moslem invaders never
penetrated, the marriage age for girls was much higher than in
the Hindu community generally.[12]

Whether or not the Hindu custom was influenced by Moslem
depredations, it soon became a Moslem practice. "Like a conta-
gious disease, child marriage obtained a powerful and deadly
grip on the Mohammedan people too, soon after they came in contact with us about the tenth century."[13] According to Eleanor
Rathbone, in 1931 the proportion of child wives under ten was
actually higher among the Moslem population of India than among
the Hindus themselves.[14]

In the *Mother India* controversy, the point was repeatedly made
that what was called child marriage in India was really no more

than betrothal. The Census Report of 1921 explains that "the figures contain a large number of unions which are little more than irrevocable betrothal. A Hindu girl-wife as a rule returns after the wedding ceremony to her parents' house and lives there until she reaches puberty, when another ceremony is performed and she goes to her husband and enters upon the real duties of wifehood. At the younger ages, therefore, wives are not wives at all for practical purposes, though their future lives are committed."

This may be true. But as Katherine Mayo and others rightly contended, it did not much alter the case. The evils of too early pregnancy, and of widowhood in the event of the husband's death, remained.

So far as premature sexual exploitation is concerned, attempts were certainly made to guard against it. The *muklava* ceremony, which permitted consummation, was supposed to be performed only when the bride was "fit to be undressed"—that is, she should have reached a stage of physical maturity appropriate to cohabitation. However, much evidence has been adduced to show that consummation before puberty was by no means uncommon. "It exists," reported the Joshi Committee, "to a far greater extent than may be ordinarily supposed and requires a drastic remedy."[15] In Bengal, for instance, the father-in-law might order the betrothed girl to be sent to his home at any time he liked; if his order was not carried out, the girl's husband was entitled to marry again.[16] Katherine Mayo, in *Slaves of the Gods*, quotes many instances of pre-puberty consummation.

Child marriage undoubtedly had much to do with the high death rate among Indian girls. "The female infant," says the Census Report of 1931, "is definitely better equipped by nature for survival than the male; but in India the advantage she has at birth is probably neutralized in infancy by comparative neglect and in adolescence by the strain of bearing children too early and too often."

Sir John Megaw, when he was medical adviser to the India Office, estimated that one of every ten girl-wives was doomed to die in childbirth. Eleanor Rathbone, who made a careful study of the problem, comments, "Such deaths are nothing less than deaths on the rack, due to the straining of muscles and sinews, nerves and tendons, in the body's effort to perform a function for which it is too weak, immature, or ill-formed."[17]

It is clear that the Indian custom of child marriage was a thoroughly undesirable institution. But it was by no means a universal institution. Miss Margaret Cousins, India's first woman Honorary Magistrate, stated that as many as two hundred million Indians did not practice child marriage at all.[18] The northern tribes—Punjabis and Sikhs—had no such custom. Neither had the coolies and agricultural workers of most provinces. It seems to have been found most frequently among the most orthodox Hindu groups—particularly the powerful Brahmins.

However, the practice was common enough, as the census figures show, and evil enough, as the facts demonstrate, to shock the civilized world. Once the facts were widely known, something had to be done about it.

*   *   *

Long before Katherine Mayo startled the reading public with her sensational report, the first efforts had been made, by both Indian and British reformers, to end the abuses of child marriage. The impression sometimes conveyed during the *Mother India* controversy, that Indians were indifferent to the evils of this custom, was a grave injustice. It is true that the dead weight of tradition, supported by ignorance and prejudice, blocked the way. But sensitive Indian leaders had already made heroic and strenuous efforts to bring about a change. So did some progressive British legislators, although they also encountered culpable indifference among government officials, both in India and back in Britain. The truth is that there existed an enlightened concern to institute reforms, together with a conservative attitude of prejudice and indifference, among Indians and British alike.

The story of the struggle to end this custom and the abuses it brought in its train is a tragic record of muddle and mismanagement.[19]

Both the Hindu and Moslem traditions enacted severe penalties for rape outside marriage. In 1846, in drafting the Indian Penal Code, the Law Commissioners extended this principle to marriage in which the wife was a child. The law took final shape in 1860, and the age limit was ten years. Violation of the law could be punished by deportation for life.

In 1891, several cases of serious bodily injury, and even of death, were reported in Bengal as a result of marital intercourse with child brides. The scandal that resulted led to the raising of the age of consent, for married and unmarried girls alike, from ten to twelve.

Unfortunately, the Act was not enforced. Indeed, it remained practically unknown except to judges, lawyers, and court officials. It was often difficult to prove that injury or death had resulted directly from sexual intercourse. It was difficult also in many cases to establish the precise age of the girl. Relatives of the husband, who were normally the only persons likely to know the facts, were reluctant to disclose them. The submissive nature of the Indian girl generally led her to suffer in silence.

Nevertheless, attempts were made to improve the situation. At first these took the form of legal action to raise the age of consent further still. In 1925 this became thirteen for a married girl and fourteen for an unmarried one.

In 1927 an Indian reformer called Sarda drafted a bill to prohibit child marriage altogether. This focused attention on the real problem. The government responded by appointing, in 1928, a committee to examine the whole situation. All but one of its ten members, a British woman doctor, were Indians. It was named for its chairman, Sir Moropant Joshi.

The Joshi Committee made a thorough investigation. They interviewed four hundred witnesses, gathered in eight thousand questionnaires. Their evidence occupied nine volumes of small print. The report concluded: "Early maternity is an evil and an evil of great magnitude. It contributes very largely to maternal and infantile mortality, and in many cases wrecks the physical system of the girl and generally leads to degeneracy in the physique of the race." The evidence suggested moreover that "consummation soon after marriage is almost universal. The fitness of a girl for consummation is hardly taken into consideration."

The Report made two recommendations:

1. That the age of consent be raised to fifteen for married girls and to eighteen for the unmarried.

2. That even the celebration of a marriage involving a girl under fourteen should be prohibited and penalized.

This looked like real progress. The Sarda Bill, amended to conform to the recommendations of the Joshi Report, after vigorous debate in the Legislative Assembly, became law on October 1, 1929.

The Act prohibited all marriages involving girls under fourteen and boys under eighteen. But it was enacted that it would not come into force for six months. Presumably the intention was to use this interval to make it widely known and to issue due warning.

What happened? Priests and marriage brokers saw their livelihood threatened. They decided to make the best of it while the going was good. Distorting the facts to suit their ends, they announced that a law would come into operation on April 1, 1930, forbidding all marriages—in one case the report said that no further marriages would be allowed for fourteen years! So hurry, they proclaimed to harassed parents, and get your daughters off your hands while you can!

The result was catastrophic. All over India, the number of marriages swelled into a vast flood. Everywhere ceremonies and festivities were organized, and girls from infancy upwards were swept into matrimony to the frantic beating of drums.

The dimensions of this vast marital stampede were not fully realized until, in 1933, the 1931 Census was published. The acknowledged number of wives under fifteen years of age had leapt from eight and a half to twelve and a half million, husbands under fifteen from three and a quarter to five and a half million! The number of infant wives under five years of age had quadrupled!

Even so, the census figures showed a million more husbands than wives. Considering the practice of polygamy by some groups, this simply did not make sense. There was only one conclusion to be drawn. The Census Commissioner estimated that from a million to a million and a quarter girls, registered as unmarried, were really married. The false returns reflected the parents' fear of prosecution.

This frightful debacle was a shattering result of the well-intentioned efforts of the reformers. "The Act," commented Eleanor Rathbone, "has been indirectly the occasion of a colossal increase in the evil it sought to remedy."[20]

The only crumb of comfort was that, by the time the Act became law, its existence was widely known throughout the country. How, in fact, did it work?

The condition was made that courts could take action only when formal complaints were lodged. Moreover, the complainant was required to deposit security for the payment of one hundred rupees—a considerable sum to the average Indian—in case the prosecution should fail.

What this amounted to was the strongest discouragement to those who were in a position to report breaches of the law!

Just four days before the Act went into force, twelve thousand Moslems assembled in the Jama Masjid, the great Delhi mosque, for the marriage of a boy of thirteen to a girl of nine. The public attitude to the new law was clearly one of defiance.

More than two years after the law had been enforced, it was reported that there had been, in all, 437 prosecutions, of which only 167 had been successful. In the successful cases, only 17 persons had been sent to prison.

In Bengal, two Moslem brothers, aged forty-five and fifty, were convicted of marrying girls of two and four respectively. They got off with a fine. In Bombay, the threat of legal action prevented a boy of twelve, in very poor health, from marrying a second wife. However, his parents merely transported him outside British territory, and the marriage was contracted. Almost immediately afterwards the boy died, leaving two child widows.

What did the successful prosecutions achieve? According to the Act, marriages contracted under age, though illegal, were not invalid. So, when the husband's family had been duly punished, the young wife, a helpless victim of their spite, had to endure the recriminations heaped upon her innocent head.

The sad truth was that the Sarda Act was well-intentioned but deplorably unrealistic.

Deeply imbedded customs are not easily changed in any culture. And laws cannot change them unless the laws are supported by enlightened public opinion.

Nearly a generation has now passed since these early efforts at reform. Child marriage has dwindled to minor proportions in India today. Dube, in his study of an Indian village published in 1955, found only 14 child marriages in a total of 380 first marriages that were investigated.[21]

The Hindu Marriage Act of 1955 set the minimum legal age for marriage at eighteen for the boy and fifteen for the girl. Betrothals may, of course, take place earlier, and do. But we were told that in India generally public opinion today has almost completely accepted the undesirability of child marriage.

*   *   *

In other countries in the East, child marriage has not been favored. In China the minimum ages were set, at the beginning of the Imperial Era, at sixteen for a boy and fourteen for a girl,[22] although Legge says that in the pre-Confucian period the usual age was between twenty and thirty for young men and between fifteen and twenty for young women.[23] Betrothal, however, was practiced widely, though illegally, in childhood and even before birth.

In Korea, during the period 1219–59, King Kojong was obliged to send consignments of beautiful women to Mongolia, as tribute following the invasion of his country. Before these consignments were rounded up, and also at times when mates for members of the royal family were being sought, marriage was temporarily prohibited. This system of rounding up attractive maidens by state officers led to the practice of marrying girls at an early age in order to prevent them from being seized and taken away.[24]

Later, in the fifteenth century, the minimum age for a bride in Korea was set at fourteen, as in China. This, however, meant thirteen, since the Chinese reckon age from conception and not from birth. In special cases when the parents were over fifty or seriously ill, a daughter could be legally married at twelve, meaning eleven. However, public opinion was opposed to these early unions, and the legal age was later changed to sixteen, and finally brought down again to fifteen.

In practice, however, these laws have not been observed. In the period 1921–30, it was found in Korea that 6.2 per cent of girls under 15 were already married.[25]

In Japan, the minimum age at which marriage was legally permitted was seventeen for a boy and fifteen for a girl. A girl who reached the age of twenty-five, and whose parents had not found her a husband, was free to find a marriage partner for herself.

* * *

By way of postscript, it may be added that in medieval Europe betrothals could take place between a boy and a girl, provided both parties were not under seven years of age.[26] R. H. Bainton gives some specific instances. "The daughter of Count Roger of Sicily was still a child when her hand was given to King Conrad in 1095. Adelheid was eight when in 1110 she was engaged to Henry V. Eleven years was the age of Gettrud, daughter of King Lothair, when betrothed to King Henry of Bavaria in 1127. King Louis of France betrothed his daughter when yet in the cradle to the thirteen-year-old son of King Henry of England in 1158. The son of the Count of Brabant was only just born when he was affianced in 1207 to the daughter of Philip of Swabia."[27]

These were betrothals. Child marriages, however, were not unknown either. During the so-called Age of Chivalry it was common in England and Europe to marry little girls of five years. The Church struggled unsuccessfully to raise the age limit to twelve years. "Wardships and marriages were bought and sold as a matter of everyday routine, like stocks and shares in the modern market. Thomas, Lord of Berkeley (1245–1321) counted on this as a regular and considerable source of income."[28]

The matter can be brought more directly home to us. "It is something of a shock to discover the number of girl and boy weddings in our own enlightened United States. A study of child marriage by the Russell Sage Foundation in 1925 showed that there were in this country 343,000 women married before they were 15 during the last 36 years (no record further back). In 1921 there were in this country 18,388 girls under 16 who had been married when 15 years old or less."[29]

So the West has had its child wives, too.

Chapter 9

WHO KEEPS CONCUBINES?

Olga Lang tells the story of a Chinese general in the province of Shensi. The general had four wives. Being a methodical man, he had them well organized, and their duties clearly defined. Number One took care of the children. Number Two managed the household. Number Three, an educated girl who had studied abroad, acted as her husband's private secretary and interpreter, and helped him to entertain his guests. Number Four was his glamour girl. Her duty was to provide for his sexual needs.[1]

In a man's world this appears to be an efficient and pleasant arrangement. And since China, for long centuries, was a man's world, polygamy was accepted as a good idea. It is said that when Sir Robert Hart was in China, a local official, newly appointed, made a formal call on him in order to get acquainted. He said he wished also to pay his respects to Lady Hart. Sir Robert explained that she was in England, educating their children. He himself had not seen her for several years.

The official then asked if he could be introduced to Sir Robert's second wife. Sir Robert explained that his country did not allow a second wife. He would even be imprisoned if he had one.

"Indeed!" was the reply. "Your honorable country does not appreciate the advantages of some of the customs of my miserable country."[2]

Even in a man's world, however, polygamy cannot be widely practiced—for reasons of simple arithmetic. In West Africa we encountered natives who sincerely believed that a beneficent providence had arranged that several girl babies should be born for every boy baby. However, anyone with a capacity for the most elementary scientific observation will soon discover that this is not so. Only in warlike societies where men kill each other off in large numbers can it become practicable for most males to have more than one female. The position of a general with four wives is clearly one of unusual privilege!

A human society that believes in polygamy must therefore decide which of its men are to be permitted this right. It cannot be accorded to many of them.

Although all the great Eastern civilizations accepted the possibility of polygamous marriage, it would be quite a mistake to imagine that they approved it in principle. It would be more accurate to say that they accepted its inevitability with some reluctance.

What makes polygamy inevitable is the nature of the patriarchal family. A man must have a son in order to continue his line. His hope is that his wife will produce an heir to gladden his heart. But supposing she should be childless?

In that event the man's obligation to beget a son is more important than any obligation he may feel not to introduce a rival to his wife's affection. She herself, knowing that she has failed to fulfill her primary function as a wife, is fully aware of her husband's predicament and eager to rescue him from it.

This situation, when it arises, makes it impossible for any patriarchal society to insist on strict monogamy. In the Old Testament we read, "Now Sarah, Abraham's wife, bare him no children; and she had a handmaid, an Egyptian, whose name was Hagar. And Sarah said unto Abraham, Behold now, the Lord hath restrained me from bearing: I pray thee, go in unto my maid; it may be that I may obtain children by her. And Abraham hearkened to the voice of Sarah, and he went in unto Hagar, and she conceived."[3]

In this story we find a picture that would be completely intelligible to Eastern tradition. The wife of the childless man takes the initiative in providing him with another woman who can make good her deficiency. By this means his problem—and hers—is solved.

Theoretically, of course, it would be possible for the man to discard his childless wife and replace her with the more fruitful woman. Sometimes this was in fact done. But proper consideration for the wife required, in all humanitarian traditions, that she be spared the humiliation of such a rejection. The outlook for any woman so treated would have been grim. She would return to her family, branded as a failure. No other man would want to marry her, since she was known to be barren. Polygamy, in these circumstances, was kinder and more ethical than divorce.

So, with the necessity to arrange for two women to share intimately the life of one man, the stage is set for polygamous marriage. In a strictly patriarchal setting no other solution is really practicable.

*   *   *

In families where women's rights were respected, every effort was made to manage the polygamous situation without injustice.

"If there is need of a handmaiden to bear children, she shall be taken into the homestead quietly. A wife cannot be degraded to the position of a Green Skirt, nor the Green Skirt raised to the position of wife, so long as the wife is alive."[4]

So ran Section 102 of the General Summary of the Laws of the Chinese Empire. In China a man could have only one legal wife. Apart from divorcing the first, he could not marry a second woman. If he tried to do so, the second marriage would be declared invalid. In general the same was true among the Hindus, although Dubois says that for one reason only—"to pay the debt to his ancestors"—he might take a second fully legitimate wife, provided his first wife was in agreement.[5] In Japan, likewise, more than one legal wife was not permitted.

What we find in these cultures, therefore, is not polygamy in the technical sense of the term. Any other woman a man took occupied a subsidiary position. The Green Skirt, or concubine, on being introduced into the home, must not be allowed to usurp the wife's privileged position. The danger of this is great. In the story of Abraham, we read, "And when Hagar saw that she had conceived, her mistress was despised in her eyes."[6]

Concubinage was carefully regulated from the time of Confucius. The status of the concubine, who often had previously been a slave girl or prostitute, was lower than that of the wife. In the household, the wife had dominion over all concubines. Sometimes the husband could not even have sexual intercourse with a concubine without his wife's permission.

Professor Headland tells the story of a Chinese neighbor of his in Peking—a great scholar and a perfect gentleman. One of the slave girls in his home was found to be pregnant, and responsibility for her state pointed clearly to the head of the house. The gentleman's wife, who was the daughter of the governor of a province, was outraged, and proposed to give the girl away to anyone who would take her. To this the husband objected, and a serious disagreement followed. What was significant was that the wife felt scandalized, not because her husband had had sex relations with the girl—that was a matter of little or no account—but because he had omitted to ask his wife formally to give her to him.[7]

The concubine, therefore, had a clearly defined position. No stigma was attached to her. She had a recognized status in the household, into which she had been introduced for an acceptable purpose, normally with the full approval of the wife. Her position was much better than that of a man's mistress in our own society. She and her children were entitled to maintenance. Usually they had their own private apartments in the household. So long as she remained in favor with the husband, her position could be pleasant and indeed privileged.

However, she had no real security. She could not claim protection since she was not legally married. She might be discarded at will—no divorce procedure was necessary. She had therefore to keep her wits about her in order to retain her position. The two best ways to do so were to make herself sexually attractive to the husband, and to bear him sons. If she remained in favor until the death of the wife, she might find herself promoted to succeed her as mistress of the household. This, for a concubine, was the classic success story.

Occasionally a married man would take a concubine, not because his wife was childless, but because her children were all daughters.

There was once a Chinese prince who lived in a palace in Peking. His wife, the princess, bore him three girls, one after the other. This was discouraging, because princes have a special need for sons and heirs. The prince got nasty about it, and blamed his wife for an apparently incurable propensity for producing female offspring. The princess, hurt and humiliated, gave her husband one of her maids. In due course the girl produced a daughter!

It now looked as if it might after all be the prince's fault. But the maid was pregnant again, so judgment was withheld. The child was born—yet another daughter! Now the prince was shaken and miserable. It did look as if he was the cause of all the trouble.

Finally the maid had a third child. It was a boy! Everyone—the prince, the princess, and the maid—was delighted. Success at last![8]

*   *   *

With the door to polygamy ajar, it was not hard to push it wide open.

Although the proper reason for taking a concubine was the failure of a wife to bear sons, other reasons were easily concocted to justify it.

Headland suggests one of these. When a Chinese woman became pregnant, he says, she was expected to separate herself from her husband until after the birth of her child. "Where in the world can you find another female mammal that will allow any such association with the male during the gestation of her young? The Chinese hold this view, and the wife, in order to satisfy her husband and protect herself, gives him a concubine during this period."[9]

Again, a wife might decide to encourage her husband to take another, younger woman because she found his sexual demands exacting.

"Mother's health was not sound after the birth of my third brother. She could not give adequate attention to Father. Mother felt sorry for Father because he had to work hard at the Court, and, when he returned home, she could not give him the needed cheer and comfort. Father was ordinarily a healthy man, steady and calm. But now he appeared nervous, quick-tempered, and restless. Mother urged him to look for a second wife. He tried to conceal his emotion and act as if he was not at all enthusiastic over her generous suggestion. But he soon accepted her consent with deep gratitude.

"Father chose the daughter of one of his clerks as his new wife-to-be. He had never seen the girl except from the picture which her father showed him. She was in Bangkok, supposedly studying in the Rajini School for Girls. Father gave the clerk 400 ticals to send for his daughter, who turned out to be a disappointment. She was illiterate and not as bright as she appeared in her photograph. But Father was a good natured person who was easily satisfied. The woman had some physical attraction. I think he liked her age. She was then nineteen."[10]

The best way to avoid conflict, when a husband hankered for a concubine, was for the wife to choose one for him, or to approve of his choice. Then both husband and concubine would feel indebted to her for making the way smooth. If the wife seriously thwarted her husband's wishes, he might divorce her and supplant her with another.

So the taking of a concubine became the accepted right of the Eastern husband. If he wanted another woman in the house and could afford to maintain her, he was likely to have his way. In the middle and upper classes, any wife might have to face this possibility. Eastern wives, trained to submission, were usually philosophical about it. In China and Japan they had very little option. Jealousy was a recognized ground for divorce!

Of one thing the wife could be sure. She knew that, so long as she did not provoke her husband to the point of divorcing her, she was secure in the enjoyment of her legal rights. Concubines need not get in her way. They would not invade her private quarters. They were under her authority, and she could appoint their household tasks so as to ease her own burdens. It was not ideal —but she could make it tolerable. And anyway, it was life!

So the polygamous household became the rich man's privilege. Indeed, it was sometimes the badge of his prestige. To have many attractive women at his disposal was the recognized mark of opulence. In China particularly, where the labor of women was not much used outside the home, keeping many females was a decidedly uneconomic proposition. The man who could afford to do it had obviously enough and to spare of this world's goods. He had arrived.

The wife of Wang Lung's uncle cried out, "Now Wang Lung is seeking to pluck a flower somewhere." And when O-lan looked at her humbly, not understanding, she laughed and said again,

"And it is not to be thought, poor fool, that one woman is enough for any man, and if it is a weary hard-working woman who has worn away her flesh working for him, it is less than enough for him. His fancy runs elsewhere the more quickly, and you, poor fool, have never been fit for a man's fancy and little better than an ox for his labor. And it is not for you to repine when he has money and buys himself another to bring her to his house, for all men are so."

And Wang Lung went out and motioned secretly to the wife of his uncle and he said,

"I listened and heard what you had to say in the courts and you are right. I have need of more than one and why should I not, seeing that I have land to feed us all?"

She answered volubly and eagerly,

"And why not, indeed? So have all men who have prospered. It is only the poor man who must needs drink from one cup."[11]

*   *   *

If a prosperous farmer or merchant could afford to take a concubine, or even two, and so make himself the envy of his neighbors, how could a potentate or prince demonstrate his vastly superior social status? To outdo the relatively little man, he had to accumulate many attractive women and maintain them in idle ease and splendid luxury.

Thus there emerged the institution known to the Moslem world as the *harem* or *seraglio*—the segregated quarters strictly forbidden to all intruders, where an important and prosperous Eastern ruler kept the many women who were retained for his exclusive pleasure. The supreme mark of a monarch's splendor was reached when so many beautiful young women were available to him that a fresh virgin, like a tasty dish, was served up to him every night.

"Now when the turn came for each maiden to go in to King Ahasuerus, after being twelve months under the regulations for the women, since this was the regular period of their beautifying, six months with oil of myrrh and six months with spices and ointments for women—when the maiden went in to the king in this way she was given whatever she desired to take with her from the harem to the king's palace. In the evening she went, and in the morning she came back to the second harem in custody of Shashgaz the king's eunuch who was in charge of the concubines; she did not go in to the king again, unless the king delighted in her and she was summoned by name."[12]

From the girl's point of view, this was obviously a life of limited horizons. The Book of Odes has a plaintive little song of the concubines, in which they bemoan the fact that whereas his wife can spend the whole night with the prince, they may visit him only for a short time, going and returning in the dark; and only occasionally with her express permission.

> Small are those starlets,
> Three or five of them in the east.
> Swiftly by night we go;
> In the early dawn we are with the prince.
> Our lot is not like hers.
>
> Small are those starlets,
> And there are Orion and the Pleiades.
> Swiftly by night we go,
> Carrying our coverlets and sheets.
> Our lot is not like hers.[13]

The great man's women are normally under the care of eunuchs, who supervise and organize the details of their lives. It is said that in China all officers, dignitaries and servants attached to the imperial household were eunuchs—some three thousand in all, not including the women. In this vast household, the Emperor was the one and only male whose sex organs were intact.[14]

The Frenchman, Matignon, has described the careful records that had to be kept of the Emperor's nightly cohabitations. This was necessary in order that the legal rights of his children might be properly recognized.

Each night His Highness decided which concubine he would summon to share his couch. He wrote her name on a tablet and gave it to the chief eunuch. The tablet was then delivered to the concubine concerned, who kept it as her personal record.

When the time came for the Emperor to retire, the concubine he had chosen was conveyed by her eunuch attendants, in a magnificent sedan chair, to the royal bedchamber. After spending the night with him, she was taken back at dawn to her own quarters.

In the morning, the name of the concubine, and the date, were entered into the special register kept for the purpose. Each entry was countersigned by the Emperor himself.[15]

The concubines of a royal personage enjoyed great prestige. In *Dream of the Red Chamber*, when a daughter of the household, Cardinal Spring, was appointed Imperial Concubine of the second rank, the family treated this as a great honor.[16]

Some time later, Cardinal Spring was allowed to pay a visit to her home. She came with all the pomp of a princess, preceded and attended by eunuchs from the imperial palace, who supervised every detail of her visit. Among other arrangements they made, nuns were summoned to offer special prayers on her behalf.[17]

The pampered concubines of an Oriental potentate enjoyed high status of a sort. But it was something far removed from the status of a wife. "A chieftain's women," Edward Thompson says of the Indian scene, "were toys and dolls. Chosen for their physical loveliness, they were moths who led a twilight existence that ended in the bewildering pomp that brought them to the flame."[18]

*   *   *

When Chinese ladies heard that a woman was giving her husband a concubine, they said that she was "going to eat vinegar."

From the woman's point of view, polygamy is by no means as attractive as it looks to the man. Almost invariably, says Olga Lang, it means lowered status for *some* women in the culture, and often for all of them.[19]

There is a story of a Chinese wife who, in her prayers, asked the gods to make the family prosperous.

"Vouchsafe to bestow upon us a hundred rolls of silk—a hundred, but no more, please."

Her husband, who was listening to his wife's devotions, asked, "Why no more than a hundred rolls?"

"Because," replied his wife sadly, "if you get more than that you'll want to buy a concubine."[20]

"Polygamy," said Ryder Smith, "is inherently factious."[21] Eastern experience would eloquently confirm this. Instances are found of two or more women who live peaceably together with one man. But there are innumerable instances where the atmosphere is anything but peaceful. The eternal struggle of the Chinese family, says Olga Lang, was to prevent the women from fighting each other, and to prevent the young people from falling in love. She adds that both efforts met with dismal failure![22]

The *Dream of the Red Chamber* provides many illustrations of the rivalries that can develop. When Phoenix becomes aware of a rival to her husband's affection, she plots ruthlessly to worst her. She finally succeeds in stirring up the whole family against her, and driving her out. On another occasion, when her husband takes a concubine, Phoenix succeeds in making life so miserable for the girl that she commits suicide. In these intrigues, Phoenix is simply exercising her prerogative, on the principle that all is fair in love and war, and that love turns to warfare when two women compete for the same man.

Evidently, therefore, the Chinese rule that wives should not give way to jealousy was something of a counsel of perfection!

A comparatively modern variation of the old Chinese custom of taking a concubine is suggested in Pearl Buck's novel, *Letter from Peking*. Here the American wife of a half-Chinese husband was forced to leave China when the Communists entered Peking. Still passionately longing for a reunion with her husband, she heard that he was being forced, for political reasons, to take a Chinese wife. From the latter she received a letter. Here is part of it: "At my former request, he wrote to you asking your agreement to my coming to his house as wife-in-absence. You know this is quite common, no more second wife or concubine, as before, which is too old fashioned, but wife-in-absence. Of course if you come back some other time, I will go away if you wish. To you I have respect as younger to elder. Please permit me, and tell me how everything should be in caring for our husband."[23]

Perhaps the only way for two women involved with the same man to get along harmoniously together is for them not to meet!

Conflict in the household becomes further complicated when there are several concubines who are not only competing with the wife but also vying with each other for favors. A wife in Thailand, seriously ill at the time, thus remonstrates with her husband's concubines, "The duty of a good wife is to see that her husband is happy. The Great Master is not happy when you two start quarreling.

"If I die, one of you will take my place. I shall have a word with the Great Master and ask him to promote the one who is more kind to my children, more considerate of his happiness, more understanding about life, and more capable of not disgracing the Great Master in his social relations."[24]

Concubines, it seems, were notoriously troublesome persons to handle. Even the great Confucius found them so. He said, "Of

all people, concubines and servants are the most difficult to behave to. If you are familiar to them, they lose their humility. If
you maintain a reserve toward them, they are discontented."[25]

Even the men of the household, therefore, were not unaffected
by the disturbances that concubines created. Indeed, these disturbances not only set up conflict between brothers, but even between father and son. In the Tso Chuan we read of fathers having
sex relations with their sons' wives and sons with their fathers'
concubines. In "The Three Kingdoms," Lu Pu actually murders
his father, the tyrant Tung Chou, for having taken from him a
beautiful dancer whom he had acquired.[26]

A group of Chinese students, all of whose fathers kept concubines, were asked in 1923 by Dr. Ava Milam what they thought
of the custom. As a result of what they had experienced, they
were overwhelmingly opposed to it.[27]

Long ago, a Chinese observer wrote these words about the institution of keeping concubines:

> The tribulus grows on the wall,
> And cannot be brushed away.
> The story of the inner chamber
> Cannot be told.
> What would have to be told
> Would be the vilest of recitals.[28]

*   *   *

In India the keeping of women by a man took a special form
known as *purdah*. Though *purdah* did not necessarily imply
polygamy, they frequently went together. The word *purdah* literally means a curtain. It is used to describe the custom by which
the women of a household were strictly segregated and locked
up out of sight in the *zenana*, or women's private quarters.
Originally a Moslem practice, it was taken over by many Hindus
also, especially in the North.

Hilda Wernher writes, "Here I am, driving across the parched
plains of India . . . to call on a princely family from Rajputana,
who keep their women in a *purdah* stricter than that of any Mus-
lims. In the Sangwar clan, as in those of many Rajput rulers, a
father-in-law never beholds his son's wife, nor can a daughter-in-
law appear with her husband before his mother. It is the most
severe segregation I've ever heard of."[29]

The fierce Moslem insistence on the strictest chastity and fidelity of their women led to the conclusion that the only way they could be kept safe—from marauding males and from their own impulses—was to lock them up. The system may have begun with captive women in the period when Islam was expanding by ruthless conquest.

It has been argued that this custom was originally necessary for the physical safety of the women themselves. Eleanor McDougall takes this view. "*Purdah* was not devised as a means of oppression. It grew at first as a protection for women in early days when there was perpetual petty warfare between neighboring places, and it was not safe for women to be seen except by their near relatives, or to venture beyond their own homes."[30]

Whatever its origin, the practice led to many evil consequences, especially to the health of the women concerned. Here is a report of the Health Officer of Calcutta in 1913: "To secure privacy, efficient lighting and ventilation are absolutely disregarded, the zenana being usually the most insanitary part of the house. No wonder that tuberculosis, which thrives in damp, dark, airless corners, plays havoc in the zenanas." On the same theme Hester Gray comments, "Indian women are just beginning to realize that the lack of fresh air and sunlight, from which secluded women suffer, is directly responsible for phthisis, osteomalacia, gross pelvic deformity, and deaths of thousands of mothers and children in childbirth."[31]

It has been estimated that, at the close of the eighteenth century, there were as many as forty million Indian women in *purdah*. While enlightened Indians tended to give up the practice, others were adopting it, because unfortunately it conveyed social prestige. A man who could keep several women shut up, doing no useful work, was obviously a man of substance. *Purdah* was seldom practiced by the poor, for the simple reason that it was a luxury they could not afford.

Often the women themselves were persuaded that it was good to live in *purdah*. One Indian Moslem lady put it this way, "We lead a quiet, peaceful, protected life within our own homes. And, with men as they are, we should be miserable, terrified, outside." Clearly she was indoctrinated to believe that the predatory male was a terrifying creature, and that lifelong imprisonment was to be preferred to the prospect of meeting him in public.

This is not surprising when we remember that, in recent years, Moslem women who have been persuaded to walk abroad without a veil have undergone all the sensations of terror that a Western woman today would feel if she were obliged to walk down the main street of her home town stark naked.

*　　　*　　　*

Today polygamy in the East is withering away. It is not being defeated by the imposition of new laws, though recent legislation in India, China and Japan requires monogamy of all but Moslems. It is not being overthrown by ardent reformers, though there have been some who have attacked multiple marriage. What is happening is that the old polygamous systems are dying a natural death. The emancipation of women, and the rising costs of living, simply make it impracticable. Public opinion, also, is opposed to polygamy because it degrades women. It therefore has no prestige value any more.

Even in Islam, which permits a man to have four wives, it is becoming fashionable not to demand this privilege. Community leaders who take more than one wife find their popularity waning. Interpreters of the Koran are suggesting that the right to four wives was a grudging concession made by the Prophet to the evil conditions of his own day, and that he looked for the time when monogamy would be practiced by the faithful.

The old habits die hard, however. Freedman, in his study of Singapore,[32] notes that while the traditional system by which prosperous men kept concubines under one roof, or in adjacent courts, is almost gone, the system of the "kept woman" is taking its place. The counterpart of the oldtime potentate today may have two or more women installed in apartments in different areas of the city. By thus distributing his women in different areas, he can make his polygamy less conspicuous.

So perhaps all that is happening is that the East is giving up its harems, only to adopt instead the distinctively Western forms of polygamy—temporary free liaisons, the keeping of mistresses, and the periodic exchanging of wives by divorce and remarriage. Whether this will prove to be progress is anybody's guess.

Chapter 10

MARRIED LIFE AND MARRIED LOVE

In Japan there was once a tenderhearted husband who, out of pity for his wife, helped her one day to do the week's washing. The criticism of the neighbors was so violent that in the end the family were forced to leave the district![1]

This incident dramatizes for us very clearly the fundamental facts about traditional husband-wife relationships in the East—that the wife is expected to occupy a subordinate position, and that attempts on the part of the individual couple to put their relationship on a basis of equal comradeship are likely to meet with trouble.

Eastern literature on marriage is full of rules and injunctions intended to discourage anything resembling equality in the status of the partners. The husband is constantly reminded of his superiority, the wife of her inferiority.

A Hindu husband who adheres strictly to his religion does not speak his wife's name. Instead, he refers to her in such deprecatory terms as "my servant" or "my dog."[2] The Japanese husband, likewise, is enjoined never to speak appreciatively of his wife. The correct procedure is to refer to her as "my old hag," or in similar terms calculated to devalue her in the ears of his listeners.

In conversation the Japanese use a number of words for "you." There is a very polite and respectful one that is used by the wife in addressing her husband. There is also an impolite one that a husband should always use in speaking to his wife. If he were to use the polite word, his friends would say he was henpecked, and he would become a laughingstock.

Ruth Benedict tells the story of a prominent Japanese gentleman of liberal views who returned from a period abroad. In a speech he made a statement that caused a public scandal. "He spoke about how happy he was to return to Japan, and mentioned reunion with his wife as one of the reasons for his pleasure. He should have spoken of his parents, Fujiyama, of his dedication to the national mission of Japan. His wife did not belong to this level."[3]

There is a widespread tradition throughout the East that a man should not eat in his wife's company. Manu says expressly that it is forbidden to do so. The husband eats first, and helps himself to all the tasty morsels. When he is finished, and has departed, his wife may pick up what she can out of what remains. If a Japanese husband is entertaining guests, he should regard his wife as on a level with the servants, and treat her accordingly.

A husband should consider his wife's work as menial, and beneath his dignity. (The well-meaning Japanese husband learned this the hard way!) There is no discourtesy in the husband standing by while his wife toils and slaves. "For him there is no ill-conscience as he basks in the sun on the verandah while his women folk pound the rice, prepare the curries, and perhaps bring him betel to chew. There is no toil in which the husband assists the wife, yet she may assist him in many explicitly male tasks."[4]

If his wife is refractory, there is no reason why the husband should not chastise her. The Artha Shastra gives the correct Indian formula—three strikes on her hips either with a bamboo cane, with a rope, or with the palm of the hand. We may be sure that these precise directions were framed as a plea for moderation. The evidence suggests that husbands were sometimes wont to go to unreasonable extremes in punishing their wives. Gandhi acknowledged this. "Hindu culture," he admitted, "has erred on the side of excessive subordination of the wife to the husband. This has resulted in the husband usurping and exercising authority that reduces him to the level of the brute."[5]

Is it any wonder that the Eastern boy, surrounded from early childhood by the influence of such ideas as these, naturally accepts the concept of his status as a superior being when he comes to marry?

*   *   *

The conditioning of the Eastern husband to the concept of his superiority is mild compared to the indoctrination of the wife concerning her subservient role.

The Padma purana, with the full authority of the Hindu religion behind it, thus instructs the Indian wife concerning her duties:

"There is no other god on earth for a woman than her husband. The most excellent of all the good works that she can do is to seek to please him by manifesting perfect obedience to him. Therein should lie her sole rule of life.

"Be her husband deformed, aged, infirm, offensive in his manners; let him also be choleric, debauched, immoral, a drunkard, a gambler; let him frequent places of ill-repute, live in open sin with other women, have no affection whatever for his home; let him rave like a lunatic; let him love without honour; let him be blind, deaf, dumb or crippled, in a word, let his defects be what they may, let his wickedness be what it may, a wife should always look upon him as her god, should lavish on him all her attention and care, paying no heed whatsoever to his character and giving him no cause whatsoever for his displeasure. . . .

"A wife must eat only after her husband has had his fill. If the latter fasts, she shall fast, too; if he touch not food, she shall not touch it; if he be in affliction she shall be so, too; if he be cheerful she shall share his joy. . . .

"If he sing she must be in ecstasy; if he dance she must look at him with delight; if he speak of learned things she must listen to him with admiration. In his presence, indeed, she ought always to be cheerful, and never show signs of sadness or discontent."[6]

Tradition forbade the Hindu wife to speak her husband's personal name. To do so would be highly disrespectful. When addressing him directly, she should call him "my lord." When referring to him in the presence of others, he is "the master of the house."

Frieda Hauswirth describes an unsuccessful attempt to break an Indian wife, who was widely read in Western literature, of this traditional habit. "No question sprung in surprise, no trick I tried in sheer fun, could ever induce her to overcome the Hindu wife's inhibition against letting the name of her husband cross her lips."[7]

The wife's demeanor in her husband's presence should be of humility and obeisance. As a symbol of this, she must not raise her eyes when he addresses her, but listen attentively and respectfully.

Savitri Devi Nanda describes her mother's departure to her husband's home. Her three aunts bade her farewell.

"The two eldest gave instructions to my mother on how to behave in her husband's home. The eldest said, 'Respect your husband as you would a god. You are but a shadow and he the substance.'

"The second said, 'Humility, my child, is a great Dharma.'"[8]

The traditional Chinese wife was instructed in the same vein. "The woman's duty," said Confucius, "is to prostrate herself submissively before her husband, in such a way as to have no will of her own, but to demonstrate a perfect form of obedience. There is no place for independent action on the part of any woman." Mrs. Mary Bryson[9] describes the improving books and pamphlets written for the edification of Chinese women—with such titles as "Counsels," "Instructions," "Admonitions for the Inner Apartments." There is much about household duties, dress, and manners. But the recurring *motif* is that a wife must strive constantly to cultivate respect, modesty, docility and a submissive demeanor in all relationships with her husband.

Even in making her toilet, the good Chinese wife should accompany each action with appropriate thoughts. "While powdering the face, remember that the heart must be kept clean and white; in arranging the head-dress, remember that the thoughts must be carefully regulated; in oiling the hair, resolve to make the heart pliable and docile."

It is said that in olden times the first three months of a Chinese marriage were a period of probation in which the young wife was being closely observed. If her behavior toward her husband failed to comply with what the tradition required, she might be sent back to her parents with the label "not approved."[10]

The Japanese wife was no better off. She was completely under her husband's thumb. Setsuko Hani describes how, under the Civil Code, the wife had no personal freedom. In any matter relating to her private life, the management of property, or the conduct of business, she could not make a move without her husband's permission. Anything she did without consulting him could be cancelled at his behest. "According to the Civil Code, an unmarried woman of over 20 years of age is a competent person just as a man is; but marriage turns her into an incompetent person. This stipulation can be interpreted only in the light that marriage produce as its effect the incompetency of a wife as a means to impose upon her complete submission to her husband."[11]

The picture is clear. For the Eastern wife, the road to marriage is not one that leads toward personal fulfillment and enlargement. It is a vocation calling for self-surrender and self-sacrifice. "As the river loses itself when it blends with the ocean, so the bride becomes one with the family of her husband."[12]

*   *   *

The domination-submission pattern traditionally prescribed for Eastern marriage is hard to understand for those accustomed to the freedom and equality that characterize husband-wife relations in the West today.

To understand what it really meant, several points must be made clear. The married couple, for example, did not normally live together in the sense that a Western couple do. They lived in an extended family group along with many others. The men and women were engaged in different tasks, had their meals apart, even slept in separate quarters. Husband and wife might therefore see very little of one another for long periods. Gandhi, in his autobiography, describes how in his early married life, in the large household to which he and his wife belonged, virtually the only time when they were alone together was at night when they had sex relations.

The development of any close relationship among Indian married couples was even actively discouraged. "It is an unwritten law among our clans that young brides and grooms should not see too much of each other, for, they say, 'New love is delicate, and gets easily destroyed, unless nurtured with care.'"[13]

In China also, "the parents exercise close supervision over their married children, for the young wife is kept in the women's apartments and the young man in the men's, and there is but little chance for them to be together in many of the ordinary homes."[14] It is customary for a recently married young man to be teased and ridiculed if he takes too much notice of his bride or wants to be with her for a great deal of the time.

Denied the opportunity to be alone together in the crowded household, the married couple could not solve their problem by

going out of the home. It was against tradition for husband and
wife to walk and talk together in public. Even when they went
to some outside function—a wedding or funeral, for instance—they
would not sit together, but with the men and women respectively,
at opposite sides of the room.

Even when husband and wife had a rare opportunity to be alone
together, they often had no real language of communication.
Neither of them had learned to feel at ease with members of the
opposite sex. Even today, in social gatherings in the East, we have
noticed how hard it is to get boys and girls to mix—the separate
sex groups usually huddle together nervously in different parts of
the room. And if as groups they are so reticent, imagine the para-
lyzing embarrassment an individual would suffer if left completely
alone with one person of the opposite sex.

Remember, too, that the married couple came to each other as
complete strangers. There had been no ice-breaking courtship
period in which they could get acquainted. The idea of shyness
between husband and wife may sound unconvincing—yet often
each was to the other a mysterious and unknown being, encountered only in the silent sexual intimacies that took place between
them under cover of darkness.

This extreme reticence was actually encouraged. "Korean husbands addressed their wives in the formal style, and extreme
modesty amounting to an excessive shyness was the accepted
manner of every lady throughout the land."[15] The easy intimacy
of the Western married couple had no part in Eastern custom.
Manu sternly warns the Hindu husband that he must never look
at his wife while she is eating, sneezing, yawning, sitting carelessly
at her ease, or baring her bosom to feed her child. It is highly
improper for him to see her naked. A Hindu man will not appear
completely unclothed in the presence of another man, let alone
in the presence of his wife.

The idea that husband and wife should talk together about
their innermost feelings would come as a surprise to many Eastern
couples. In a series of seminars conducted in widely separated
regions in India, we repeatedly asked about traditional attitudes
toward communication between husband and wife. We were told
again and again that the man regarded his wife as the means of
securing sons, as a source of sexual pleasure, and as a house-

keeper; and that the woman sought in her husband security and protection, and the fulfillment of her womanhood in becoming a mother. When burdened with some personal trouble or anxiety, their natural impulse would be to seek understanding and counsel, not from each other, but from a relative or friend of the same sex. There are exceptions, of course, but this is the general rule.

There is a Chinese saying that a man needs a wife to keep house, a concubine for sexual enjoyment, and a friend with whom to share ideas, dreams, and hopes. Many a husband may have to look to his wife to combine the first two functions. But for the third he would naturally seek out someone of his own sex. How could a woman understand the workings of a man's mind, or a man the workings of a woman's?

* * *

"Son of Heaven directs inherent principle of Yang essence. She-who-is-equal regulates Yin qualities. Son of Heaven rules all without. She-who-is-equal rules all within."[16]

This statement in the Chinese "Record of Rites" gives us a valuable clue to the superiority and inferiority concepts of the functions of marriage partners in the East. The idea is that these distinctions are not intended to rank husband and wife according to their respective worth. They are intended to symbolize the separateness, and the reciprocal nature, of their functions. The Yang-Yin principle certainly implies superiority and inferiority. But what is meant, as Father O'Hara has expressed it, is "the superiority of activeness and the inferiority of receptiveness."[17]

It would be unrealistic to suggest that this noble concept has been prominent in the minds of the average Asian peasant and his wife. Again and again, they have interpreted their roles as expressions of domination and subservience. But it would be equally unrealistic to suggest that the fundamental purpose behind the Eastern conception of marriage is merely to enable the husband to bully his wife.

As a matter of fact, it is quite a mistake to consider that in the East only the wife was submissive. The husband was equally submissive toward those who were above him in the hierarchy. The obedience of the wife to her husband was no more abject than was the obedience of that same husband to his father in the home, or to those above him in rank in the community outside the home. If we single out the husband-wife relationship and interpret it as exploitation of the woman, we gain an entirely false picture. In the rigid hierarchy of patriarchal society, everyone exploited someone else, and was in turn exploited by someone else. When this is clearly grasped, the word "exploitation" is seen to be the wrong term. It was simply that relationships in the East hardly ever operated horizontally as between two people on the same level. Almost invariably, they operated vertically—looking up toward a superior, or looking down toward an inferior.

It would have been completely out of keeping with all the rest of Eastern thinking about human relationships, therefore, if marriage had been conceived of as a fellowship of equals. Instead, it was seen as the interaction of two different types of persons, who by a reciprocal operation brought into being the fundamental unit of human society—the family. The idea of leveling the differences that existed between them was not only absurd—it was dangerous—because it was as a result of their differences that the Yang-Yin principle was able to operate and to sustain the purposes of Creation. To suggest that the differences between men and women were of no significance was to fly in the face of Heaven.

So the functions of husband and wife were sharply differentiated. In China, the woman is called *nei jen*—the "inside person." In the outside world she may have had no power or influence. But that was not her province. In the inside world of the home, her power and prestige were considerable.

Here is how a Chinese farmer expressed it:

"The house is woman's sphere. Here she reigns supreme. As man's authority is confined to the outside world, so he needs to have no responsibility about the work inside the courtyard walls. The female must cook, and spin, weave, braid, and sew all of the stuffs—the hemp, the jute, the flax, the silk, the straw, and the cotton that the male has brought to her."[18]

And here is the testimony of an Indian woman who had seen the position of the women in her own family, "The creed of my great-aunts and great-grandmothers, like the ancient wisdom of my race, had been that the husband is the substance and the wife the shadow. But by some strange law it seemed to have worked out the other way. In the older generations of our family the wives were the substance and the men the shadow. The menfolk had flitted about on the outskirts of life while the ancient dames had taken the fulness of it. Each was the sun of her house; around her moved the others like the greater or the lesser planets."[19]

To the Western mind, the home may be considered a narrow sphere in which to operate. But we are thinking of the suburban house of today, to which the husband and father returns to eat and sleep from the great metropolis where the real work of the world is done. In the agrarian society of the ancient East, the world's life and the world's work revolved around the home. The wives who had the power to influence and fashion the life of the home shaped the destinies of men and of nations. They knew and recognized their limitations, and respected the frontiers they might not cross. But to think of them as inferior and unimportant members of society is greatly to underestimate their power.

* * *

The beginning of an Eastern marriage is like the awakening of children on Christmas morning.

"What will he be like?"

"What will she be like?"

These are the questions that have continually been occupying the minds of bride and bridegroom for weeks and months past.

Happy indeed are they if they feel as this Chinese couple did:

> Round and round the firewood is bound;
> And the Three Stars appear in the sky.
>   This evening is what evening,
>   That I see this good man?
> O me! O me!
> That I should get a good man like this!

> Round and round the thorn is bound;
> And the Three Stars are seen from the door.
>   This evening is what evening,
>   That I should see this beauty?
> O me! O me!
> That I should see a beauty like this![20]

Whatever their first impressions, however, the way ahead for the couple is clear and plain. They are united for life. They have

portant task to fulfill together. It is obviously desirable
should strive to make their married life a pleasant one.

Waln, soon after her marriage, received the following
ge from Shun-ko, her adopted Chinese mother.

"Kuei-tzu is inviting you to join our annual procession of worship to the sacred mountain. As your mother by affection I command you to refuse this first year of your marriage. Make yourself secure now in your husband's esteem. Then in later years you may do all things as you choose."[21]

Since the Eastern idea was that love came after marriage, the early months together as husband and wife were the time of courtship.

"After the marriage, the wedded ones court each other slowly, by pleasing, and by giving and taking happiness. Each seems only to look upon the lovely things in the other, forgetting or not seeing the unlovely things. Thus in time they would mould each other to the one common way, which is their way of life. Once given, the love of a Hindu girl can never be taken back. Her husband is her only love."[22]

Fortunately, in the East ideas about love are not distorted by romantic illusion. "Perfect harmony between two beings who are in love on the Earth," said Tagore, "is as rare as the meeting of two stars in the Heavens." So the young couple do not ask too much, but are content with the simplest tokens of affection. Their opportunities to be together, as husband and wife, are probably much more limited than those of a courting couple in the West. So they must make the best of those opportunities as they come.

Demonstrations of affection must, of course, be strictly private. Even to touch hands in the presence of others would be a serious offense. It would be a mark of disrespect toward elders, and a bad example to the young. More lavish displays of affection—"smelling the face," as the Chinese say—would be highly improper.

So, inevitably, expressions of love must be confined to the times when the couple can retire behind the curtains of the marriage bed. This fact has led the Chinese to coin a quaint saying:

> Ascend to bed, husband and wife.
> Descend from bed, reserved gentlefolk.[23]

An Indian woman remembers this incident from her childhood:

"I was allowed to go to my newly-married aunt and uncle's rooms. They did not mind my being there. While I examined things they flirted with each other, and I had seen them kiss too. My aunt would say 'Careful! The child!' But my uncle would laugh. They were foolish.

"One day I asked my mother why my uncle and aunt were so friendly in their rooms and so aloof outside among the family. She was angry with me and threatened to forbid me their rooms if ever I repeated things. So I became very careful and silent, for I liked my aunt's rooms."[24]

Even the strictly formal Japanese could unbend in private. "The Japanese man . . . loved, fondled, and petted his wife, no less than our Western husband does. But the laws of morality forbade him to pay much respect in the outward manner."[25]

*   *   *

The curtains that conceal the Eastern marriage bed have not, as in the West, been penetrated to a great extent by scientific research, at least of the Kinsey type. In some other respects, however, Asians are more communicative about their marital relationships than Westerners are.

The Kama Sutra, by Vatsyayana, is one of the great classics in the literature of sexual love. Written with engaging frankness, it lacks completely the prurient flavor of so many of the sex manuals of the West. Vatsyayana writes of the sex relationship of husband and wife with the enthusiasm and warmth of an artist.

It is too much to expect every Eastern married couple to approach sex in this enlightened spirit. There is much crudeness and much clumsiness in the sexual approach of the Asian husband to his wife, for he is often very ignorant. On the other hand, however, the Eastern bride is not so hypersensitive as many sheltered and overprotected Western girls have been. The girl in the East knows what sex means. It is the gateway to the great goal of her entire life. She has no dread of pregnancy or of childbirth. She longs ardently for both. If in the process of attaining her heart's desire she should suffer a little physical pain or discomfort, what matter? The Eastern wife, in short, is not susceptible to sexual trauma.

There is plenty of evidence that the Eastern wife enjoys her sex

life. Manu indicates her husband's duty to cohabit with her.
"Reprehensible is the husband who approaches not his wife in due
season."

The Indian woman is not generally inhibited about her sexual
needs. Mira Bai, the Hindi poetess, expresses thus the wife's longing for her absent husband's lovemaking:

> Apart from Rama, sleep does not come to me,
> Through the sufferings of separation no sleep comes,
> And the fire of love is kindled.
>
> Without the light of my beloved, the temple is dark;
> The lamp does not please me.
> Apart from my beloved, I feel very lonely;
> The night is passed in waking,
> When will my beloved come home?[26]

Exactly the same situation is described in a Chinese folk song
translated by Florence Ayscough:

> Alone I keep watch in empty bedroom,
> I sleep wrapped in my clothes,
> And going out into the dream-world
> I enjoy union with you.

As the story unfolds, her husband returns.

> Happiness, delight, cannot be expressed!
> Together within bed-curtains of transmuted gold,
> We confide our inmost thoughts.
> A saying runs, "Return from far distance
> Is better than joy of new marriage."[27]

In India it is often said that among the hard-working peasants
in the villages, living in grim, desperate poverty, the sexual union
of husband and wife is the only means of recreation, and that its
enjoyment is enhanced because of the lack of other pleasures. An
Indian sociologist has thus expressed the man's need:

"The average Indian is a rather frustrated individual. His ego
is completely deflated by the conditions under which he lives. It
is a psychological necessity that this man become master of some
situation in which he can assert his biological dominance. Just so
long as these people are forced to meet drudgery, famine, and

economic depression, so long will they be nightly driven into the conjugal embrace."[28]

However, the conjugal embrace cannot be a nightly event for the orthodox Hindu. Manu raises a warning finger:

"Sixteen days and nights in each month, with four distinct days neglected by the virtuous, are called the natural season of women: of those sixteen, the four first, the eleventh, and the thirteenth, are reprehended: the ten remaining nights are approved."

So it comes down to ten nights in the month—six only for the virtuous. And Manu is not yet finished:

"He who avoids conjugal embraces on the six reprehended nights, and on eight others, is equal in chastity to a *brahmachari.*"

To those husbands who wish to gain spiritual merit, therefore, it comes down to two nights a month. And if they would follow in the footsteps of Gandhi, they must eschew sex relations with their wives altogether. "It is not proved to my satisfaction," he says, "that sexual union in marriage is in itself good and beneficial."[29]

Gandhi was a very great man and is justly revered throughout India. But even a great man can be mistaken on one point. And when he seeks to deny to married couples the joy of sexual union, the wisdom and experience of the East are against him. On this subject, Vatsyayana is a better guide.

*   *   *

"Your wife is your closest friend."

This statement is hardly typical of the Eastern concept of marriage. Yet it comes from no less a source than a Siamese work on Buddhism, in a chapter entitled "How to Live in This World."[30] It was probably written by a celibate priest with no personal experience of married life.

Eastern marriage is weak in the development of interpersonal relationships between husband and wife. The difficulty is that the unquestioning obedience of the wife, and the rigid separation of their spheres of action, prevent any dynamic interplay between the two personalities.

At one of our Indian seminars we were trying to explain marriage counseling. It seemed hard to convey the idea.

"What happens," we asked, "when an Indian husband and wife get involved in a serious quarrel?"

"It doesn't happen," was the reply.

"Put it this way then," we tried again. "What happens when an Indian husband and wife disagree about something?"

"It doesn't happen," was the reply.

Baffled, we asked why it didn't happen.

"Because," they explained, "the Indian wife has been trained from childhood to look up to her husband as a god. So in her eyes he can say no wrong and do no wrong."

We gave up. Marriage counseling, in such a situation, requires redefinition.

All Eastern marriages are certainly not like that. But many are. A Burmese friend put it to us like this:

"A husband sees a white bird flying over his head. He says to his wife 'Look at that black bird.' She looks and says 'Yes, I see the black bird.' For her the bird *is* black, because her husband says so."

This kind of unquestioning obedience in the wife makes a marriage dull. That is what the Japanese husband has found out. His completely submissive wife bores him, so he seeks the stimulating company of the geisha, who is clever and provocative.

"Japanese women," says Professor Chamberlain, "are not ill-used; there is probably little of wife-beating in Japan, neither is there any Zenana system, any veiling of the face; rather it is that women are all their lives treated as babies."[31]

This is no doubt true. But Japanese women are treated by their husbands as babies because they are trained to act as babies; and they are trained to act as babies because it is considered that this is the attitude in a wife that will be most appreciated by a husband. So long as this state of affairs remains true, marriage cannot develop on the basis of comradeship; comradeship isn't the kind of relationship into which one enters with a baby.

The other hindrance to comradeship in marriage is the strict separation in the East of the husband's and the wife's functions. The greatest care is taken to see that they do not overlap. For example, a Japanese gentleman who was old enough to be a grandfather declared that never in his entire life had he been in the kitchen of his own home! It was not his province, and he had no need, and no right, to enter it.

When the spheres of wife and husband are almost completely

separated, the couple are provided with little or no opportunity to interfere in each other's affairs. This makes for harmony—but it is the kind of harmony that is achieved by keeping at arm's length.

These elaborate arrangements have clearly been devised to prevent conflict between husband and wife. They have succeeded remarkably well. But in the process, they have deprived marriage of the very quality that, in the West, we value most highly—the rich, deep comradeship that grows up between a man and a woman who have learned to share life as free and equal partners. Oddly enough, it is only through the acceptance of conflict, or at least of potential conflict, that this kind of relationship can develop its fullest possibilities.

* * *

"When my husband is angry, I keep calm. You see, when one becomes fire, the other must be water."[32]

The Siamese wife who said this had hit on a technique that Western couples might find useful.

What we wanted to know, however, was whether the Eastern wife ever became fire; and if so, what happened?

We raised this question in a Bombay seminar. An Indian psychiatric social worker, trained in the U.S.A., had investigated the matter.

"It is almost impossible," she said, "for an Indian wife to express criticism of her husband. To do so would be to go completely against all her training. She does sometimes develop strong feelings of frustration and hostility—we know that. But she bottles them up. The only way we can find out about her internal frustrations is through the psychosomatic symptoms she produces."

In short, when the Indian wife becomes fire, she does not break out in flames. She smolders inwardly until it makes her ill. Indian physicians have told us that when the situation becomes intolerable she commits suicide.

Suicide was, of course, the traditional way out of intolerable trouble for unhappy Chinese and Japanese wives. Indeed, the threat to take her life was the strongest card a wife could play in an effort to secure justice. A family tended to lose face when the wife of one of its sons committed suicide.

However, these are extreme cases. Most wives saw to it that

their situation did not become desperate. In the East and West alike, every astute woman knows that there are subtle ways of getting round her man. The Eastern woman, for whom subtlety was the only method available, has acquired great skill in this art. As a wife in Ceylon expressed it, "A woman need not be educated to know how to get on harmoniously with her husband. If she is gentle about it he will come around to her point of view."[33]

Though he is a rare bird, the henpecked husband is not wholly unknown in the East. A Chinese vendor of cakes, in the effort to make his wares specially attractive, offered them for sale to the accompaniment of this little song:

> The man who eats fears not his wife,
> And the woman works better all her life.[34]

The Chinese name for a submissive husband is *kuei che ting teng*, which means "Kneel and hold a candle on his head." The idea is that he prostrates himself on the ground and acts as a candlestick for his wife while she works.[35] A more humiliating picture of a husband would be hard to imagine.

There is a delightful old Korean folk tale about a magistrate who, feeling that his wife's domination was becoming intolerable, summoned a meeting of all the men under his jurisdiction.

He then asked all those who felt that their wives were dominating them to take their places at his right hand, while those who held undisputed authority in their homes stood at his left.

All but one of the assembled company went to the magistrate's right side. He then praised the one man who was master in his own home, and urged the others to emulate him.

After a moment the object of his praise, a weak-looking individual, interrupted the magistrate's speech.

"Your Excellency," he said, "I do not know what this is all about. All I know is that my wife, when I left home this morning, commanded me at all costs to stay away from crowds. So when I saw everyone moving to your right, I naturally obeyed her orders and moved over to your left."[36]

An Eastern husband dominated by his wife is in an absurd and impossible position. His masculine status is gravely damaged. In Burma they have a special term for the dignity and sanctity of a man's status. They call it his *hpon*. It is a wife's solemn duty not to damage her husband's *hpon*, and she will do so only in extreme circumstances. A Burmese writer illustrates this with a story of an aunt of hers who, after a serious quarrel with a brother-in-law, threw over him a basin of water from the maternity chamber in the house. This was a double blow at his *hpon*—the throwing of any water would have been humiliating, but it was rendered particularly so by having come from the room that no man could enter without defilement.[37]

A wife was likely to lose far more than she gained if she tried to play a dominant role in the marriage. An Indian illustration of this is given by Savitri Devi Nanda:

"I observed that the long struggle between Aunt Tara and my Uncle Yog was over. After winning a complete victory over that lover-of-peace-at-any-price, she had found its fruit empty and without meaning; for the peace-loving ones have a way of eluding the victor. The power that she had gained over him had proved worthless as a goal in itself, losing the most valued object, the love of her husband. Both seemed resigned. I never knew what they were thinking, for elders do not speak their minds before the young. But this I did find out, that all things went half and half in their house. Half of it was furnished as he wished and the other half as she liked. There were two cooks, cooking in separate kitchens. There were separate baths and separate drawing rooms; one for her and the other for my uncle."[38]

Aunt Tara's policy was disastrous. Her story is a solemn warning to Eastern wives. Perhaps to Western wives, too.

*   *   *

The supreme manifestation of a wife's devotion to her husband was her fidelity to him. An unfaithful wife was not considered fit to live.

"Should a wife, proud of her family and the great qualities of her kinsman, actually violate the duty which she owes to her lord, let the king condemn her to be devoured by dogs in a place much frequented."

This is Manu's approach to the subject. Elsewhere, however, he prescribes some lighter penalties—perhaps for cases where there were extenuating circumstances.

In China, the woman was expected to deal with the matter herself. Any wife known to have committed adultery was expected to take her own life. In Korea, the adulteress was not put to death, but lost her status as a wife and became a slave.[39]

For the Japanese wife, suicide was considered the proper action after infidelity had been established. Thomas Rundell tells the story of a nobleman who left his wife at home while he was away on a journey. During her husband's absence, another gentleman of rank seduced her.

On her husband's return the wife gave a grand feast, to which her seducer was invited as one of the guests. After all had eaten, the wife narrated the whole story to the assembled company, but without naming the seducer. She then begged to be put to death, declaring that she was unworthy to live.

Her husband and the guests tried to pacify her. But, suddenly breaking away from them, she rushed to the edge of the terrace and threw herself over the parapet.

In the confusion that followed, the seducer escaped and rushed down the stairs. When the party arrived, they found his corpse alongside that of the wife who had been his victim. He had expiated his crime by sharing her suicide.[40]

The dramatic nature of this story makes its accuracy questionable. As a cautionary tale, however, it would meet with the fullest approval. It records the actions that are considered to be correct.

Laws requiring the execution of persons involved in adultery are seldom carried out in actual life situations. They do, however, demonstrate the grave nature of the offense in the eyes of the community.

Wives were expected to safeguard themselves from possible violation. The Eastern wife should avoid being alone with any other man—even a relative. Special precautions should be taken when her man is away from home. "While her husband is absent, a wife shall sleep with one of her female relatives, and not alone," says the Padma purana.

The devoted Japanese wife was even expected to blacken her teeth and shave her eyebrows, in order to make herself unattractive and to demonstrate her fidelity to her husband.[41] Faust says that the custom of blackening the teeth was still in vogue in some country areas in Japan in the 1920's.[42] We ourselves have encountered it recently in northern Thailand. We suspect, however, that the black enamel was intended to cover up the disfiguring stains caused by the chewing of betel nut!

As a rule, the preservation of her fidelity was not left solely to the wife. It was her husband's duty to protect her from danger. Says Manu, "Women must, above all, be restrained from the smallest illicit gratification; for, not being thus restrained, they bring sorrow on both families. Let husbands consider this as the supreme law; and let them, how weak soever, diligently keep their wives under lawful restrictions. For he who preserves his wife from vice, preserves his offspring from suspicion of bastardy, his ancient usages from neglect, his family from disgrace, himself from anguish, and his duty from violation."

We have seen how the evil custom of *purdah* was employed in India to attain this end. Fortunately for Eastern women, their jealous husbands do not appear to have gone to such lengths as in the West, where girdles of chastity were at one time in vogue. Eric Dingwall has described these monstrous iron structures, fastened round the woman's waist to cover her genitals. The departing husband locked the girdle in place and took away the key. However, some ingenious wives managed to secure duplicate keys, and the girdles were even broken. One medieval writer complains that it is easier to keep a swarm of fleas in a basket than to keep the virtue of a woman under lock and key![43]

A more appropriate comment might be that, if a man regards his wife in this light and puts her under lock and key, he deserves to be outwitted!

* * *

In the East, marital infidelity did not mean exactly what it means in the West today.

"Adultery is only a feminine vice. Copulation on the man's part is not his wife's concern, unless he sires a child. Then she must accept the child as one of her own household. . . . No child in China can ever suffer bastardy, as no man's offspring is an illegitimate child."[44]

In Japan, also, husbands are free to indulge in sex relations outside the home. Indeed, the Japanese recognize a cleavage between marital responsibilities and romantic love. As Ruth Benedict puts it, one is the man's major obligation, the other his minor relaxation.[45]

Yoko, a seventeen-year-old girl, learned about this from her uncle. "It will sound funny to you, but we men have a tendency to take to outside amours at times. The period is up to the individual, but when he has money and time to spare, he feels like making love to some other girl, some geisha perhaps, even if he still loves his wife as much as when they married."[46]

He went on to advise her that, if her future husband ever behaved in this way, Yoko should treat it like an attack of the measles. "If you leave it alone it is cured and gone in a short time. So you'd better ignore it."

This is easy advice for a man to give—but harder for a woman to follow. Behind the impassive mask of the Eastern wife's stoical expression, the sorrow and humility of rejection gnaw at her heart, just as they do at any woman's heart the world over.

> You feast with your new love,
> And think me not worth being with.
> My person is rejected;—
> What avails it to care for what may come after?
>
> You cannot cherish me,
> And you count me even as an enemy.
> You disdain my virtues,
> As a pedlar's wares which do not sell.[47]

There is a widespread idea that it is easy in the East for a man to find extramarital sexual outlets. In the large cities that is true, but not necessarily elsewhere. Hilda Wernher, from her close knowledge of Indian life, thus describes the situation:

"If it is true that F. (a Muslim) can't live with his wife on account of her health, then it is either a life of continence or a second marriage for him. There is nothing in between.

"In the West such a problem wouldn't arise—there'd be many outlets for a man, whether he particularly liked them or not. In a small town in India there aren't. A man is supposed to stick to his wife, and that is that. If he were to launch some amorous adventure, he'd lose his social standing, his job, his friends, and maybe his caste. If Indian men want what is called a fling, they go to the nearest Westernized city, or more often to Bombay, to

Europe, or the U.S. The average ones, I mean. Princes or rich men's sons have other ways at their disposal."[48]

A clear distinction must be made between a married man's amours with concubines, prostitutes, and geishas, and any attempt on his part to seduce another man's wife. Only the latter brands the Eastern husband as an adulterer. He cannot sin against his own wife. But he can very definitely, and very seriously, sin against the husband of the woman whom he seduces.

This is a grave offense, because it is one man violating another man's rights. "Nothing is known in this world so obstructive to length of days," says Manu, "as the culpable attention of a man to the wife of another."

The man found guilty of adultery comes under the harsh judgment of the law. Manu again says, "Let the adulterer be placed in an iron bed well heated, under which the executioner shall throw logs continually, till the sinful wretch be there burned to death."

Indeed, even death does not necessarily end his torments. In the Buddhist *Sankoha,* or Myth of Hades, the man who had committed adultery has to climb a tree covered with prickly thorns, while a vulture continually attacks him and feeds upon his flesh.[49]

Men of adulterous disposition are strongly disliked in the East. They are like known robbers. They disturb the peace, and put the married men in the community in a state of perpetual anxiety.

Manu gives some indications by which such men may be recognized:

"He who talks with the wife of another man at a place of pilgrimage, in a forest or a grove, or at the confluence of rivers, incurs the guilt of an adulterous inclination. To send her flowers or perfumes, to sport or jest with her, to touch her apparel and ornaments, to sit with her on the same couch, are held adulterous acts on his part. To touch a married woman on her breasts or any other place, which ought not to be touched, or, being touched unbecomingly by her, to bear it complacently, are adulterous acts with mutual assent."

When such men are identified, the community should be rid of them:

"Let the king banish from his realm men who commit overt

ulterous inclination, having punished them with such
rks as excite aversion."

* * *

There are marked differences between the marriage relationship in the East and in the West. How do they compare in terms
of the happiness which husband and wife find together?

This is a very difficult question to answer. We have seen that
not more than half of all marriages in the United States today
bring happiness to those involved in them.[50] That is a very poor
record. It is greatly influenced by the distorted and unreasonable
expectations that millions of young Americans are bringing to marriage. As Pollock has said, "Marriage suffers most from our regarding it as a failure whenever it falls below a perfect score."[51]

In the East, men and women are more realistic. They do not
marry primarily for happiness, but to fulfill their family and
social obligations. Any happiness that marriage brings is, therefore, accepted as a gift and not as a right. This being so, the prob-
ability is that far more couples are satisfied with their marriages
in the East than in the West.

On the other hand, because of the serious limitations under
which Eastern marriages suffer, fewer of them are likely to bring
the richness and depth of fulfillment that our good Western marriages achieve. Nevertheless, there is plenty of evidence that the
East has produced, in good measure, the qualities that mark truly
and deeply happy marriages the world over.

There is in the West a striking dearth of literature that extols
the joys and delights of married life and married love. The subject of marriage is featured more frequently as a theme for syni-
cism and ribaldry than for panegyrics. The East has its cynical
writing too—*Dream of the Red Chamber* would probably be
placed in that category—but on the other hand, some very heartfelt and tender praise of marriage has come from Asian sources.
It is quite possible that, in a competition in which material on
this theme was submitted and judged in terms of its depth and
sincerity of feeling, the East would win first place. This may come
as a surprise to Western readers.

We conclude this chapter with selections gathered from four

different Asian countries, to add to those that have already been given in the earlier chapter on love.

The Mahabharata, from India, has this passage in praise of a good wife:

> A wife is half the man, his truest friend;
> A loving wife is a perpetual spring
> Of virtue, pleasure, wealth; a faithful wife
> Is his best aid in seeking heavenly bliss;
> A sweetly speaking wife is a companion
> In solitude, a father in advice,
> A mother in all seasons of distress,
> A rest in passing through life's wilderness.

From the Chinese here is a simple lyric describing how the wife of some great officer of state bewails her husband's absence and longs for the joy of his return:

> *Yaou-yauo* went the insects,
> And the hoppers sprang about.
> While I do not see my lord,
> My sorrowful heart is agitated.
>> Let me have seen him,
>> Let me have met him,
> And my heart will then be stilled.
>
> I ascended the hill in the south,
> And gathered the turtle-foot ferns.
> While I do not see my lord,
> My sorrowful heart is very sad.
>> Let me have seen him,
>> Let me have met him,
> And my heart will then be pleased.
>
> I ascended that hill in the south,
> And gathered the thorn ferns.
> While I do not see my lord,
> My sorrowful heart is wounded with grief.
>> Let me have seen him,
>> Let me have met him,
> And my heart will then be at peace.[52]

From Japan comes a husband's description of how he took leave of his wife. A soldier, he is going to war. He does not expect to return.

"Then my wife cut off her hair at the neck, as is the custom of a woman when her husband dies in Japan. One half of this we buried near the moon-gate in our garden; the other half she put carefully away to be kept until her death. She was to wait until she could give my ashes honourable burial. Then she would be at liberty to lay her own weary body and confused mind to rest.

"We do not kiss in Japan. When I came away my wife and I bowed to each other many times. I could feel each one of her heart throbs."[53]

From Thailand here is a description of a husband's controlled but heartfelt tribute to his dead wife:

"Eight Buddhist priests gathered round my mother's body, which was resting peacefully on a rosewood dais in the huge hall. Her palms were closed together above her bosom, holding a small bouquet of flowers and two sticks of incense, as if she were showing reverence to Lord Buddha. She was in her favorite dress, the combination of light green and yellow. On her face I could still detect the habitual gentleness of her kindly smile.

"After the priests had finished their prayer to send her soul to the place of everlasting happiness, relatives and friends stepped in one by one to lay flowers around her and to wish her an eternal blessing. Father was the first to say his farewell. There were signs of grief on his face, but, being a learned man, he was well controlled.

"'You have been my faithful and beloved wife. I shall always be proud to have you in this world or in the next. May your soul find the path to righteousness.'"[54]

Chapter 11

THE WIDOW'S FIERY SACRIFICE

All marriages that come to an end are terminated either by divorce or by death. In the East, apart from a period in Japanese history when the divorce rate reached phenomenal proportions, the vast majority of marriages have ended with the death of one of the partners.

The Hindu view of divorce springs from the religious nature of the marriage bond. In some respects it resembles the Roman Catholic attitude in the West:

"Because marriage is said to be sacred it is irrevocable. The parties to the marriage cannot dissolve it at will. They are bound to each other until the death of either of them."[1]

That is the theoretical position. However, in practice the Hindu husband could and did put away his wife for many reasons—for adultery, for drunkenness, for bad behavior, for disease, even for wastefulness. She remained legally his wife, but she was "superseded." He could then take another wife, since polygamy was not forbidden. So he had the advantages of divorce and remarriage in everything but name.

No doubt Moslem influence played a part in bringing about this state of affairs. All a Moslem man has to do, in order to be rid of his wife, is to say "I divorce you" three times. Something very like this seems to have been the practice in some Hindu communities:

"In Hindostan the husband may divorce his wife at pleasure. Says the divine Manu, 'The woman who speaks unkindly to her husband may be superseded by another without delay.' Let him address her by the title 'Mother' and the marriage covenant is dissolved. This is the only bill of divorce requisite."[2]

Attempts were made, however, to restrain a husband who tried to put away his wife for insufficient reason. Such a husband could be required to put on the skin of an ass, with the hairy side out, and to beg alms from seven houses, saying, "Give alms to him who forsook his wife."[3] No husband would wish to be involved in such a humiliating procedure.

For the Hindu wife, there were no loopholes. Said Manu, "Neither by sale nor by desertion can a wife be released from her husband: thus we fully acknowledge the law enacted of old by the Lord of creatures. Once is a damsel given in marriage: this is done once for all and irrevocably."

What this meant was that the principle of no divorce was applied to discriminate against the woman. The unhappy Hindu wife, however badly she was treated, had no honorable way out.

Frieda Hauswirth tells the story of a girl of sixteen who sought her help thirty years ago. Married three years previously against her will, she had been kept in *purdah* ever since. Her husband had infected her with venereal disease but refused to let her have treatment.

"She said 'I hate him, and I won't live with him. If you won't help me I will run away.'

"She looked me squarely in the eyes and I could see that she knew what that would mean, and that she held it over me, the free Western woman, as a sort of desperate threatening appeal. Such running away without help and preparation, from a sheltered niche in Hindu society, could not possibly mean anything else but being driven to prostitution."[4]

Assistance was given her, and later this sheltered Hindu girl helped to organize the passive resistance movement in her province. In 1930 she was reported to be in another kind of seclusion, namely prison, for her activities!

Happily all this has been changed by the Hindu Marriage Act of 1955. Section 13 of the Act states: "Any marriage solemnized, whether before or after the commencement of this Act, may, on a petition presented by either the husband or the wife, be dissolved by a decree of divorce." The grounds on which a petition may be presented then follow.

In our copy of the Act, given to us in New Delhi by a Supreme Court lawyer in 1956, the following note is added:

"This section is revolutionary in character so far as Hindu society is concerned. It introduces a sweeping change in the law governing Hindu marriages since time immemorial, as laid down from age to age by the ancient law-givers and commentators dating back to the era of Manu. These provisions cut at the root of the sacramental character and irrevocability of a Hindu marriage, bringing it into line with the modern conception of marriage with a vengeance."

* * *

For the Chinese, marriage was not sacramental. Thus there was no difficulty in accepting the principle of divorce. "If the husband and wife live together according to righteousness, they remain together; if righteousness is no more, they should separate," said a noted philosopher of the Sung dynasty.

Confucius laid down seven reasons for which a wife could be put away. These were incorporated into the legal code of the Manchu dynasty. They are:

1. She is rebellious toward her parents-in-law.
2. She has failed to produce a son.
3. She has been unfaithful to her husband.
4. She has shown jealousy toward her husband's other women.
5. She has a repulsive and incurable disease.
6. She is given to hurtful talk and talebearing.
7. She is a thief.

There were, however, three circumstances in which, even though grounds existed, the wife could not be put aside:

1. She has mourned three years for her husband's parents.
2. She has no family to which to return.
3. She married her husband when he was poor, and now he is rich.

These limiting conditions were obviously designed to safeguard the wife from exploitation. If she had mourned her husband's parents, this gave her an established place in his family. If she had no place to go, it would have been dire cruelty to cast her out. And it would have been a gross injustice if she had supported her husband in adversity, and he now wished to discard her in his prosperity.

There is evidence that in feudal and early imperial times, before the dawn of the Christian era, divorces could be arranged on the wife's initiative. But later her wishes were regarded as of little importance, and only the husband could act.

When we speak of the husband acting, however, we need to realize that he was often merely the tool of his family. It was much more important for him to please his parents than to please his wife.

"If the son very much approves of his wife, but his parents do not like her, he should divorce her; if he does not approve of his wife, and his parents say, 'She serves us well,' he should behave to her in all respects as a husband—without fail even to the end of his life."[5]

In China arrangement of a divorce did not involve any kind of court procedure. "If a man and a woman are incompatible of temperament they may separate, with the mutual consent of their two homesteads, and the woman return to her father's house. In such cases there is no need to refer the matter to the civil authorities. It is a family affair, arranged by mutual good-will on the part of the only parties concerned."[6]

No doubt many abuses were made possible by this informal arrangement—yet probably not any more than take place in divorce-court procedures. It was left to the husband and his family elders to decide whether one of the seven legitimate grounds for divorce existed. But clearly they would not wish to offend the wife's family, as would certainly happen if they sent her back without good reason. So in practice a wife had some protection against exploitation. Her family could champion her if she was threatened with divorce on a trumped-up charge. On the other hand, if she was badly treated in her husband's home, her parents could put pressure on the family to arrange a divorce. Although the law formally allowed a wife no rights of divorce, therefore, it was possible for her to force the issue through her own family's intervention.

The evidence suggests that divorce in old China was not common. A wife who returned to her parents had little or no chance to remarry, and her future prospects otherwise were bleak. Her children belonged to her husband's family, so she had to leave them behind.

The poor man had little incentive for sending his wife away, because he would probably be unable to afford to marry another. The rich man could take a concubine and let his discarded wife remain. Polygamy and divorce are alternative means of achieving the same end. In old China polygamy was much the more humanitarian course of the two. That this was recognized is evident from the existence of a strong public disapproval of divorce.

With the coming of the modern era, divorce became more frequent in China. When a married man went to live and work in the city, and met a girl there to whom he was attracted, she would hold out for marriage to him. No city girl wished to accept the status of concubine. So, to meet her wishes, the man would be forced to make his traditional wife submit to the cruelty and humiliation of divorce.[7]

In Korea the "seven reasons and three restraints" governed divorce, as in China. But divorce procedures were strictly supervised. Any man who put away his wife without adequate cause was liable to be publicly disgraced and beaten with eighty strokes. A wife, as in China, had no rights. If she left her husband, even with just cause, she could receive one hundred strokes. If she ran away and remarried, death by hanging was the legal penalty.[8]

* * *

In the early years of the present century, Japan had the highest divorce rate in the world, with the United States in second place.

One reason for this was that the system for registering divorces was similar to that for marriages. All that was necessary was for the head of the family to remove the wife's name from the family register. It was therefore possible for the girl's in-laws, on the slightest whim, to terminate her marriage. In some cases, a young wife would discover that her divorce had been registered and that she had not even been informed!

Here is an actual account of such a case:

"A certain girl whom I knew was married some time ago to a man belonging to a farmer family in a rural village. Before one week had passed since their wedding ceremony took place, she was ordered by her family people to pay a visit to her parents' house, according to the custom pertaining with marriage. When the innocent bride, however, was visiting her parents and other dear ones, she unexpectedly found her trousseau, which she had brought with her to her new home, being sent back to her parents' house. Following it, a messenger came to her parents' house from the bridegroom's house, informing her that she had been divorced.

"The reason for her divorce was explained by the messenger: she was not in harmony with the family tradition. This story was told to me nearly one month after the incident. To my question of how the bride's family had negotiated with the bridegroom's family on this matter, I was informed that, although they asked the go-between several times to negotiate with the other party, the matter was still standing unsettled. She was 23 or 24, and was still of marriageable age, and this was her first marriage. She was half resigning herself to her fate, with her qualification for marriage mercilessly negated in only ten days or so."[9]

Another factor that encouraged divorces in Japan was that a married couple of twenty-five or over could terminate their marriage by mutual consent. No court procedure was involved. All the couple had to do was to record their agreement to divorce in the Family Registration Office.

This meant that when a couple were married by arrangement and did not feel inclined to accept each other, all they had to do was to wait until they had reached the age of twenty-five, and then bring their union to an end.

When divorce courts were set up in Japan, the main grounds were adultery, crime involving three years or more of imprisonment, cruelty, malicious rejection, and insulting behavior on the part of near relatives of the other party.

It is significant, however, that adultery as an offense justifying divorce applied only to the wife. There was some criticism of this unequal standard, but public opinion was opposed to any reform. The discrimination against the wife was explained on the ground that adultery committed by the husband does not directly affect his lineage, but that adultery on the wife's part is generally a stain upon the family line.

The informal approach to divorce has persisted in Japan. In 1951 it was reported that about 90 per cent of all divorces take place by mutual consent, without court action. When the couple fail to reach agreement, they may take the case to a Family Court, consisting of a judge and two or more "conciliators," selected from citizens from all walks of life. Here they may be reconciled, or they may reach agreement to divorce by mutual consent. Of the 10 per cent of divorces submitted for legal action, about 9 per cent are handled in the Family Court. The remaining 1 per cent are dealt with by the processes of litigation in the District Courts.

The frequency of divorce in Japan has led to some ingenuity on the part of husbands. When the new laws made it possible for women to own property, men who were in business difficulties discovered a happy solution to their troubles. The husband would settle all his worldly goods on his wife and then divorce her. He would then inform his creditors that he had nothing with which to pay his debts, which was perfectly true. When the creditors gave up the chase, the man would move to some other part of the country, remarry his wife, and repossess his property!

The custom of adoption is also very widespread in Japan. A tenderhearted husband, having divorced his wife and finding her hurt and disgruntled, has been known to show his good will toward her by adopting her as his daughter!

Examples of ingenuity in manipulating divorces are found all over the world, and are not lacking in the East. In Thailand, a man who wanted to divorce his wife could resort to the simple expedient of entering the Buddhist priesthood, which had the result of leaving her high and dry. Later, when the coast was clear, he could revoke his priestly vows and return to the world with the status of a single man!

In India, the new Hindu Marriage Act gives as one ground for divorce the fact that the marriage partner has ceased to be a Hindu by conversion to another religion. We found that this provided a convenient way out of marriage for some couples. One would agree to become, for the time being, a Moslem. The other would then undertake divorce proceedings. After one or both had remarried, the "convert" would decide to return to the faith of his fathers!

Divorce has not, except perhaps in Japan and Java, become as yet a major social problem in the East. Compared with the United States, in which half of all the reported divorces in the entire world take place,[10] Eastern rates are low. Asians find the ease and frequency of American divorces perplexing. Here is the report of a student from Thailand writing home from a college in the United States:

"Divorce cases are as numerous as traffic accidents. In traffic accidents the insurance companies cover the damages. But in a divorce case, the husband is held responsible for alimony. There is no insurance company for divorce compensation. I do not think it is possible to establish one, if it is established it will soon go bankrupt. Many women earn their living by divorcing and re-marrying. Every time they find a richer husband, their alimony capacity increases respectively."[11]

*   *   *

Among the many examples of unjust discrimination against the female sex the world over, it would be hard to find anything more ruthless than the traditional treatment of widows in some Eastern communities.

A widow's troubles could begin early in life. Incredible as it may seem, it was even possible to be *born* a widow! In Korea, as in China, pregnant mothers sometimes formally betrothed their unborn children. If the boy died before the girl was born, this made her technically a widow. If married later in life, her status would be that of a remarried widow, and not a maiden.

This was, of course, very unusual. But in India particularly, child widows were by no means rare. Here are the figures given in the Census Report of 1921.

Widows aged	1–5	11,892
Widows aged	5–10	85,037
Widows aged	10–15	232,147
	Total	329,076

It can be confidently assumed that these were most conservative figures.

The prevalence of Indian child widows was, of course, easily explained. As in Korea, the custom of early betrothal, in a land where infant mortality rates are high, meant that a girl's husband could die while he was cutting his first teeth. At the other extreme, the Hindu readiness to marry young girls to much older men meant that a husband could die of old age while waiting for his child wife to reach puberty.

Mrs. Hate, in an extensive study of Hindu women published in 1948, gave some revealing facts about the widows in the group.

The average age at which they had become widows was twenty. The lowest age was eight, the highest fifty-four. The average period of their married life was seven years. Sixteen per cent of them had enjoyed no married life as such at all, and another 14 per cent had lived with their husbands only one year.[12]

It would seem hardship enough to involve a mere child in the bewildering experiences of widowhood. But that was only the beginning of her troubles. In addition, she might be held responsible for her husband's death, and the possibility of remarriage might be denied her for the rest of her life.

In India there was a persistent tradition that a husband's death could be caused by sins committed by his wife in a previous incarnation.[13] It is hard to quote authentic sources in Hindu literature for such an idea, but we find it clearly expressed in the lament of the king's widow in a "tale from days of yore" quoted by Johann Meyer:

"Henceforward, O king, pitiable, heart-withering agonies of soul will come upon me, that am without thee, thou lotus-eyed one. It must be that I, a wretched one, have [in an earlier existence] sundered some that were mated; therefore it is that this parting from thee has befallen me. I have in a former body torn asunder those that were intimately bound together; hence, O king, has this sorrow taken me in its grasp, springing from my separation from thee, and heaped up in earlier bodies through evil deeds."[14]

Quite clearly, if the dead husband's family really believed that the widow was responsible for the loss of their son, she would be in an unenviable plight. And even if the idea of her guilt was a vague one that did not amount to a conviction, it could be a powerful weapon in the hands of spiteful people who disliked the girl and wanted to penalize her.

* * *

Whether for this cause or for some other, the Hindu widow's lot was often a miserable one in her former husband's home.

"She becomes the menial of every other person in the house of her late husband. All the hardest and ugliest tasks are hers, no comforts, no ease. She may take but one meal a day and that of the meanest. She must perform strict fasts. Her hair must be shaven off. She must take care to absent herself from any scenes

of ceremony or rejoicing, from a marriage, from a religious celebration, from the sight of an expectant mother or of any person
whom the curse of her glance might harm. Those who speak to
her may speak in terms of contempt and reproach."[15]

Mrs. Hate, in her study, gives the following case histories of
widows:

1. "I was only 15 when I unfortunately lost my husband. Immediately I was tonsured. My husband owned a piece of land.
I was entitled to its rent, but my brother-in-law deprived me of
it. After one year I went to stay with my sister. According to the
ideas of those days every year they used to tap my veins, so that
I became weak. I am now 70, and have passed all my life working
for others, with prayer as my only consolation."

2. "My step-sister arranged my marriage with a man 37 years
older than myself. I became a widow three years after marriage.
My father-in-law settled a sum of money on me, but I am entitled
to its meagre interest only. Moreover my husband owned two
shops which were taken by my nephew. He promised to give me
an allowance every month, but never kept his word. How am I
to maintain myself?"

3. "I was only nine when my present misfortune fell to my lot.
Though young, I was tonsured and had to beat my chest for the
whole year. My mother-in-law and husband's sister pocketed the
money that had been settled on me by my father-in-law. If I had
refused to give my consent, they would have given me poison!
After some months my parents brought me to their house. I trained
myself and became a teacher. Now I am independent."[16]

These were particularly unfortunate cases. They illustrate, however, how the widow was open to exploitation by her former
husband's family. It is significant that, in the group of widows
investigated by Mrs. Hate, only 16 per cent had continued to live
in the homes of their former husbands. Forty-eight per cent had
returned to their parents. The rest were living alone, some of them
in desperate poverty.

The devout widow was not expected to complain under these
hardships. On the contrary, she should welcome them. Says Manu,
"A faithful wife, when her lord is deceased, should emaciate her
body, by living voluntarily on pure flowers, roots, and fruit. She
should not even pronounce the name of another man.

"Let her continue till death forgiving all injuries, performing harsh duties, avoiding every sensual pleasure, and cheerfully practising the incomparable rules of virtue."

The young widow might endeavor to follow this ascetic rule and avoid sensual pleasure. But the matter was not always entirely in her own hands. In a rescue home in Bombay in which there were 188 widows, it was found that seventy of them had been seduced.[17]

Giving evidence before the Joshi Committee, Sir P. C. Ray, of the University College of Science and Technology in Calcutta, said that when a man dies, leaving a young widow, she becomes "the common property of the entire village caste."

Many cases are on record where a widow was sent out to beg. If she was youthful and in any way attractive, this was only one short step removed from a life of prostitution.

When, as a result of such exploitation, a widow became pregnant, she was in a dire predicament, for her husband's family would consider this a terrible disgrace. The Abbé Dubois says that, in this dilemma, the widow would if possible bring on an abortion. If this failed, she would appear to set off on a pilgrimage to some distant religious shrine. In reality she would seek refuge in some nearby village where she had a trusted friend, and remain there till her child was born. She would give the child to anyone who would take it—or destroy it if she was desperate—and then return to her home.[18]

*   *   *

For a young girl deprived of her husband, the logical course of action would seem to be remarriage. This we take for granted in our modern Western culture.

To the orthodox Hindu widow, however, this was out of the question. Manu says plainly, "A widow who, from a wish to bear children, slights her deceased husband by marrying again, brings disgrace on herself here below, and shall be excluded from the seat of her lord. A second husband is not allowed, in any part of this code, to a virtuous woman."

This applies not merely to the mature woman who has lived with her husband. It includes the betrothed child who has not even seen her intended spouse. The underlying principle was that you could not make a gift of the same thing twice over. A girl who had been given to a man, even if she was at the time too young for him to live with as a wife, belonged absolutely to him and could not at any later time be given to another.[19]

Not only did a remarried Hindu widow suffer severe censure. All her relatives were likewise disgraced. In a list given by Manu of people who are to be shunned, and which includes the unchaste and the adulterous, we find "the son of a twice-married woman," and "the husband of a twice-married woman."

To reinforce this point, Manu sternly warns men against any idea of marrying a widow. A Brahmin who did so would put himself in the category of "base, inadmissible men." He would find himself boycotted and excluded from religious and social privileges in his community. Life could be made well-nigh intolerable for him. Cases are on record in which men who married widows have had to seek police protection.[20]

Frieda Hauswirth tells the story of a case that had a happy ending. A poor Indian youth, whom the fathers of eligible local girls carefully avoided, found a man in a distant village who was willing to give him his daughter in marriage. In due course she bore him a daughter.

The relatives concluded that, since the first-born was a girl, the gods must be angry for some reason. Someone investigated the young wife's background and was horrified to discover that she had been a widow. She had been married at three years of age and widowed at four—a fact that her father, anxious to dispose of her, had concealed.

Now the husband was threatened, unless he sent his wife away, with exposure. "Such exposure would inevitably have brought about outcasting, which means the loss of all social intercourse, of work—in fact, virtual starvation and death for his child, wife, and himself."

The poor husband was placed in a terrible dilemma.

"Stunned by the revelation, Kiron could not find it in his loyal heart to cast aside these two beloved beings and retain for himself the privilege of caste; nor could he face the terrible consequences of ostracism."

In his predicament he sought the help of a famous athlete, of great popularity, who lived in the district and was known to have progressive ideas. The athlete announced a great feast in his house and invited all the prominent Brahmins in the community. When the final dish of curry was served, it was brought to the guests by "this mortal sinner, the remarried widow."

The Brahmins were in consternation. To accept food from the girl's hands and eat meant being outcast along with her. The alternative was to insult their host and leave the house. At this point the athlete placed himself threateningly in front of the door that was their only way of retreat.

The stratagem worked. "Without a word they sat down again, and ate. There was never again any talk of outcasting the woman."[21]

Obviously this story was not typical. Otherwise it would never have been told.

As early as 1856, the Widow Remarriage Act was passed in an attempt to end the hardships of young girls forbidden to marry. Sustained efforts throughout the years that followed met with some response. In 1887, the estimated number of widows in India was forty million. In 1925, it was twenty-seven million.

In 1926, Gandhi used his great influence to attack this evil. In *Young India*, he wrote:

To force widowhood upon little girls is a brutal crime for which we Hindus are daily paying dearly. . . . There is no warrant in any *shastra* for such widowhood. Voluntary widowhood consciously adopted by a woman who has felt the affection of a partner adds grace and dignity to life, sanctifies the home and uplifts religion itself. Widowhood imposed by religion or custom is an unbearable yoke and defiles the home by secret vice and degrades religion. And does not the Hindu widowhood stink in one's nostrils when one thinks of old and diseased men over fifty taking or rather purchasing girl wives, sometimes one on top of another?[22]

Despite such vigorous championship of the cause of the widows, progress was painfully slow. "The movement languishes," wrote Hester Gray in the 1930's, "and the idea of a widow, even of a child widow, remarrying is still extremely repugnant to Hindu thought."[23] Mrs. Hate, in her group of 111 widows, found that only two of them had remarried. Even today, and even in educated circles, the prejudice still lingers. An Indian woman, writing in 1950 about a girls' school reunion, relates this incident:

"Krishna was accompanied by her beautiful elder sister called Vedvati, whom I had known in the early years in school.

"Vedvati was a widow and dressed in widow's white robes. It made me almost afraid to look at her: cut off from moving and throbbing life, she had the serenity of one carved in stone. It seemed to me that, standing apart from life, she was watching us with the wisdom of all her 25 years. Krishna told us that she had refused all further offers of marriage in fear that her second love might die just as her first one had."[24]

So much for the widow. What about the Hindu widower?

Manu says, "A man whose wife dies before him must kindle sacred fires, and perform funeral rites. He may then marry again, and again light the nuptial fire."

In fact, the devout Hindu was strongly *encouraged* to remarry. The three aims of marriage were *dharma* (religious duty), *praja* (offspring), and *rati* (pleasure). *Dharma* came first. It was the duty of the husband to offer the daily sacrifice in company with his wife. "It was only on the death of the householder that these obligations ceased. They were interrupted on the death of the wife, and hence the householder was enjoined immediately to take a second wife."[25]

For the widow, no remarriage under any circumstances. For the widower, remarriage as soon as possible, as a religious duty. Such was the teaching of Hinduism.

Public opinion in modern India is in general sympathetic toward the remarriage of widows. But among strict orthodox Hindus, we were told, tradition still rules.

*   *   *

In China and Japan there was no legal or religious prohibition of the remarriage of widows. But there was a strong public opinion that, in many cases, had virtually the same result.

"Widow remarriage in China is discouraged. It is virtuous to refuse to 'drink the tea of two families.' If the widow insists, she 'goes through the gate with empty hands.' She leaves her sons, and her property, behind. She may take her daughters, but if she does they lose all rights in the home into which they were born."[26]

The idea is that a wife should be so absorbed in her duty of pleasing her husband that when he dies life has no further meaning for her. "Woman is born for the service of man with her person, so that the wife draws out her life with her husband, and should die with him. Hence when her husband dies, she calls herself 'The person not yet dead.' She henceforth is simply waiting for death, and ought not to have any desire of becoming the wife of another."[27]

The duty of the wife not to remarry is emphasized in some of the stories collected by Lu Hsin-wu in 1591 A.D. The purpose of the stories is to exalt the virtues of good women, and there are several that praise the faithful widow. One concerns a very beautiful girl who, after the death of her husband, was urged by her family to remarry. She refused, and emphasized her determination by cutting off her long tresses of black hair.

After a time, disorder broke out in the kingdom. Again her relatives strongly urged the girl, for her own protection, to take another husband. But her resolution not to remarry remained firm. In order to settle the matter, she cut off her nose and her ears![28]

Notice the difference of emphasis here. The Hindu girl, even if she desired remarriage, would be restrained by her parents. But in China it is the girl herself who is expected to turn a deaf ear to all pressures, even from her parents, to marry again.

This conflict between the widowed girl and her parents who urge remarriage is the moving theme of an old Chinese lyric:

> It floats about, that boat of cypress wood,
> There in the middle of the Ho.
> With his two tufts of hair falling over his forehead,
> He was my mate;
> And I swear that till death I will have no other.
> O Mother, O Heaven,
> Why will you not understand me?[29]

The fact that remarriage was not actually forbidden, but only considered to show lack of virtue in the widow, meant that there were inevitably some defections. Very different in spirit from the above lyric is the cynical Chinese rhyme:

> A maid weds to please her clan,
> But a widow pleases herself.
> So if Heaven wants to rain
> Or your mother to marry again,
> Nothing can prevent it.[30]

All the same, if there was not prevention, there was active discouragement. Some parts of the Chinese countryside abounded in monuments erected to the memory of faithful widows who had refused to remarry. Thus the dead made their mute appeal to the living.

In Korea, as in China, there was no legal prohibition of remarriage. But a widow who married again was considered guilty of a decidedly unfilial act against her husband's family. One way in which this sentiment was expressed was to declare sons of such second marriages legally unfit to occupy any official position. After the death of King Sung-Jong in 1894, however, full freedom of remarriage, without censure, was accorded to widows.[31]

The Japanese call the widow *mibojin*, which means literally "the not-yet-dead-one." This reflects the Chinese idea of the brokenhearted wife waiting for death because life has no meaning for her apart from her husband. It is even interpreted to mean that she ought to have killed herself in order to follow her husband into the other world, and that by failing to do so she has proved unworthy of him.

A Japanese widow was not under any obligation not to remarry. She might, however, freely decide not to do so. If she so decided, she would cut off her hair. This was a sign that she had taken a vow to live alone for the rest of her life, as a tribute to her husband's memory.[32]

If these ideas should seem strange and harsh, we had better look into our own Western tradition. Lecky, the historian, tells us that the Romans regarded second marriage as a sign of intemperance, and greatly praised the widow who did not remarry. "The affection a wife owes her husband is so profound and so pure that it must not cease even with his death; that it should guide and consecrate all her subsequent life, and that it never can be transferred to another object. . . . Examples are recorded of Roman wives, sometimes in the prime of youth and beauty, upon the death of their husbands devoting the remainder of their lives to retirement and to the memory of the dead."[33]

Even in our Christian heritage similar attitudes may be found. Tertullian thundered about the iniquity of the *digami*, or twice-married. And St. Jerome wrote, "She who has been twice married, though she be an old, and decrepit, and poor woman, is not deemed worthy to receive the charity of the Church. And if the bread of charity is taken from her, how much more that bread which descends from heaven!"[34]

*   *   *

In traditional Eastern thinking, the duties of a widow follow logically from the duties of a wife. These are epitomized in the story of Savitri in the Mahabharata:

What befalls the wedded husband still befalls the faithful wife,
Where he leads she ever follows, be it death or be it life.

The widow, in short, had really no right to be alive at all. With her husband's departure, her claim to continued physical existence was at best tenuous. She belonged to him, was an integral part of his being, and apart from him she had no true existence. The sacrament of marriage bound her to him irrevocably.

Out of this concept, deeply rooted in Hindu thought about marriage, sprang one of the most awful rites ever practiced in any human culture—that of *suttee*. The woman who took part in the rite was the *Sati*—the True One. As a token of her complete devotion to her dead husband, she ascended his funeral pyre and voluntarily perished in the flames that cremated his dead body.

The Western mind cannot understand *suttee*, and the psychology behind it, if it is merely viewed as a disgusting pagan practice. To the Hindu it appeared as a supreme act of heroism and spiritual devotion, like the noble self-sacrifice of the early Christian martyrs. The following story, going back little more than thirty years, eloquently makes the point:

"The head of one of the few colleges for women in India retired after 25 years of service. In a country where fewer than two women in a hundred can read and write, graduates of this college represent a high degree of selection. Her girls represented for this American teacher her life's achievement. They joined together to give her a farewell present.

"One group bought a painting. It represented, they said, the highest ideal of Indian womanhood. It would carry a message from her students to her friends in America.

"It was a picture of a *Sati*. Lurid crimson flames writhed and coiled about an Indian woman whose face was set in an ecstasy of renunciation."[35]

The veneration of these educated Indian girls for the *Sati* can best be interpreted by reproducing an eyewitness account of the rite itself. Major-General Sir W. H. Sleeman, in his memoirs, related the following story:

On Tuesday, Nov. 24th, 1829, I had an application from the heads of the most respectable and most extensive family of Brahmans in this district to suffer this old woman to burn herself with the remains of her husband, Ummed Singh Upadhya, who had that morning died upon the banks of the Nerbudda. . . .

On Saturday, the 28th, in the morning, I rode out ten miles to the spot, and found the poor old widow sitting with the *dhajā* round her head, a brass plate before her with undressed rice and flowers, and a coconut in each hand. She talked very collectedly, telling me that "she had determined to mix her ashes with those of her departed husband, and should patiently wait my permission to do so, assured that God would enable her to sustain life until that was given, though she dared not eat or drink."

Looking at the sun, then rising before her over a long and beautiful reach of the Nerbudda river, she said calmly: "My soul has been for five days with my husband's near that sun; nothing but my earthly frame is left; and this I know you will in time suffer to be mixed with the ashes of his in yonder pit, because it is not in your nature to prolong the miseries of a poor old woman."

Having satisfied myself that it would be unavailing to attempt to save her life, I sent for all the principal members of the family, and consented that she should be suffered to burn herself if they would enter into engagements that no other member of their family should ever do the same. This they all agreed to, and the papers having been drawn out in due form about mid-day, I sent down notice to the old lady, who seemed extremely pleased and thankful.

The ceremonies of bathing were gone through before three, while the wood and other combustible materials for a strong fire were collected and put into the pit. After bathing, she called for a *pān* (betel leaf) and ate it; then rose up and, with one arm on the shoulder of her eldest son and the other on that of her nephew, approached the fire.

I had sentries placed all round, and no other person was allowed to approach within five paces. As she rose up fire was set to the pile, and it was instantly in a blaze. The distance was about 150 yards. She came on with a calm and cheerful countenance, stopped once, and, casting her eyes upwards, said: "Why have they kept me five days from thee, my husband?"

On coming to the sentries her supporters stopped; she walked once round the pit, paused a moment, and, while muttering a prayer, threw some flowers into the fire. Then she walked up deliberately and steadily to the brink, stepped into the centre of the flame, sat down, and, leaning back in the midst as if reposing upon a couch, was consumed without uttering a shriek or betraying one sign of agony.[36]

* * *

Controversy has raged as to whether or not *suttee* was an ancient Hindu practice, enjoined in the sacred writings.

The soldiers of Alexander the Great, in the fourth century B.C., are reported to have found widow-burning practiced in the Punjab. From then until modern times, according to Edward Thompson, instances have been cited by a long sequence of eye-witnesses.[37]

Hindu pundits say that in their *shastras,* or sacred books, *suttee* is not commanded, but only commended. There is one case of a *Sati* in the Ramayana and several in the Mahabharata. But Meyer considers these to have been added by later editors. "Assertions that it is the duty and nature of a good wife to follow her lord in death can be found often enough in both poems, but they yield no proof, since they all might be referred to later revision."[38]

Other passages from the sacred writings seem to encourage the widow to follow her husband's body into the fire. But the view of the best scholars is that the original text has been tampered with. As one commentator says dryly, "Few false readings have had consequences so fearful."

There were several reasons that, once the custom of *suttee* was established, gave it support. One ancient authority, at the time when wives were apparently given to poisoning their husbands on a disturbing scale, considered it to be a strong deterrent against such dastardly practices. There is no doubt that a wife, if she knows that her husband's death would also be the occasion of her own, would have the strongest possible incentive for keeping him alive!

Another reason often given was the husband's fear that his wife or wives might be taken by some other man after his death, which would be humiliating and disturbing to his spirit. There is evidence that the dead man's relatives sometimes put pressure on the widow to submit to *suttee* because they were afraid of the vengeance of his ghost if his property was thus withheld from him.

But the main reason was undoubtedly the idea that the husband needed his wife's ministries in the other world, and that it was her duty to follow him and continue to serve him there. "We may look on *suttee*," says Edward Thompson, "as almost inevitable from the premise of Hindu sociology and religion, that the husband stands to the wife in place of the Deity."[39] Dubois makes essentially the same point when he says that "it was considered an effrontery to the memory of the deceased, and as an evident mark of the want of that ardent devotion which a woman owes to her husband, when she showed any reluctance to accompany his body to the pile."[40]

One reason that may have prompted the widow to choose *suttee* was that the alternative was so uninviting. An English lady who saw for herself the abject misery of Hindu widows considered that it would be merciful to revive the custom of *suttee* as a humanitarian reform! Rather than languish in humiliation and destitution for the remainder of her days, a spirited woman might prefer to perish gloriously. And the *Sati* did indeed end her life in a figurative, as well as a literal, burst of dazzling limelight:

"The widow who mounted the pyre passed from the condition of a sinner to one of beatification: her dying curse or blessing had absolute power and unfettered course. After her death prayers were made to her spirit, and those prayers were sure of fulfillment. Her dying redeemed her ancestors from hell, and she enjoyed everlasting communion with her lord.

"Everything conspired to point the widow along one path—that which led to the red glow of the funeral pyre. After the death of a *Sati* there was so much pomp and noise of applause, and about the memory of one, such praise and exaltation, that often a psychological intoxication upheld her till she had passed beyond the reach of succor. The intoxication was of the spirit, not of the body; and the compulsion was terrible, being the whole tremendous, impalpable weight of familiar tradition and of expectation. These things hid from her the fate awarded her. And the upward race and roar of the flames and the shouts and music of the spectators drowned any voice of agony from the fire."[41]

In 1867, a gentleman named Mr. Ewer was quoted by the *Cal-*

cutta Review as neatly summarizing the benefits of the custom:

"The son was relieved of the expense of maintaining a mother; the male relatives came in at once for the estate which the widow would have held for her life; the Brahmins were paid for their services and were interested in the maintenance of their religion; and the crowd attended the show with the savage merriment exhibited by an English crowd at a boxing match."

He might have added that even for the unhappy lady this was a glorious, if painful, hour.

* * *

A rite that was attended with so much pageantry, religious fervor, and public enthusiasm was not easy to suppress.

The British Government, however, could hardly be indifferent to such practices. In South India particularly *suttee* was a source of embarrassment because the funerals of rajahs were events of almost unbelievable excitement, with hundreds, and even thousands, of wives and concubines being dragged shrieking to the immense funeral pyre and consigned, struggling, to the devouring flames. Some Portuguese missionaries reported one mammoth *suttee* at which they claimed that eleven thousand women were sacrificed; despite the respect due to their religious position, the figure was believed to be greatly exaggerated.

A disturbing fact, too, was that *suttee* was by no means always a voluntary act of renunciation on the part of the widow. Sometimes it was forced upon her unwillingly.

Such a case was reported in detail in 1796. A Brahmin had died, and his wife was taken along to be burned with his body. "All the previous ceremonies were performed; she was fastened on the pile, and the fire was kindled; but the night was dark and rainy. When the fire began to scorch this poor woman, she contrived to disentangle herself from the dead body and, creeping from under the pile, hid herself among some brushwood. In a little while it was discovered that there was only one body on the pile. The relations immediately took the alarm and searched for the poor wretch; the son soon dragged her forth, and insisted that she should throw herself on the pile again, or drown or hang herself. She pleaded for her life at the hands of her own son, and declared that she could not embrace so horrid a death—but she pleaded in vain. The son urged that he should lose his caste, and therefore he would die, or she should. Unable to persuade her to hang or drown herself, the son and the others present then tied her hands and feet and threw her on the funeral pile, where she quickly perished."[42]

Another feature that occasioned much concern was the age of the wives who were being involved. Three cases, reported early in the nineteenth century, involved child wives only eight years old.

Within the Portuguese territory of Goa, *suttee* had been strictly prohibited as early as the year 1510. But the British had hesitated and taken no decisive action.

Even when action *was* taken in 1813, all that was done was to insist that *suttee* would be permitted only if the rite was performed in strict accordance with the *shastras*. Each case had to be announced in advance, and government officers had to attend to ensure that all was done decently and in order.

To the embarrassment of the British, this apparent seal of official approval gave the custom a great boost. In the Bengal Presidency, the figures went up steadily. In 1815 there were 378 cases, in 1816 there were 442, in 1817 the total leaped to 707, and in 1818 it reached 839. In four years, under British supervision, the number of *Satis* had more than doubled!

When the Hindus were taken to task for thus abusing their privileges, they put all the blame on the Moslems. Unattached women were so unsafe, they declared, that it was best for them to preserve their honor by being burned to death after their male protectors had died.

Clearly, firm action was necessary. After some delays, a policy emerged. In 1829, two years after his appointment as Governor-General of India, Lord William Bentinck issued Regulation XVII, which made it a homicidal act to burn widows or to bury them alive.

The reference to burial was intended for the Telugu-speaking area of South India, where a curious variation of *suttee* was practiced. Instead of placing the dead husband's body on a funeral pyre, he was seated at the bottom of a deep pit dug in the earth. On an adjoining seat his widow took her place. Composed and calm, she remained seated thus while the earth was shoveled back into the pit. In one case that has been described, the widow raised her hand above her head. After her head had been covered with earth, she continued to wave her hand to the spectators above, until finally the moving hand was covered also.

The Regulation of 1829 was immediately successful, mainly because the weight of enlightened Indian opinion was on the side of the reform. However, a few illegal *suttees* continued to be practiced, and cases were reported every year up to 1913. Even after that there were occasional secret celebrations of the ancient rite, and reports of such celebration come in sporadically even at the present time. Here is an account of several recent cases:

"A lady in Gwalior who was 22 and happened to be a third wife of Mangilal became a *sati* on his death on 17 April 1951. All persuasions to move her from her resolve—even an appeal in the name of her young son—were of no avail. A crowd estimated at several thousand gathered at the cremation ghat and stories of miracles about the incident started. Another very recent case was reported from a village in Jaipur district. Men were reported to have garlanded the woman and her path to the pyre was strewn with flowers. In order that the hand of the law should not come down too heavily on the persons concerned, a child of 7 was made to set fire to the pyre."[43]

The strange practice of *suttee* may now be said, for all practical purposes, to have vanished from the Indian scene. Yet the idea still holds a peculiar fascination for the Indian woman who takes pride in her Hindu traditions—the idea of wifely devotion that goes to the utmost in self-sacrifice. Here is how one educated Indian woman expressed it in 1950:

"I am a descendant of *Satis* and proud of them: they were not those who buried themselves alive, for that had been forbidden, but those who had survived their widowhood only for a space of a few days, then died slowly because the will to live had ceased with the death of the beloved. To them love had come as something terrible but lovely. My grandmother said in old days they did not talk of being in love nor of faithfulness, nor did they swear eternal love; she said that the *Sati* died as she had lived, inseparable in death as in life from her husband.

"There were two *Satis* on my father's side and one on my mother's, but we still had a living *Sati* in our house, an aunt. About 18 years ago, in an epidemic of plague, the news arrived that her husband's sister lay ill. Her mother-in-law in a frenzy of fear sent her son to go and visit his sister. The sister recovered but next day the brother lay ill, and the day after he died. My aunt, his wife, has kept his rooms just as he had left them the day before; his turban lies in a glass case, as he had laid it; so also the clothes and the cane. A lamp burns night and day under the painting of a tall young man about 28 years old; beside it in the evenings can be seen the middle-aged wife with greying hair; once a beautiful young woman, now a shadow. The young man in the painting seems more alive than his wife, the living dead."[44]

* * *

Nowhere else in the East can the religious fervor or vivid pageantry of the *suttee* ceremony be matched. Yet it would be a mistake to assume that the devotion unto death of the Indian widow has no counterpart elsewhere.

"Should a girl in China lose her betrothed, or a young wife her husband, she is highly commended if she takes opium or in some other way contrives to follow him into the unseen world. Outside the walls of many Chinese cities, as well as in some public streets, I have frequently seen monumental arches erected to perpetuate the memory of young women who have killed themselves sooner than outlive their betrothed or their husbands."[45]

The story of Chang Shih, a betrothed Chinese maiden, is worthy of a place alongside the noblest example of a Hindu *Sati's* devotion:

A girl of 18, Chang Shih by name, was shortly to be married. Her bridegroom, to whom she had been betrothed in early childhood, suddenly died. The parents dreaded to tell her of this sad fact, but Chang Shih, sensing that something was wrong, asked what the trouble might be. Her mother replied, weeping, that he, who was to have become son-in-law of the house, had closed his eyes in death.

The young girl turned quietly and left the room, expressing no emotion. Presently she reappeared. Gold hair ornaments, powder, and rouge, had been laid aside. She wore, instead of silk gauze skirt and brocaded jacket, a long white coarse cotton gown. Black hair hung loose upon her shoulders; her pale face was strained and set. The mother, horrified, exclaimed: "How is it that you who are still a maid, appear thus as a widow?" She tried then to comfort her daughter explaining that a new marriage would shortly be arranged. Chang Shih replied: "My mother's voice speaks, the thoughts are not my mother's. Can I, your daughter, give myself to another man when my husband has gone, all lonely, to the Yellow Springs?" Continuing she begged that the wedding be not cancelled, that at the time appointed, seven days later, she might sit in the bridal chair and, escorted by the spirit of her husband, go to his home.

Marriage of two spirits or of living girls to the spirits of dead men are not rare in China and always bring renown to the families concerned. In this case everyone was delighted and preparations for the wedding were completed.

In Shantung, where these events took place, it is customary for the groom to proceed to the house of the bride seated in the scarlet bridal chair. This is followed by a green official chair which he uses on the return journey. The groom is received with great ceremony, and is introduced to everyone present except the bride, whom he is not allowed to see. When she is ready to start, the farewell ceremony is accomplished, the red sedan chair containing the bride is carried first, the green, now occupied by the groom, follows, and the procession returns to the house of the groom where the marriage ceremony takes place.

On Chang Shih's wedding day all was accomplished according to ritual, the only difference being that, instead of a living bridegroom, the p'ai wei, a strip of white paper, bearing his name and age and the important words, ling wei—seat of the soul—was placed in the red chair for the first journey, and occupied the green chair on the way back. Arrived at the groom's house the p'ai wei was placed in the great hall where family and friends were waiting to receive the young girl, and the wedding ceremony joining the living to the dead was performed. Chang Shih, elaborately dressed as a rich young bride, paid the necessary reverence to Heaven, Earth, to the ancestral tablets of her new family, and finally to the living members of that family in order of seniority. Then, retiring to what should have been her bridal chamber, she laid off the wedding dress and appeared in the sack cloth of a widow.

Weeks filled with sad and onerous duties passed. They were devotedly performed by the virgin widow of a man whom she had never seen. Finally the burial day dawned. A long file of white clad mourners accompanied by the widow threaded the fields to a newly made grave. The coffin was lowered. To the surprise and horror of all, the widow threw herself into the grave and lay face down upon the coffin. Puzzled, the mourners stood at first in silence, respectful of grief; finally relatives urged the young woman to arise. She merely replied: "My place is by my husband. Fill up the grave." Thinking to humor her each mourner, according to custom sprinkled a handful of earth upon the coffin and the prostrate form. Having done this everyone went away leaving the widow to her strange vigil.

An hour or two later relatives returned to supervise the filling of a grave which they expected now to find occupied by the coffin only. They were mistaken. Chang Shih, prone in the grave, lay dead.[46]

Three hours' journey by train from Seoul, Korea, near the resort town of Yusong, is a place known as the "Rock of the Falling Flowers." The story goes that, more than a thousand years ago, Korea was divided into three kingdoms, struggling with each other for supremacy. Finally one kingdom, with Chinese military aid, conquered and overran the others.

In the ruined castle on the rock three thousand women assembled. Their husbands had been killed or taken to China as slaves. They knew they would never see them again. As a demonstration of their devotion, the three thousand, decked in their gayest garments, marched to the edge of the precipice and threw themselves into the river below.[47]

When it comes to suicide, the Japanese yield to no other people. Stories of Japanese widows who chose death, rather than to live on after their husbands, are not lacking. Indeed, some wives have demonstrated a zeal that went even further:

"One or two women committed suicide when their husbands were posted abroad to Manchuria or China on active service. Their spirit was highly commended, since their purpose was to free their husbands' minds from any worries which might have distracted them from serving the Emperor."[48]

The tragic and terrible story of the devotion of the Eastern widow to her dead husband raises many searching questions. We are wont to describe our marriage in the West as "love marriage," and to consider many Eastern unions as arrangements of mere convenience. Yet what is love? Although custom and duty left many widows in the East no alternative but to suffer and even to die, it would be a grave injustice to explain all their sacrifices in these terms. In many, many cases the widow walked into the fire proudly and by deliberate choice. This was her way of showing the depth of her affection, her devotion, her fidelity. It was a strange way, and to us a gravely mistaken one. But leaving aside the inappropriateness of the action, and looking at the motive, dare we say that these women of the East knew less of true love than their Western sisters?

* * *

Let us conclude this rather somber chapter on a lighter note.

There were, of course, perfidious widows in the East. To illustrate their subtle ways, here is a story told about Chuang Tzu, one of China's ancient philosophers, and a contemporary of Aristotle.

Out walking one day, he encountered a woman in widow's garb. She was busily employed in fanning a newly made grave. Chuang Tzu turned aside, and asked her what she was doing. She replied that her late husband had made her promise that she would not take a second husband till the earth on his grave was dry!

The philosopher, who was also a magician, flicked the fan a few times and, presto, the grave was dry! The woman thanked him profusely and hurried eagerly away.

On his way home, Chuang reflected on this incident and found himself assailed with torturing doubts as to whether his wife might not behave in a similar way. He decided, for his own peace of mind, to put her to the test.

He feigned death, and was in due course put in a coffin. He then magically changed himself into an attractive young man, approached his wife with flattering advances, and proposed marriage to her.

She accepted him and began at once to make preparations. She put on the red wedding robe and prepared wine for the celebration. At this point Chuang, in the role of the young man, feigned illness, and appealed to her to get him medicine, or he would die. The only cure for his condition, he assured her, was the brain of a man recently dead.

The distracted lady rushed to her husband's coffin to procure the essential ingredient for the medicine. As she opened the coffin lid, the young man vanished, and Chuang sat up and looked reprovingly at his wife. What did she mean, he asked her sternly, by this behavior?

The quick-witted lady was equal to the occasion. With reassuring smiles she explained everything. She had found herself unable to believe, she said, that her husband was really dead. She thought that, if he revived, it would delight his heart if she were to welcome him back to life in her wedding garments. So she had donned the red robe before opening the coffin.

And the wine, what was that for? he asked bitterly. That, she replied immediately, was a precautionary measure. If she had been mistaken, and the body was decomposed, the wine would have served as a disinfectant!

Chapter 12

ABOVE ALL, GIVE US CHILDREN!

"The purpose of marriage is creation. No matter how blessed with happiness the man and the woman are in their relation, the marriage is a failure if it is childless."[1]

This Chinese saying would apply equally to all traditional Eastern communities. Marriage that turns out to be unfruitful defeats its primary purpose. As we have seen, it is of supreme importance that a man should have a son. "Then only is a man perfect," says Manu, "when he consists of three persons united; his wife, himself, and his son."

Until this vastly important event occurs, everyone waits anxiously. Not only the young married couple. Not only the members of the family. In the unseen world, the ancestors wait too. "Nothing can be more unfilial than to be without posterity. This is the unforgivable sin against the spirit of the ancestors. The dead rule the living with an iron hand."[2]

From the wedding day onward, the idea of fruitfulness is uppermost in the minds of the couple. Nora Waln describes the Chinese custom of serving the nuptial supper for bride and groom, before they settle down for the wedding night, on a baby's bath basin turned upside down. The supper itself includes "son and daughter dumplings."[3]

If the bride does not soon become pregnant, an awkward situation arises. Something is wrong. The ancient Hebrews believed that pregnancy was not simply the result of sexual union, but required also direct divine intervention. God opened the womb, showing thereby His favor toward the wife.[4] Confucius, in "Spring and Autumn," expresses the same idea: "There has never been a birth without the collaboration of Heaven. God is the Creator of all men."

The wife who does not bear children, therefore, is in serious trouble. At worst, she may believe that a divine curse rests upon her, since the supreme blessing bestowed upon womankind is withheld from her. At best, she will be embarrassed and uncomfortable, knowing the disappointment her husband and his family are bound to experience.

Millicent Pommerenke writes of Indian wives being stoned by the people of their community because of their inability to bear children.[5] That is certainly not typical. It is not unusual, however, for a childless wife to be returned to her parents.

Into view on the horizon came two figures, moving very slowly. I went on with my pounding. The figures grew larger every time I looked up, and then when they were still a fair distance away I recognized my daughter. I had seen her only once since her marriage, and since then over a year had passed.

They approached slowly, as if their feet were somehow weighted. Something is wrong, I thought. Young people should not walk thus. And when I saw their faces the words of welcome I had ready died unuttered.

In silence Ira knelt at my feet. I raised her up quickly, with hammering heart. "Let us go in," I said. "You must be tired."

Ira entered obediently. Her husband stood stiffly outside.

"Mother-in-law," he said, "I intend no discourtesy, but this is no ordinary visit. You gave me your daughter in marriage. I have brought her back to you. She is a barren woman."

"You have not been married long," I said with dry lips. "She may yet conceive."

"I have waited five years," he replied. "She has not borne in her first blooming, who can say she will conceive later. I need sons."

Ira was sitting with her face in her arms. She looked up, and her mouth moved a little, loosely, as if she had no control over her lips. She was lovely still, but strain and hopelessness had shadowed her eyes and lined her forehead. She seemed to back away as I went to her.

"Leave me alone, Mother. I have seen this coming for a long time. The reality is much easier to bear than the imaginings. At least now there is no more fear, no more necessity for lies and concealment."[6]

It is good when the rejected childless wife can go home and find refuge there. Otherwise, the streets await her. "Our houses," said a Bombay procuress, "are filled to capacity with young girls who have been forced into our profession because society has no other place for them. To be sterile is the only shame; you bear the world within your womb."[7]

*　　*　　*

The childless do not give up easily. Too much is at stake.

Religion is the first natural source to which the wife turns. Perhaps, if she can find favor in the eyes of her gods, they will grant her conception. Praying women are a characteristic feature of Eastern temples. They pray, no doubt, for many blessings. But most of all, they pray for fertility. With pathetic fervor they make their offerings, spending their slender resources freely in the hope that this great bounty may be vouchsafed them. The priests who direct the sacrifices of childless women are seldom idle.

In former times, according to Dubois, the priests occasionally intervened more directly. "There are few temples where the presiding deity does not claim the power of curing barrenness in women. On their arrival, the women hasten to disclose the object of their pilgrimage to the Brahmins. The latter advise them to pass the night in the temple where, they say, the great Venkateswara, touched by their devotion, will perhaps visit them in the spirit. . . . The following morning these detestable hypocrites, pretending complete ignorance of what has passed, make due enquiries into all the details; and having congratulated the women upon the reception they have met from the god, receive the gifts with which they have provided themselves and take leave of them, after flattering them with the hope that they have not taken their journey in vain. Fully convinced that the god has deigned to have intercourse with them, the poor creatures return home enchanted, flattering themselves that they will soon procure for their husbands the honor of paternity."[8]

If religion fails to have the desired effect, the despairing wife may give her husband a concubine, thankful that he is in a position to retain her as well, despite the fact that she has proved herself to be a liability.

A particularly serious difficulty arises when the husband dies without issue. The worst of all disasters has befallen him. His line is cut off in the land of the living.

Yet all may not be lost. Desperate situations call for desperate remedies. One solution has been to bring in a brother or other near kinsman of the husband to beget a child on his behalf. This is the explanation of the curious custom of the "levirate," of which we find instances in the Old Testament. The widely misunderstood story of the sin of Onan, in Genesis 38, is an excellent illustration of this custom. Er, the firstborn son of Judah, is dead. Tamar, his wife, is left without an heir.

"And Judah said unto Onan [Er's younger brother], Go in unto thy brother's wife, and perform the duty of a husband's brother unto her, and raise up seed to thy brother. Now Onan knew that the seed should not be his; and it came to pass, when he went in unto his brother's wife, that he spilled it on the ground, lest he should give seed to his brother. And the thing which he did was evil in the sight of the Lord; and the Lord slew him."

The sin of Onan has been variously interpreted. Some have identified it as masturbation; others as coitus interruptus. Clearly it was neither. His sin was that he practiced a wicked deception. He pretended to perform the sacred duty of the *levir*. But by practicing withdrawal he avoided giving Tamar a child—because if she had borne a son to Er, this child would have taken precedence over Onan and his own wife's children in the line of succession. Thus he committed the dastardly act of cutting off his dead brother's line in order to secure a better inheritance for himself.

The story goes on to describe how Tamar, thus thwarted, in the end succeeded, by disguising herself as a common harlot, in becoming pregnant by Judah himself. In this way, to her great credit, she secured progeny for her dead husband, and saved his line from extinction.

The levirate has been widely practiced in some parts of the East.[9] The Law of Manu gives the following directions:

"On the failure of issue by the husband, the desired offspring may be procreated, either by his brother or some other *sapinda* [near kinsman], on the wife, who has been duly authorized; sprinkled with clarified butter, silent, in the night, let the kinsman thus appointed beget one son, but a second by no means, on the widow or childless wife."

In China and Japan, it was a common practice to adopt into the family a boy who would count as the son of the childless man, and would be willing to perform the necessary sacrifices to the ancestors. This was straining the principle of succession a good deal. While it is logical to suppose that a brother's seed might serve a man who could provide none of his own, since both have the same original ancestry, it is quite another matter to bring in alien seed to continue the family line. However, where nothing else can be done, a poor solution may be better than none at all.

If a Chinese or Japanese wife produced only daughters, her husband, having no other means of begetting sons, might adopt as a son the prospective husband of one of his daughters. Such a boy was called *yoshi*, or foster son. He came to live in his wife's home, and was integrated into the life of the family. In many instances, however, once the *yoshi* had done his duty and produced a son, he was cold-shouldered out of the household and finally persuaded to agree to a divorce, for which if necessary he was suitably rewarded. In recent years the function of *yoshi* has become so unpopular that young men willing to perform it are harder and harder to find.

One relatively modern Chinese couple, whose union was not blessed with children, were repeatedly urged by the husband's old mother to bring in a concubine in order to meet the deficiency. This they did not wish to do. They preferred the idea of adoption. So the wife announced that she was at last pregnant, and went off on a long visit to her mother's distant home. On returning to her husband, she padded herself well to suggest that the arrival of her baby was imminent. Arrangements had meanwhile been made with a doctor that, as soon as a foundling child was available, the wife would go to the hospital. The appropriate day came, and she departed with her mother-in-law's best wishes. When the wife returned with the foundling child, the old lady was in the seventh heaven of delight, and exclaimed, "He is a charming boy, and exactly like his father!"

These complicated arrangements all introduce awkward and disturbing elements into the life of the family, and have often been the cause of much trouble. That they have been necessary at all testifies eloquently to the central importance of the fact that has been the very foundation stone of the patriarchal system—that at all costs a man must have a son, and that every other consideration in the life of the family must yield to that paramount necessity.

*   *   *

The expectant mother in the East is a very happy person. Her ideas about what is taking place within her body would, however, strike a modern Western mother as decidedly quaint.

"The woman," said Manu, "is considered as the field, and the man as the grain. Vegetable bodies are formed by the united operation of the seed and the field. . . . Whatever be the quality of the seed, scattered in a field prepared in due season, a plant of the same quality springs in that field, with peculiar visible properties.

"Certainly this earth is called the primeval womb of many beings; but the seed exhibits not in its vegetation any properties of the womb.

"On earth here below, even in the same ploughed field, seeds of many different forms, having been sown by husbandmen in the proper season, vegetate according to their nature. That one plant should be sown, and another produced, cannot happen."

In other words, the wife is carrying her husband's child—quite literally. She contributes the substance for its growth, but not its essential, individual essence.

This concept is widespread—and not only in the East. It was basic to Hebrew thought about reproduction.[10] Lecky, the historian, finds it among the ancient Greeks, and sees in it the basis for the concept of woman's innate inferiority. "The inferiority of women to men was illustrated and defended by a very curious physiological notion, that the generative power belonged exclusively to men, women having only a very subordinate part in the production of their children."[11] Roman and Christian writers (including St. Thomas Aquinas) refer to the same concept.

Fortunately, Eastern women do not take too much to heart the idea that their function in motherhood is little more than that of an incubator. The vessel is an honorable one, and shares in the glory of that which it contains. "In some cases," says Manu, "the prolific power of the male is chiefly distinguished; in others, the receptacle of the female; but, when both are equal in dignity, the offspring is most highly esteemed."

The pregnant wife enjoys great prestige. Of China, Nora Waln says, "Strangers seeing that a woman carries a child, congratulate her. At such times, the most honorable place at every table is hers by right."[12]

A pregnant woman who procures an abortion is included by Manu among those who must be shunned, and is classified along with the wife who has struck her husband—a monstrous action for any Hindu woman. Even if a pregnant wife has committed some serious fault, or even broken the law, she cannot be punished until her child is born. A pregnant widow, for example, cannot become *Sati* until she has been delivered.

Although the Eastern mother-to-be believes that she contributes nothing of her essential self to the child, she considers that she has vast and awesome potentialities for influencing it while it is in her womb. Consequently, many rules, some of them based on the wildest superstition, are carefully observed. In China the wife was taught never to lie on her back, and not to laugh loudly. She should not eat food with a bad flavor, or anything not properly cut up. Hashed-up food is liable to give the child a careless disposition. The mother should do nothing carelessly. She should not sit on a mat that was not straight, or look at clashing colors, or evil sights, or obscene pictures. She should hear no obscene sounds, listen to no gossip. She herself should use only refined language. She is urged to read good poetry, and particularly to be told beautiful stories before she goes to bed at night, so that she may dwell on them as she sleeps. She should think lofty thoughts and take great care not to lose her temper. If she fulfills all these requirements, her child will be born physically, mentally and morally perfect.

In particular, a pregnant woman must be kept away from anything that has to do with death. Nora Waln gives an illustration of this:

"I found the women of the Wong homestead in tearful agitation because their Elder had given the order for his burial clothes to be stitched. While I waited, he came in through the Orchid Door.

"On the approach of the Elder, his wife motioned the two young women of the Family, who were pregnant, to leave the court where we were gathered, as women concerned with the beginning of life must not loiter where consideration is given to the end of life's pilgrimage."[13]

Nowadays we are sophisticated enough to know that most of these ideas have little validity, because the mother's mental influence upon her unborn child is virtually nil. Most of us, however, would agree with the man who said, "I would rather be borne by a mother who had followed these rules than by one who had disregarded them." And we can understand the dilemma of the Chinese lady, offering suggestions for her daughter's behavior during pregnancy, when she remarked, "There are many creeds and many religions. We do not know what is really helpful to the soul about to be born. So it is best to use all the advised methods to safeguard a child's entry into the world."[14]

However, not all the methods advised were harmless. A mother-in-law in India, for example, might starve her son's young wife, in the belief that this would result in a smaller fetus and so make birth easier. The result, all too often, was the enfeeblement and even the death of both mother and child.

*   *   *

Dignified is the status of the pregnant wife. But when her hour is come, she is a dangerous person to be near.

Throughout the East the idea of malevolent influences associated with childbirth is widespread.

A highly qualified Indian physician of a generation ago, Dr. H. Suhrawardy, gave a vivid account of how these superstitious ideas hindered the processes of nature: "In a great many homes in India, especially among the Indians of the higher castes, the puerperal woman is looked upon as unclean. Her touch necessitates a bath of purification, and therefore the worst and the oldest beds, and such bedding as could be thrown away after the event, are used, and the most useless lumber-room of the house is chosen as the lying-in apartment. Sepsis, puerperal fever, infantile tetanus, and other microbe diseases take their heavy toll. After childbirth the poor mother is denied God's light and fresh air, and even cold water. The windows and doors, such as there may be in that small room, are kept shut and securely fastened; and although ventilation is totally obstructed, and there are no fireplaces and chimneys in Indian houses, yet a fire is constantly kept going inside, and a small taper is kept lighted day and night to ward off the evil spirits. Instead of a clean accoucheur or a midwife, a dirty low-class woman, with long and filthy nails and fingers cramped with dirty rings, made of base metals, is requisitioned to usher into life the helpless infant who is the hope and future of the country.

"In the vitiated and unhappy surroundings which I have attempted to describe, the poor woman who has undergone the travails of childbirth is incarcerated and given hot fomentations to her body and made to drink decoctions of various "heating" vegetables and dried fruits from three weeks to forty days. During this period the infant is never brought out of the room of horrors, for fear of the evil eye, the Dain or village witch, and the evil spirits. It has always been a wonder how, under such conditions, mothers have ever escaped cent per cent mortality, and why our very manhood has not been exterminated or dwarfed to the lowest possible ebb by the blight of these harrowing surroundings."[15]

One of the most curious of all Asian customs is the "mother-roasting" practiced in Thailand. Here is a description by an English physician: "They called it *yu fai* (to stay with the fire), and it consisted of bringing a brazier of lighted charcoal to the bedside and keeping it as near to the patient's stomach as she could bear. It was said to 'dry the womb.' Often it raised huge blisters, and when the skin was covered with them and the patient could stick it no longer, they turned her over and blistered her back. This treatment went on for two or three weeks. It caused great suffering but it was the custom, and custom to them was sacred. That anyone should dispute it would never have entered their heads."[16]

A native of Thailand describes the procedure in more detail: "We built a bed out of bamboo strips. Underneath the bed we kept the charcoal dimly burning. Mother, lying on the bed, appeared like a fish being roasted. I could not see the reason why she had to torture herself thus. But the people at that time believed that a maternity patient had lost a considerable amount of blood, and in order to keep her body warm, she must stay near the fire for a week. Mother became weak on account of the heat, and the baby was not healthy. We feared that it might not live. But fate is unpredictable. The baby survived."[17]

Notice that, in these two accounts, the reasons given for the mother-roasting custom are different. It is very likely that the original reason was not based on health or hygiene at all, but had something to do with keeping away evil spirits. These demonic beings, according to Eastern tradition, take a peculiar and excessive interest in the process of childbirth.

Nowadays, fortunately for Thai women, a hot-water bottle applied to the mother's stomach is usually considered an acceptable method of satisfying this curious old custom!

All these crude and barbaric processes the Eastern wife endured, as she endured childbirth itself, with stoic resignation. "A Chinese woman who approaches childbirth with fear of the birth-pains is considered a coward not worthy of life. Birth is a woman's career."[18] Chinese and Japanese women were expected to deliver their children in complete silence. A woman who cried out would suffer a serious loss of face.

"She would have no one with her when the hour came. It came one night, early, when the sun was scarcely set. She stopped and stood up then, her scythe dropped. On her face was a new sweat, the sweat of a new agony.

"'It is come,' she said, 'I will go into the house. Do not come into the room until I call. Only bring me a newly peeled reed, and slit it, that I may cut the child's life from mine.'

"When he reached the house he went to the door of their room. She came to the door and through the crack her hand reached out and took the reed. She said no word, but he heard her panting as an animal pants which has run for a long way.

"Wang Lung stood listening at the door to those heavy animal pants. A smell of hot blood came through the crack, a sickening smell that frightened him. The panting of the woman within became quick and loud, like whispered screams, but she made no sound aloud."[19]

Such grim, solitary endurance is not always the rule. The Indian wife, as we have seen, was attended by a midwife, though judging by some descriptions of the obstetrical techniques employed, she might have been better off without this assistance! It was also her prerogative to have her mother in attendance.[20]

Because of the ceremonial uncleanness associated with child-birth, in some Eastern countries it was the custom in wealthy homes to set aside a special room as the family birth chamber. There all members of the family, throughout successive generations, first saw the light—or more accurately, became dimly aware of the darkness.

Some interesting customs are associated with the disposal of the placenta. There is a widespread belief that this should be buried under the entrance to the house. Various reasons are given for this, and several of them were quoted to us in answer to inquiries we made. One was that this kept away evil spirits—a useful reason for any Eastern custom for which no other good explanation is available. A more plausible idea was that the presence of the placenta at the door of the family home created a mystical link that, later in life, would always tend to draw the child back to his or her birthplace.

In a Japanese variation of this custom the placenta is put in a jar and buried at the gateway that opens into the grounds of the family home. In the case of a son, it was buried inside the gateway, because he would remain in the family. The placenta of a daughter was buried just outside the gate, because she would go forth from her home and become a member of some other family.

Among some simple Indian peasants there is a curious belief about babies born in the West. The reason their skin is white, they say, is because immediately after birth the infant is plunged in a bath containing a special secret ingredient. Westerners guard the secret of this ingredient closely, so it is not available to other people, whose skins are therefore of darker colors!

*　　*　　*

"Everywhere, the women and children with babies strapped on their backs; the pregnant mothers of what I call a three-in-one—one topside, one alongside, and one inside . . . the children sent out to play with a big fat baby fastened to them like a crustacean shell; the smaller children with dolls strapped on their backs to prepare them for later responsibilities—and the occasional woman who wears a child who wears a doll."[21]

This picture from Japan could have a counterpart anywhere in the East. Only some of the details would be different. In India the mother carries her child astride on the hip, and not on the back. But physical closeness to the mother, or to the elder sister who is deputizing for the mother, is considered essential for young children in the East; and for the first year at least, the infant is with his mother almost all the time. This constant loving protection produces a deep sense of security.

In our travels in the East we were impressed with the extent to which fathers shared in the general cuddling and fondling that are bestowed on small children. Though to his older children the father may be distant and aloof, he often has no inhibitions about lavishing warm and tender affection on the infant. We have watched Eastern fathers playing with their babies with a freedom and spontaneity that would be rare among fathers in the West.

In the early years of life the child is not much subjected to demands or disciplines. The tyranny of schedules has not yet invaded the world of the Eastern mother. She feeds her baby at the breast whenever he wants it, and is not embarrassed if this is in a public place. Weaning is late in many cases. Children may be given the breast for as long as five years. But often the arrival of another baby compels the previous one to stand aside in favor of the newcomer.

There is little rigidity in toilet training. It is not expected that a small child will behave like one who is old enough to follow directions. So little or no pressure is applied to the child in the attempt to make him "clean."

The small child's freedom from inhibitions is encouraged by the fact that he is free to run about naked. The climate of some Eastern lands, and the poverty of the people, conspire to favor this arrangement. Up to as much as seven or eight years of age, children of poorer parents may run about the streets and play without benefit of garments of any kind.

There is a story, told with minor variations throughout Asia, about the Westernized parents who took their small son from the city to visit country relatives. While the grownups sat and talked, the little boy in his city clothes was allowed to go out with his cousins and play in the village street. On the way home his parents asked him if he had enjoyed himself.

"Yes," he replied, "I had lots of fun. The children were very nice, and let me play their games."

"Were you playing with little boys or little girls?" he was asked.

"I don't know," was the reply. "You see I couldn't tell, because they had no clothes on!"

Early childhood is a time of ceremonies. There are rites connected with birth, with the naming of the child, with the shaving or cutting of the hair. Manu says the child should be carried out of the house for the first time at four months, to see the sun; and fed with rice for the first time at six months. In Korea a family celebration is held when the child is three weeks old, and another when he has completed the first hundred days of his life.[22]

The really important occasion, however, is the first birthday. This is usually celebrated by a party with many guests. Gifts are brought for the child, who is dressed up for the occasion. In China this is often the time when the child is expected to give the first indication of his future career. Beside him are placed objects symbolizing the various trades and professions. The one he grasps first will show the field in which he will later specialize. Ambitious mothers are not beyond offering a little vocational guidance at this point. They will put a writing brush in a very accessible position in the hope that the little boy will be induced to pick it up. If he does, this is a sign that he is destined to be a scholar!

At each of these milestones in the child's life the parents express their gratitude that he is still alive. In the West today the death of a child has become, thanks to our admirable health and sanitation services, a rare event. But the picture in the East is, alas, very different. Even in a relatively modern city like Rangoon, we were told that three out of ten children die during the first year of life. In rural areas the rate may be decidedly higher.

In Indian cities, especially Calcutta, we have watched the steady stream of bearers carrying the dead on rough litters to the burning ghats, and noticed how often the still form was that of a child. In earlier days, when health services were less efficient and famine came often, the child mortality must often have been appalling.

Professor Headland, who lived in Peking, described the daily collection of dead babies that was once a feature of the city services:

"If a baby happens to die, he is carefully wrapped up in a piece of old matting, if his parents are poor, and tenderly placed on some street corner, where he is picked up by the driver of the big black cart, to which a gentle but very big black cow is hitched, and taken outside the city, where he and a large company of other small unfortunates are buried side by side or one on top of the other in a common hole, without a monument to mark his resting place.

"I have seen that big black cow come down the street in Peking, morning after morning at about nine o'clock, and I have seen the man who went with the cart picking up the pathetic little packages, and sticking them into the back end of the cart as we used to put wood on the farm wagon."[23]

When a child dies, it is a common belief that it has been taken by the evil spirits. To prevent this, protective religious rites are performed, and charms given to the child to wear. Superstitious parents will be careful never to praise their child as clever or beautiful. He will be spoken of with contempt so as to encourage the predatory spirits to seek a victim elsewhere. "My brother was named the Red Lotus. But everyone called him 'the ugly one' in order to fool the devils with the idea that he really was no good and that it was not worth their trouble to take him away."[24]

*   *   *

The value placed on a child in the East is inevitably influenced by its sex.

"Wang Lung stood listening at the door. When he could bear no more and was about to break into the room, a thin, fierce cry came out and he forgot everything.

" 'Is it a man?' he cried importunately, forgetting the woman. The thin cry burst out again, wiry, insistent. 'Is it a man?' he cried again, 'tell me at least this—is it a man?'

"And the voice of the woman answered as faintly as an echo, 'A man!'

"He shook the old man's shoulder.

" 'It is a man child!' he called triumphantly. 'You are grandfather and I am father!' "[25]

The desire for sons led to speculation as to the possibility of sex determination. "Some say," reports Manu cautiously, "that on the even nights are conceived sons; on the odd nights daughters; therefore let the man, who wishes for a son, approach his wife in due season on the even nights; but a boy is in truth produced by the greater quality of the male strength; and a girl by the greater quality of the female." The idea that the vigor of the husband's performance in intercourse tends to encourage the production of male offspring seems to recur in many cultures. We have encountered it also in Africa.

The Chinese had further ideas as to what influences the sex of the future child. One gentleman in Peking, whose wife had borne him four daughters in a row, called in a geomancer to inquire into the reason. The Chinese have a belief in what they call *feng shua*, a Taoist concept of the fitness and balance of things in nature, which they believe creates the conditions needed for favorable events. The expert consultant examined the gentleman's house in detail and found everything in order.

Baffled, he went outside. Suddenly he spied the chimney of the mission compound across the street. "Ah," he exclaimed. "There is your trouble. The foreign devils have put up a chimney, and that has destroyed your *feng shua*. Until that is pulled down, you'll have nothing but daughters."

The gentleman, with great politeness, called on the missionaries and explained his distressing predicament. What could they do? The chimney was dismantled. This had the desired result. The gentleman's wife bore him two fine sons![26]

Since sons were so eagerly desired, the arrival of a first-born daughter was inevitably something of a disappointment. This led to the idea, in Hindu thinking, that being born a girl was the penalty for some sin committed in a previous incarnation. "We are girls because we did something wrong when we were living before. S—— is trying to get merit so that she may be a man next time."[27]

Dr. Reddi, Deputy President of the Madras Legislative Council, spoke of the low estimation of daughters in a speech in 1928: "The birth of a girl is looked upon as a great piece of misfortune, especially if the parents are poor; the responsibility of finding a decent, suitable husband for her is already felt so keenly as to kill even the paternal and the maternal love, with the sad result that in many poor families girl children are neglected from the moment of their birth. In a few instances I have seen the girl babies allowed to die of sheer neglect by their parents."[28]

This appears to have been specially true of Rajputana. According to Pandita Ramabai, when the Rajput father heard of a daughter's birth he announced to his friends that "nothing" has been born to him. The friends then "go away grave and quiet."[29]

The Book of Odes describes the similarly contrasting attitudes of Chinese parents to male and female births:

> A son is born.
> He is placed upon a bed,
> And clothed with brilliant stuffs.

> A daughter is born.
> They place her on the ground,
> They wrap her in common cloths.[30]

In dire necessity, as we have seen, female children were disposed of by being put to death. However, this must not be taken to mean that they were unloved or regarded as useless. It was a desperate measure resorted to when all the mouths simply could not be fed, and someone had to be sacrificed. Under these circumstances a girl, being of lesser value, was more expendable than a boy.

The Suzuki family was in desperate straits. "There were already four children, and in spite of the father's working hard from early till late the family was always hungry, and they were desperate at the prospect of an additional mouth to feed. There was no way to get more land. Or to extract more from the land they had. It was a problem to which there was no solution.

"So they decided to ask the midwife to kill the child if it was a girl.

"When the mother was in labor the midwife prepared a piece of wet paper and waited for the child to be born. If a girl, the wet paper would be spread over her face, preventing breathing, and death would come.

"It was a boy. And because of the idea of the predominance of men over women, the baby could not be killed. But there was no rejoicing, and the family was weighed down with a dark shadow as they thought of their increased burdens."[31]

Whenever possible, however, a girl baby would be sold rather than killed. Not only did this bring a little sorely needed cash; it also gave the child the chance to survive.

The sale of older girls by poverty-stricken families has continued in Japan until very recently. Millicent Pommerenke reports a discussion in which she asked what price was paid for these girls. One figure quoted was $5.60. An instance was given of a girl sold for a sack of potatoes. But a pretty girl, who could sing, dance, or speak English, could bring in as much as $40.[32]

Strictly speaking, the word "sale" is misleading here. What happens is that the parents surrender total rights over their daughter in exchange for money or goods paid in respect of her future earnings. Freedman, writing in 1957, reported finding this practice still carried on in Singapore.[33] Girls thus disposed of are often employed in sweat shops, or as prostitutes. Even when these transactions are illegal, they are very difficult to control in practice.

The real problem is, of course, the economic one. Families able to feed their daughters would never wish to part with them. Parental love in the East is as warm and strong as in the West, and it would be a grave injustice to think of these fathers and mothers as callous and unfeeling when they have to part with their daughters.

Indeed, apart from the question of their status in the hierarchy, daughters are loved for their own sake just as much as sons are. Even Manu says, "A house-holder must consider his wife and son, as his own body; his daughter, as the highest object of tenderness."

Lest there be any doubt on this point, here is a translation from the Bengali of a poem, written by an Indian mother, about her baby daughter:

"As the fruit of a thousand births, as reward for a thousand austerities, she had favor on us at break of day and came. To welcome her the dawn maiden with swift hands made blossom and bud to flower; when they heard that she would come to earth, the sweet singing birds caroled welcome with dulcet voice; the morning breeze said softly to all men, 'There comes to earth a flower from heaven.'

"Three months and six days ago she came to the dwelling of men. She knows not day and night; tears, joy, love, laughter are all unknown. Yet her own folk come running to her each moment like bees covetous of honey. When she bursts into laughter, all laugh too. What limitless power is in her little heart! In her baby babble what music pours forth; in all the world where is its like?

"Love or joy she has taken away, poetry and memory too; she has snatched away my whole heart. Without her the world is empty; vice and virtue I forget. Blessed is thy power, and thy glory incomparable."[34]

* * *

"These are the duties of parents to their children: giving food, clothing, and shelter, forbidding wrong-doing, encouraging right

conduct, giving education, assisting them in matrimony, and trans-
ferring properties to them in good time."[35]

Apart from maintenance, therefore, the chief functions of Eastern parents toward their sons and daughters during the period
of childhood are to train them in discipline and prepare them for
adult life.

The disciplinary process does not start seriously till a child is
about six or seven. Up to that time Eastern children in general
are brought up very permissively. "Indian people are as a rule
tenderly affectionate to little children, and the Indian baby suffers
more from over-indulgence than from neglect."[36] In Ceylon,
"childhood is relatively free of restraints. Even disobedience is
often treated laxly."[37] "Japanese young children are emotionally
replete in the continuing presence of the loving, serving mother
or mother substitute. In our few weeks of travel I only heard a
Japanese child cry or raise its voice contentiously on two occasions.
The philosophy seems to be that a child to the age of six should
have everything possible that it wants and be protected and
cherished in every way."[38]

However, once the child is considered old enough to learn correct behavior, the discipline applied is strict and uncompromising.
"The pressure of the family system is tremendous, and disobedience is almost impossible. A rebel against his family would have
the whole of society against him, and could find no refuge."[39]

The functions of father and mother diverge at this point. With
little children, both are equally free and permissive. Such light
correction as is needed is given by the mother. More severe punishment is seldom required.

With the increase of restrictions, however, the father assumes
his traditional role as chief disciplinarian. "Warmth is replaced
by aloofness and avoidance of bodily intimacies and other manifestations of affection. The father turns abruptly from comforter
and playmate to mentor and example, a person to be held in awe
and respect. The mother on the other hand makes no sharp transition in her role. It is to her that the growing children turn for affection, and through adolescence it is she who is the intermediary
between children and father, and the special pleader to the husband in their behalf."[40]

This emerging distinction in parental functions is well expressed by the Chinese. The mother is *chia-tze*, the symbol of kindness; the father is *chia-yen*, the symbol of dignity and sternness. The Record of Rites puts it thus, "The mother deals with the sons on the ground of affection and not of showing them honor, the father on the ground of showing them honor and not of affection."[41]

The function of the mother as intercessor was quaintly expressed by a Korean student of ours in a paper he submitted: "When children in Korea have problems, they talk with their mother. The mother intercedes them to the father when he is in the mood of cheerfulness."

The principle behind all discipline is that children owe their parents unlimited gratitude and respect. "The pain and care which a father and mother undergo in producing and rearing children," says Manu, "cannot be compensated in a hundred years." The Chinese equivalent, in the "Book of Filial Piety," is: "our bodies, to every hair and shred of skin, are received from our parents. We must not presume to injure or to wound them. This is the beginning of filial piety."

As we have seen, filial piety was regarded by Confucius as the root of all virtue. Children must be disciplined not simply in order that they may enjoy good relations with their parents. They are also being prepared for the wider life of human society, which is founded on respect for law and order. As Yu Tzo, one of the disciples of Confucius, remarks, "Few persons who have been obedient sons and younger brothers are insubordinate. We do not know of a rebellion instigated by persons disinclined to offend their superiors." Later, the Emperor Kang Hsi (1662–1722) expressed the same idea in the Sacred Edict: "If everybody is filial and brotherly, nobody will oppose the law." Even today, in Oriental communities in the West, the markedly low incidence of juvenile delinquency continues to prove the point.

So the children of the East have been taught to show the greatest respect and politeness to their parents, and to all elders.

"We went first to the Garden of Children. Shun-Yi, who was then ten years old and had an intelligent face, rose from a game of hedged-in chess which he was playing with his sister Hsung-mu. He took her left hand and the right hand of their half-brother, Wen-wu, and all bowed together. A chubby lad, Tsai-fu, thrust a shuttle-cock into the pockets of his long, turquoise gown and bent so that his forehead tapped the playground floor. Ming-chi had boots of yellow-and-black striped tiger cloth. He saluted with his feet well placed to display them."[42]

*   *   *

When children reach the age at which their character training begins, they are placed under the direct supervision of the parent of their own sex.

The mother instructs the daughters in household tasks. "Many of the minor chores fall to the growing girls in the family. It is not uncommon (in Ceylon) to see a girl of eight or nine at play with a baby brother on her hip. Firewood collection is a popular task among older girls for it offers a breath of freedom from parental scrutiny amidst other neighborhood girls who can giggle together over small gossip."[43]

The mother's aim is to mold her daughter to fulfill the traditional feminine roles. "My mother wanted me to become like the ancient daughters of her house, a true and staid woman, full of dignity, like my grandmother."[44] To this end, the girls of the family would be regaled with stories of the family tradition, and would be taught the rules of good wifely conduct. The traditions were embodied in cautionary tales, rhymes and rules to be memorized, and these were passed down from mother to daughter. We have already given examples of this oral tradition, and the literature that sometimes sought to preserve it.

Above all, the mother supervises her daughter's arrival at puberty. This in the East is an event of great importance, not an embarrassment to be concealed or evaded. Here is an account of the puberty rite in a village in modern Ceylon:

"When a mother becomes aware of her daughter's first menstrual flow, steps are taken immediately to isolate her from all male contact. . . . It is generally believed that such contact at this time would make her permanently 'sexy' and, by implication, of loose morals. That such an eventuality will not take place is further abetted by breaks in her seclusion during which elder women come to give warnings as to the proclivities of men, and the need for avoiding them in the interests of that supreme value in a bride, virginity.

"After the girl has been in seclusion for several days, and the menstrual flow concluded, her mother will go to the astrologer for a reading of her daughter's horoscope and the determination of an auspicious time to bathe her. The post-menstrual bath is invariably given by the *dhobi's* wife ("washer" caste) under the prolific yak tree. . . . Water is poured over the girl, in the usual style of a village bath, from a new pot. At the conclusion of bathing this pot is to be dashed against the yak tree by the girl herself. Then taking a knife, the girl gazes upon the tree and stabs it sharply seven times, its milky fluid oozing from the cuts. At this sign the ceremony is completed and the girl returns to her household for feasting and entertainment. Great care is taken that she see first of all as she returns to the house a good omen of fertility, e.g. a pregnant woman or nursing mother. A view of a barren wife would be disastrous. . . .

"Even in the poorest home, presents are given to the girl and special sweetmeats are prepared for neighbors and relatives who pay congratulatory calls. The beating of the great *raban,* a round drum three feet or more in diameter, by the women of the family, announces to the entire village, if the entire village is not already aware, that the little girl is now a woman."[45]

Meanwhile the father has assumed responsibility for the training of his sons. His aim is definitely not to be a "pal." "The superior man," says Confucius, "maintains a distant reserve toward his son." The traditional Indian father is held in superstitious awe by the younger males of the family. They cannot sit with him or eat with him. "In certain families, especially in South India, the young men of the house cannot even talk to him except through the medium of the oldest son or a favored individual."[46]

The belief was that plenty of stern discipline is good for a growing boy. Under Chinese law, a father could not be penalized even if he killed his son accidentally while chastising him "in a lawful and customary manner."[47] In *Dream of the Red Chamber,* Chia Cheng beat his son Pao-Yu savagely with a heavy bamboo rod until he was covered with bruises. Only the intervention of Madame Wang, who begged to be killed first, saved his life.[48]

Usually, however, the father preferred to hand over his son to someone else to undergo the severe discipline that was prescribed. "Burmese parents whose hearts suffered too much at the thought

of inflicting any punishment themselves handed their sons over
to the monks, with the plea that they would teach them to be good
and obedient, and chastise them severely if they did not obey."[49]

In India the boy, as we have seen, was put under the care of a
guru, or teacher, and became a *brahmachari.* The Chinese boy
destined for scholarship was, like the Indian lad, committed to a
teacher's supervision. This supervision was expected to be firm.

"And Wang Lung was awed by the old teacher's great brass
spectacles, and by his long loose robe of black and by his immense
fan, which he held even in winter, and Wang Lung bowed before
him and said,

" 'Sir, here are my two worthless sons. If anything can be driven
into their thick brass skulls it is only by beating them, and therefore if you wish to please me, beat them to make them learn.' "[50]

*   *   *

"The duties of children toward their parents are: taking care of
them when they are old, helping them in their work, keeping the
good name of the family, obedience, trustworthiness, using their
properties sensibly, and remembering them after their death."[51]

These obligations are never fully discharged. They continue
through the life of the parents, and beyond. To a dutiful child,
says the Book of Odes, concern for his parents always prompts
his first waking thought:

> When early dawn unseals my eyes,
> Before my mind my parents rise.

Primarily this is a matter of duty. Many Chinese sources emphasize this. The Record of Rites says, "While his parents are
alive, a son should not dare to consider his wealth his own, nor
hold it for his own use only." Mencius says, "The superior man
will not for all the world be niggardly toward his parents." And
again, "There never has been a man trained to benevolence who
neglected his parents."

In the East it has never been the custom for parents to make
provision for their old age. In most instances this would in any
case have been impossible, since most live from hand to mouth,
from harvest to harvest. But the duty of children to maintain parents is so sacred that it takes precedence over all others. In

Japanese law, for instance, a man's obligation to provide for his parents comes before his duty even to his wife and children.[52]

This duty is discharged automatically in the joint family. "The sons bring in their pay and hand it over to their mother. She knows better what is good for the family than younger women do. The earners of the clan pool their resources. Mother, the woman who brought forth the male scions of the family and the wife of the first-born of the older generation, is its domestic head and its exchequer. It is she who manages the whole establishment, who refuses or permits, withholds or distributes."[53]

To the Westerner it is curious to notice how, in the East, a grown man in his thirties will make no major decision until he has consulted his parents. But to the Eastern mind this is correct and commendable conduct. In Japan a man is still legally a "child" as long as his parents remain alive, regardless of his age and status. In the Chinese novel *Chia* by Pa Chin, the father discovers that one of his sons has a mistress. Enraged, he does not hesitate to prescribe corporal punishment, although the son is well over thirty years of age!

Ideally, however, a child's obligations to his parents are never considered merely a matter of duty. Confucius said that obedience to a ruler should be based on respect, but obedience to a parent should be based on love. The Record of Rites enjoins the performance of all duties toward parents "with an appearance of pleasure to make them feel at ease." Even if feelings of affection are absent, they are to be simulated. A wife or concubine in Korea who made insulting remarks to her parents-in-law could be hanged without delay, and a husband who spoke insultingly of his wife's parents could receive sixty strokes of the bamboo.[54]

As Eastern parents advance in years, they are treated with increasing honor. The whole culture has encouraged this. "Chinese society's orientation to age," wrote Marion Levy in 1949, "is one which invests increasing age with increasingly higher status. This is in marked contrast with the prevalent pattern in the industrialized West—which, especially as epitomized in the United States, is overwhelmingly a youth culture. . . . In China extreme age lends to judgment a weight of validity that is lacking in the West. The average Chinese would regard the situation of the aged in the United States as an example of unintelligible barbarism and lack of human feeling."[55]

Throughout the East, tradition has regarded the old as having the wisdom of knowledge and experience, which in an agricultural society counts for more than physical strength and energy. In a society based on the observance of tradition, it is the old who know what the customs are. They are the living link with the honored past, and their conservatism is a bulwark against the follies and dangers of youthful innovation. Above all, the elderly are soon to become the ancestors, wielding supernatural powers. It is wise to honor and humor them, for their power to retaliate may soon be terrifying.

Vested with such power, the elderly parents could become tyrants. But more often, it seems, the security of their status made them benevolent. They developed dignity and grace.

"The Lady in First Authority in the House of Lin sat on a bamboo divan under the cool shade of a papaya tree. She was a woman beautiful in age. In women who have filled their years well, in every race, I find age has greater charm, grace, and beauty than is ever an attribute of youth. I knelt to her as I had been taught to kneel to the home-mother in the House of Exile."[56]

A wise provision prevented aging parents from continuing to hold power too long. In all Eastern cultures, the time came when it was considered proper for the heads of the family to abdicate.

Manu says, "When the father of a family perceives his muscles become flaccid and his hair gray, and sees the child of his child, let him then seek refuge in a forest. Let him commit the care of his wife to her sons: or accompanied by her, if she choose to attend him, let him dwell in the forest with complete power over his organs of sense and action." Here follows an account of ascetic practices that he is urged to follow. Then Manu continues, "Having shuffled off his body by any of these modes, which great sages practised, and becoming void of sorrow and fear, he rises to exaltation in the divine essence."

There is little doubt that this consequence would follow the rigors described. If seriously undertaken, they would be calculated rapidly to terminate his life!

A similar but less exacting arrangement was in vogue in China. "An aging father may, after a long life of ruling his family, hand over to his son. He will then enter a monastery or become a mendicant monk, traveling about and begging for alms."[57]

Likewise in Japan. Following the royal custom, a family head could abdicate. When he did so, it was customary for him to shave his head and become a priest. This kind of retirement was called *niudo,* or entrance into religion. The idea was that he would thus spend the remainder of his days in prayer and contemplation.

At the same time, the father might retire from his business or profession. This was called *inkio.* The two steps might be taken together, or separately. It was not usual for a Japanese man to lay down his lifework and family status before the age of sixty.[58]

The idea of a final retreat into asceticism and religion was held up as a counsel of perfection. In practice, the aging parents would generally remain in the family home but hand over responsibility and authority to their eldest son and his wife. Secure, honored, and treated with the utmost respect, they would end their days in peace.

"And when Wang Lung went, and it was very seldom, into his sons' courts, they treated him courteously and they ran to get tea for him and he asked to see the last child and he asked many times, for he forgot easily,

" 'How many grandchildren have I now?' "

"Then he would sit a little while and look at the children gathering around him to stare. His grandsons were tall lads now, and he looked at them, peering at them to see what they were, and he muttered to himself,

" 'Now that one has the look of his great-grandfather and there is a small merchant Liu, and here is myself when young.' "[59]

* * *

Patterns of parent-child relationships differ greatly between the East and the West.

The essence of the difference lies in the manner of handling the inevitable conflict in ideas and wishes that exists between two generations.

In the traditional East this conflict was rigidly suppressed. The parents made the rules for the children, and the children obeyed them. Change was not acceptable. The life cycle followed repetitively its age-old pattern.

The obligation to give unquestioning honor and respect to parents and elders was a built-in shock absorber, a protection of family harmony and solidarity like the incest taboo. Suppressing hostility is not, of course, ideal. But the traditional East preferred it to an explosive disruption of family solidarity. Therefore respect from children to parents was demanded. If it could be given naturally and spontaneously, out of genuine admiration and affection, so much the better. But if not, it was demanded just the same. Thus the family remained secure.

In the West, we have removed this age-old protective mechanism, this shock absorber. We have taken this action in order to give our children freedom, and to bring realism into family relationships. When admiration and affection in the young are genuinely present, there is natural respect for parents, and all is well. But when hostility develops, we say, let it be expressed and accepted, so that the way may be cleared for better understanding. This is all right if the parent can maturely accept the hostility, as the occupants of an automobile without shock absorbers might set their teeth and let themselves be bumped and bounced about. But if the parent cannot do this, the family disintegrates. The child loses his confidence in authority figures, loses his inner security, and may become delinquent.

When family relationships are inherently good, both Eastern and Western patterns work smoothly. But in unsatisfactory situations, we have a cleavage. The East chooses to preserve the outer appearance of good relations, ignoring the hidden frustrations involved. The West allows the frustrations to be expressed, letting family stability fall apart, if necessary, in the process.

Which of these two systems is best? The question is probably purely academic. For even if we have the insight to make a choice, we probably do not have the power to put it into effect. All that we can really do is to try to understand intelligently the system of the culture to which we belong, and to make it work as effectively as possible.

Chapter 13

THE FUTURE OF MARRIAGE

As we look at marriage and family patterns in our modern world, in East and West alike, there is only one fact about them of which we can be quite sure—that they are changing.

The changes that are taking place now in the East are similar in many ways to those that have already occurred in the West. Similar, yet not identical. The causes that are producing these changes are also similar, but not identical. Change is being brought about by new factors in the social environment, such as urbanization, industrialization, the economic emancipation of women, population mobility, and so on. Change is also occurring in the climate of thought, as a result of new ideas about human personality and human relationships.

The changes in Eastern patterns broadly resemble those that have already occurred in the West. To some extent they are the result of copying Western ways. But this cause is a relatively superficial one.

In other spheres, such as technology, health services, education, and business organization, it is true that the East is frankly and eagerly copying the West, because it is convinced that Western ways are best. But this fact should not confuse Western minds into imagining that the East is trying to copy the West in *everything*. That very definitely is not true. In cultural values, in social institutions, even to some extent in political organization, the East believes it has traditions that are better for its way of life than anything the West can offer.

Certainly this is true of family life. In so far as the East appears to be adopting Western ways, it is mainly because Asians are having to adapt themselves to the changing circumstances that the

West has already experienced. All human cultures, when molded by similar external conditions, tend to react in similar ways, because human nature, beneath the cultural crust that is responsible for surface differences, is everywhere the same. Of this we became deeply convinced as a result of our counseling sessions with our Asian friends at Chiengmai.

The East has in fact many values, in its traditional marriage and family patterns, that it would like if possible to preserve. It considers these values superior to those of the West. Whether it will in fact be possible to preserve them, we consider doubtful. For Asia, we are quite convinced, is about to be subjected to increasingly powerful pressures of the kind that have already broken down our own traditional family patterns. "It would be a grave error," said our Chiengmai delegates in their published report, "to assume complacently that the East is secure against the kind of family disintegration now being witnessed in the West."[1]

Yet the East has one great advantage over the West. As it moves into a new era of cultural change, it need not do so blindly. The path has been trodden before. The mistakes of the West may be examined and studied, and valuable lessons may be learned that could save the East, as it comes to tread the same path, from needless personal suffering and social dislocation.

The West, likewise, as it moves further into the unknown future, has much to learn from the East. In Asia there can still be seen family customs and institutions that once existed in our own culture, but have now passed out of living memory. Some of these are evil, and we may be glad to be rid of them. Others were useful in a social setting that no longer exists. But there are some institutions that, we have come to feel, had great value, and their loss has proved detrimental to our modern way of life. By careful study of Eastern family patterns we may determine what these lost values are, and perhaps devise ways in which we may be able to recover them.

What seems very clear to us is that the future study of Eastern and Western marriage and family patterns should not proceed separately. There is so much that we need to learn from each other that we ought to be working in this field together. This was the greatest lesson that Chiengmai taught us.

* * *

"If there is any 'gulf' between East and West, it is where sex and the family are in question, and woman's function and her relation to man."[2]

This was the opinion of an expert on India, expressed in 1928. Since then, events have been moving swiftly. The "gulf" is being bridged.

The old family system, for example, is now in a state of decay. Speaking of Japan, Professor Nakagawa says, "Although the house was primarily a society or group formed for production, it is now being disintegrated with the increasing importance of the productive activities of individuals. It is true that some types of the house in the original sense are still to be seen in rural and fishing villages, but I believe it is no exaggeration to say that the [feudalistic] family system has, for the most part, been destroyed so far as its form is concerned. . . . Its foundations, social and economic, have already collapsed.[3]

A similar situation has been developing in some parts of India. "I discovered that though all was well with my grandparents' house, it was not so with every house of our clan. Most of the families had broken up, and the younger sons had already gone to far-off cities, taking with them their wives and children. The elder sons had built themselves small houses near the parental homes."[4]

The women of the East, long held in subjection, have gone a long way toward breaking with the past. In 1948, just before the Communist era began, a Chinese woman writer summed up the position for her country: "In not much more than half a century, women in China have passed through a series of changes that it took European women five hundred years to bring about. . . . The question uppermost in the minds of thinking women in China today is how they can become equipped to be abreast of their Occidental sisters in this new era, to share equal rights and responsibilities with men, and to relieve the miseries of the huge masses of rural women."[5]

In a similar vein, a Japanese woman writes:

"Deepest gratitude is due the Occupation from all Japanese women for giving them complete legal equality with their men, and showing Japanese men good manners toward women. It would have taken ages of hard battling if Japanese women had had to fight for these rights by themselves. 'What would have been our status,' Japanese women say thoughtfully to each other, 'if our militarists had won the war and continued to rule the country with their brutal force?' This is a candid confession of Japanese women's sincere appreciation of the Occupation. And whatever reaction may set in in the future, the time will never come again when Japanese wives, as semi-minors, will be put back under the legal guardianship of their husbands and forced to surrender all their possessions and their labor to the control of the husband and parents-in-law."[6]

Greater freedom to choose marriage partners is beginning to take the place of the traditional arranged marriage. A Korean writes, "Old traditional marriage custom now seems almost as strange to urban Koreans as it does to foreigners. The trend now is toward a greater freedom of choice in the selection of a life-time mate, and a companionship approaching the relationship of husband and wife in the Western world is developing throughout Korea."[7]

Even freedom on the wife's part to carry on extramarital affairs seems to be on the way. Hanako, a Japanese wife interviewed by Cressy, related a story of a woman friend of hers, who, unknown to her husband, was involved with another man. Hanako's comment is revealing:

"'Please don't misunderstand me. I love my husband. I value my home and I have no intention of following her example.'

"She paused, and smiled.

"'But it is a bit romantic, don't you think?'"[8]

These are illustrations only. They do not give us the full picture. Call them straws in the wind, if you will. But they show the way the wind is blowing. Yes, the gap between East and West is closing.

Our own impression is that in the East the new ideas are replacing the old most rapidly among three groups. First, among urban dwellers, the children of the first generation which moved in from rural areas. Second, among those who are enjoying the benefits of higher education. Third, among the Christians, who constitute about 3 per cent of East Asia's population.

Add these together and they total only a minority of Asians.

But they are, so far as shaping future trends is concerned, important minority. The way they live today is likely t way all Asians will be living in another generation.

It would not be too much to say that the changes taking place in marriage and family patterns in the East today are likely to build up to the dimensions of a social revolution.

*   *   *

What lies at the heart of this process of change? Is there one fundamental factor that constitutes the root of it?

We think there is. It is the concept of the freedom of the individual—his right to autonomy and self-determination.

Individual freedom can, of course, never be completely exercised, unless the individual is an absolute despot, or lives on a desert island. And individual freedom does not necessarily lead to happiness; often the reverse is true. Freedom can, in fact, only be safe and satisfying when it is responsibly exercised within a framework that protects the rights of others to *their* measure of freedom.

All human freedom, therefore, must be viewed relatively. Just as hardly anyone can have complete freedom, so nobody can possibly be deprived entirely of his freedom, humanly speaking, except by death. A bird in a cage enjoys a considerable measure of freedom, but decidedly less than the bird on the bough outside the window.

What is changing in the East is not that everyone is gaining new freedom. It is that the inequalities in the distribution of freedom are being evened out. Traditionally, men have had far more freedom of choice and action than women, and the old far more than the young. There have been other areas of inequality, but these are the two that have been especially significant for marriage and family relationships. Everywhere in Asia today—under Communist and non-Communist regimes alike—what is happening to family relationships is that the wife is being given rights she never exercised before in relation to her husband, and that children are being given, or are taking, new freedom in relation to their parents.

These are basically the same changes that have been taking place in the West for nearly a century. In the West, however, and particularly in the United States, the process has now gone so far

that it can hardly go any further. In the most progressive areas
of the West today the wife's position is now so good that frequently
she has more leisure, more power and more wealth than her husband. And we seem in some communities to be moving swiftly to
the point at which children will have so much freedom that their
parents will be powerless to exercise any great control over their
behavior. Already some of the accepted behavior patterns, instead
of being handed down from the previous generation as in the past,
are beginning to be formulated empirically by the young people
of the new generation themselves. These trends, as we shall see,
are reaching a point in the West at which some thoughtful observers are suggesting that they have gone too far, and need to be
reversed.

What is likely to happen in the East if similar trends move to
their logical conclusion? Will there be a change in the personality
pattern of the Eastern woman, for instance?

Cressy describes how a young Japanese girl, on first seeing
American movies, was deeply influenced by the types of woman
they portrayed. "It was quite clear to her that many of them were
not a good kind of woman and that much of what they did was
questionable. But that was not the point. Details and plots were
forgotten. The indelible impression that remained was that these
American women were 'bright and vivid,' had 'strong attractive
personalities,' and expressed themselves decisively."[9]

That is one point of view. Another is the attitude of the English-
man, quoted by Shingoro, who declared, "How sweet Japanese
woman is! If this be the result of suppression and oppression, then
these are not altogether bad. On the other hand, how diamond-
hearted the character of the American woman becomes under the
idolatry of which she is the object!"[10]

It could be said, in regard to the second quotation, that this is a
man's view, and that it is therefore biased. But the question cannot be as lightly dismissed as that. There is some evidence that
American men who have the opportunity to travel are expressing
a decided preference for the women of the older cultures than for
those of their own. If there is any truth in this, it is the kind of
truth that American women generally can hardly ignore. And its
implications for the future of Eastern women are of such a nature
that they will not wish to ignore it either.

It is, of course, very difficult to define with any precision what we mean by such vague phrases as "the truly feminine woman." If we mean the dumb, submissive creature the East has created by its agelong processes of "suppression and oppression," then the sooner we abandon ideals of this kind the better. One thing is clear —that in the new era upon which we are entering, the inherent right of the woman as a person must never again be subjected to her need to conform to the arbitrary criteria that men wish to lay down for their own convenience.

However, we have a suspicion that a woman's femininity never was really dependent on the binding of her feet or the denial of her right to vote or the prevention of her mind from growing. A woman does not cease to be a woman when she takes long walks or adopts an intelligent attitude to world affairs or becomes a cultured person.

What, then, decides the matter? We do not know. But we think the question is important. And we are bound to acknowledge that, in our comings and goings between East and West, we have noted a significant difference between the personalities of the women in the two cultures. There are of course notable exceptions in both directions. But in general, there is about the average Eastern woman a poise, a serenity, an impression of inward contentment, that stands out in contrast to the bewildered, restless, anxious demeanor of many Western women today.

Obviously we are not arguing for any curtailment of woman's freedom. But we are asking, in all seriousness, the question, "How ought a woman to make the right use of her freedom?" For it seems to us that, if by her use of it she becomes less womanly, she is not unlike the man who is in danger of gaining the whole world and losing his own soul.

*   *   *

For long centuries the East has been a man's world. Not only so. It has been also an old man's world. The young man has presented the appearance of a rather weak, subdued, and undignified person—good for heavy manual labor and soldiering (both of which were despised by the Chinese intelligentsia) but awkward and incompetent in the world of affairs. Young people generally were expected to do precisely what they were told, and having no alternative, they generally complied.

All this, too, is changing. Although Eastern cultures are still a long way from being youth cultures, they are moving decisively in that direction. The revolutionary movements that have been changing the face of Asia have exploited to the full the sense of frustration of women and of youth. To these two groups Gandhi made his strongest appeal. From them Sun Yat-sen and Chiang Kai-shek drew much of their support. They have been the backbone of the Chinese Communist movement.

The emancipation of youth has almost always begun among students. This is only natural. The students are the young people who have access to new ideas. They are more closely organized than other youth groups. So students in the East have tended in recent years to take the lead over, and set the pattern for, all young people of their generation. The college campus has been the seedbed of the revolution of youth against the old people and the old traditions.

To a large extent, the Eastern student has, up to now, regarded his counterpart in the West as the model to be copied. And since the equality of the sexes, and the freedom to choose a marriage partner on the basis of love, have been conspicuous features of student life in the West, they have become central issues in the Eastern students' struggle to overthrow the old order and establish a new one in its place.

The Eastern youth's struggle for emancipation has not, however, gone smoothly. Freedom can be an intoxicant, and those who take too much too quickly, or too much at a time, are liable to lose their balance. Externally, the postwar revolt of Japanese youth has looked very like the revolt of youth in the United States in the 1920's. But Japanese young people were not emotionally conditioned for independence. "They were accustomed to external controls—the head of the family, the police, the national government. It has even been said that a Japanese individual has no inner controls. This is only partly correct, but it has a measure of truth."[11]

The result of this lack of well-developed inner controls has been disturbing. Dr. Tsunehisa Takeyama, one of Tokyo's leading psychiatrists, reported in January 1959 that the suicide rate in

Japan, which averages about two and a half tim
U.S.A., is among the 15-24 age group two and a
the Japanese national average. In fact, for this age
is now the leading cause of death; and no less th
of Japanese university and high-school students admit that they
have contemplated suicide at least once. Dr. Takeyama, in explaining this, refers to the deeply ingrained pattern of obedience
to authority, and goes on, "While this remains a basic influence
in their unconscious make-up, it conflicts sharply with their conscious striving to behave in accordance with modern Western
ways."[12]

It can be argued that the hierarchical tradition has been more
rigid in Japan than elsewhere in the East, so troubles of this kind
are not likely to be as acute elsewhere. Moreover, all transition
periods are costly; if the transition is to be made, the price must
be paid.

However, the vital question is, to what extent *does* the transition have to be made? In the area with which we are here
concerned, we are by no means sure of the answer. Does the
Western pattern of romantic love and freedom in boy-girl relations commend itself as a desirable one, which we would wish
our friends in the East to adopt?

*　　*　　*

"It is in the United States that perhaps the only, at any rate
the most complete, demonstration of romantic love as the pro-
logue and theme of marriage has been staged. The explanation
lies in the relaxation of parental control over courtship."[13]

These words are taken from one of the most competent studies
ever made, by two of the leading Western authorities, of family
life in the United States. What Burgess and Locke say, in other
words, is that the more freedom young people have had, the more
they have tended to be influenced, in their concepts of marriage,
by romantic ideas.

And how have the romantic ideas been viewed by the experts?

Here is what Ralph Linton, a noted social philosopher, says
about them:

"All societies recognize that there are occasional violent emotional attachments between persons of opposite sex, but our

sent American culture is practically the only one which has attempted to capitalize these and make them the basis for marriage. Most groups regard them as unfortunate and point out the victims of such attachments as horrible examples. Their rarity in most societies suggests that they are psychological abnormalities to which our own culture has attached an extraordinary value just as other cultures have attached extreme values to other abnormalities."[14]

James Bossard and his colleague, Eleanor Boll, who have devoted years of study to marriage in the United States, suggest that modern American youth, given too much freedom, has tended to develop "a spoiled-child psychology, petulant with an almost hysterical optimism." This provides a poor basis for marriage. "If one selects a mate and marries solely for personal happiness and personality fulfillment, then, when the mate no longer serves that function, the marriage is gone." If we broaden this principle till it becomes a general pattern for living, the implications are disturbing. "The line between the individualist and the self-centered person is a very narrow one. That is why the history of individualism as a national theme is not reassuring. Whenever and wherever it has appeared as a major cultural value, untempered by the necessary antidotes, it is followed by the downfall or inner decay of a culture. The desire for personal happiness degenerates into social lassitude, and the drive for self-expression carries within itself the seeds of self-destruction."[15]

Jessie Bernard, another very competent authority on American marriage, demonstrates how the romantic approach to marriage has become a social compulsion:

"The professed reason for getting married is likely to be that 'we are in love.' This is part of the romantic myth of our culture. Love is the conventional reason for getting married; it is simulated if not felt; it is the 'correct thing.'"[16]

These are the views of some Western authorities. They are not unlike some of the opinions expressed by Asian observers who have visited the West. Here is an Eastern man's point of view:

"The complete domination of sentiment and individual desire in the courtship method of marriage is harmful to social discipline and is, as a rule, detrimental to the race. . . . People who once fall in love may after some time and for similar reasons fall out of love. Hence if the ideal basis for the union of the sexes is to be mutual passion, an arrangement must be provided so that simultaneously with a break in the fascination on either side, the marriage between the partners shall come to an end. Yet under existing conditions it would not be possible to make the marriage laws as lax as that."[17]

And here is an Eastern woman's opinion, after observing how our Western customs work out from the woman's point of view:

"Women in the West have more worries than we have here . . . whereas parents in India arrange for the marriage of their daughters, girls abroad have to find their own husbands. That must be the most nerve-racking task of all. . . . It is a terribly serious problem which continually harasses girls in the West even at an early age. Magazines and books hammer into them 'how to be popular,' how to compete with other girls, and so on. They know that if they don't find their future husbands by themselves, they'll remain alone and job-hunting for the rest of their lives. Is it any wonder that they look harassed and preoccupied?"[18]

* * *

Thoughtful observers do not appear to be enthusiastic about our system of mate selection based on romance. How does it work out in practice?

There are some wonderful marriages in the West, marriages that bring to those concerned a rich and abiding measure of deep happiness. They were based on mutual love in the first place, and the love continues and grows to the end.

No one would seriously suggest, however, that most of our marriages are like that. Measuring happiness in marriage is one of the most complex tasks for research in this field, and we have not yet learned how to do it accurately. However, we have a rough index in marriages that openly come to an end, and in those in which the couples rate themselves as unhappy. As we have already seen, these together account for about half of all marriages in the United States today.

This poor record certainly does not give the United States anything very convincing to export to other countries. If this is all that freedom to choose marriage partners achieves, in the most advanced form in which it has yet been practiced in the West, it hardly offers encouragement to the East to adopt the same patterns.

This is not, moreover, the whole picture. Freedom of choice on the basis of romantic love necessarily implies freedom of association between the sexes. You cannot choose unless you can compare. You cannot compare unless you have opportunity to experience a number of relationships with eligible members of the opposite sex. You cannot develop such relationships unless you are allowed to get acquainted.

So freedom of choice leads to experimental relationships as a preliminary to final selection. You have to discover whether you are "really in love." At first you think you are; then you discover that it was "only infatuation." So you have to have a series of these experiences, each more intense than the last, until you decide that the present one is "the real thing," and that you are now ready to marry.

In order to facilitate this process, the custom known as "dating" has developed in the United States. It is of fairly recent origin. It emerged as a result of the revolt of American youth in the 1920's, and was at first associated with a group who defied the traditional moral standards and practiced what was called "free love." Later, dating became an accepted social custom, was made respectable by playing down the sexual element, and was adopted widely by all groups of American youth. It is now so much taken for granted that many Americans are surprised to learn that it is of such recent origin.

Dating is officially regarded today as a process in which young people are prepared for marriage by gaining experience of relationships with members of the opposite sex in a socially acceptable setting. For many young people it does actually fulfill this purpose, and leads them to a wise choice and a happy marriage.

However, it has other consequences—call them "side effects" if you will. It has become a tyrannical system that demands that the social life of young people shall be established on a paired basis. This has turned much of the leisure activity of American youth into the semblance of a vast Noah's Ark, in which the animals go in two by two or not at all. In consequence, adolescents are driven into competition with their peers so that they may be sure of a date in order to be able to attend the school dance. The girls are forced to capitalize on their sexual attractiveness to the utmost, so that they will be ranked as "popular" and therefore never be in the predicament of having to stay at home on Saturday night. The insecurity created by this situation has helped to encourage the practice of "going steady," which means that a boy and girl enter into a commitment to each other in order to be sure of having a partner for each successive social event that, as a pair, they will be eligible to attend.

At the same time, dating has, with the aid of the automobile, opened up the way for extensive sexual experimentation. According to Bossard and Boll, this was how dating began. It was viewed as a period of mutual exploitation between the sexes before the final settling down. The girls exploited the boys financially, the boys exploited the girls sexually.[19]

Consideration of this aspect of dating is generally avoided in public discussion. But it seems a reasonable conjecture, on the basis of the available evidence, that about half of all American girls now experience sexual intercourse before marriage, and the number of boys who do so is considerably greater.

Another significant fact about dating is that the age at which it begins becomes progressively lower. Many boys and girls are caught up in the social pressure soon after puberty, with the result that their emotional and sexual development, instead of being restrained as has been customary in the older cultures, is accelerated.

The result is that American young people are being precipitated into marriage at an increasingly early age. The average age at first marriage in the United States is lower today than at any time since records have been kept. Nearly half of all the girls who are destined to marry are already wives before their twentieth birthday.

These young marriages show disturbingly high rates of failure. About half of all American divorces involve those who married before their twentieth year. This custom of teen-age marriages is certainly not being encouraged by parents and teachers. On the contrary, they are doing everything in their power to apply the brakes. But their power is very limited. The young people have taken the situation into their own hands. In the name of romantic love everything is permissible.

This may seem a gloomy picture. We hope we have not mis-
represented the facts. We believe that this is only a phase in the
evolution of the Western principle of freedom for youth. What
will follow next no one can say with any certainty. Our hope is
that American youth will learn to exercise the almost unlimited
freedom they now possess with an increasing measure of responsibility.

But the relevance of these facts to the rapidly changing East
must be realistically faced. If the present runaway abuse of freedom in the United States can happen among young people whose
"inner controls" should be reasonably well developed, since they
have a long heritage of democracy behind them, what might be
the result if, too rapidly, the external controls were relaxed in
the East?

*   *   *

"I believe," said Dr. Samuel Johnson, "that marriages would in
general be as happy, and often more so, if they were all made by
the Lord Chancellor, upon a due consideration of the characters
and circumstances, without the partners having any choice in the
matter."[20]

We are bound to acknowledge, after a careful appraisal of the
methods of mate selection in the East and West, that the great
Dr. Johnson was probably perfectly right.

From one extreme to the other, four patterns of mate selection
may be distinguished.

1. *Selection by the parents—the young people themselves not
consulted.* This is the traditional method employed in the East.
When the choice is carefully and wisely made, it is usually a good
one. But it is open to the grave errors caused by ignorance and
exploitation.

2. *Selection by the parents, but the young people consulted.*
This is an improvement on the first method, provided the young
people are allowed to make the final decision. In some communities, though formally consulted, they are expected to acquiesce
in the choice made for them, and have no real freedom to express
their minds.

3. *Selection by the young people, but parental approval necessary.* This pattern exists in at least two forms. The strictest is the

one in which no action may be taken by the young people until they have been given parental permission to proceed. A good example is the early American Quaker father, who was approached by a neighbor's son asking his permission to court his daughter Sarah. Unless John was approved by Sarah's father in the first place, no further step could be taken. But even if her father approved of John, Sarah still had the right to refuse him.

The other variation is where Sarah could encourage John's attentions without seeking her father's permission; but if she and John became serious, her father's approval was essential before marriage could take place. If he used his veto, she had to give up John—or elope!

4. *Selection by the young people—the parents not consulted.* This is the method that is becoming widespread in the West today. In the United States, the couple may be living away from home and unable to consult their parents. But even when the parents are formally consulted, all too often their acquiescence is nominal. They know that, even if they raise objections, the marriage is likely to take place anyway.

Which of these methods is most desirable?

We would reject the first. Even if it is efficient, we believe it denies to young people a freedom that should be theirs by right. This is the position being widely adopted in the East today.

We would also reject the last. Young people should not be dominated by their parents in this matter, but neither should their parents be left entirely out of the picture. The experience of parents can often correct and restrain the headstrong and distorted choices of inexperienced youth. The kind of freedom young people in the West today are demanding is unreasonable, and undesirable in their own best interests.

The desirable ideal, we believe, is a co-operative selection by young people and parents together. This may not always be easily achieved. But it is worth the effort that may be needed. It forges unity in the family. It balances the intense feelings of youth with the detached judgment of more mature experience. It offers, we believe, the best basis for successful marriages—especially if backed by scientific knowledge accumulated by study and research.

At the present time, the East is moving steadily toward the ideal of co-operation between parents and young people. The West, alas, is moving further away from it, as young people increasingly ignore their parents' opinions. However, there is some compensation in the fact that the results of study and research concerning the criteria of good mate selection are being made increasingly available to Western youth.

An interesting example of the use of research material is furnished by a press release that we recently received:

"A new experiment in marriage-making is just completing two and a half years of activity in New York City. It is called the Scientific Introduction Service, and it represents a serious attempt to apply modern psychological and sociological knowledge to matchmaking. The agency employs the latest techniques in personality evaluation and incorporates the findings of recent compatibility studies in making the selection of suitable partners. Prospective clients receive interviews and personality tests to uncover their personality patterns, tastes, preferences, and attitudes. Data is then coded and processed on an IBM-type electronic brain and carefully reviewed by the staff."

Here are resources put to use in mate selection such as the old-time marriage broker, or even Dr. Johnson, never dreamed of!

This is not, by any means, the only matchmaking agency in the United States. There seems to have been an upsurge of such organizations, in response to a widespread public demand, in the West since World War II. In Britain it is reported that there are now more than fifty registered marriage bureaux offering this kind of service.[21]

Is it possible that the West may, in the end, go back to the arranged marriage, modern style?

*   *   *

Throughout the East today, in country after country, new laws are being framed that stress the equal rights of husband and wife. These laws reflect the widespread acceptance of the comradeship concept of marriage.

Needless to say, an idea so revolutionary to Eastern thought is not being introduced without resistance. We have encountered many instances of violent clashes between the old concept and the new. These clashes are particularly prevalent in Japan. Sumie

Seo Mishima illustrates this from her personal involvement in two divorce cases that occurred in her own family circle:

"In both of them I have fought and am still fighting hard on the wife's side against the tenacious clinging of man to his feudal privileges. These two husbands, while applauding the democratic principles whenever these were beneficial to their own personal interests, stuck tightly to the old tradition of a husband withholding his wife's possessions in case the divorce came through the wife's choice or through her fault. In either case the wife was turned out with only her clothes, her money and some other possessions being confiscated by the husband. . . .

"I thought it was unbelievable that such husbands should and could exist in our present democratic Japan. So I tried hard to persuade them to be reasonable and manly enough to respect their wives' basic human rights. But I failed, and had to realize that it was a fight against a tradition of centuries and not against individual men. I knew that the newly democratized law was there, ready to protect the wife, but it required money, time and tedious procedure to have that law work effectively. In either case, the wife had no money to start a suit.

"The fact is that the present democracy in Japan has been framed and grafted onto Japanese soil by external agencies. It has been given a complete legislative framework on which it is expected to grow and ripen into a fully functioning organism. . . .

"These changes, however, have been mainly superficial, while the basic social relations and sentiments of the people have remained practically unchanged."[22]

In the story of Kazuko, Cressy has vividly dramatized the desperate but in this case unavailing struggle of a Japanese wife to adopt, against the relentless pressure of hostile traditions, the new democratic concept of the marriage relationship:

It seemed that Kazuko, after the frustration of her attempts to find a congenial husband on her own initiative, had given up. But after some months she began to feel the loneliness her Professor in College had told her about, and finally did what many others like her had done: let herself be persuaded by friends to seek marriage along conventional lines.

A young man was introduced to her and took her out a few times. Their meetings did not have the thrill of her date with the Wagnerian superman of her dreams, or even of the hot-shot Hollywood-character business man. In their place was a mild curiosity.

He was eight years older, a university graduate who was a member of a law firm. . . . She began to feel she might come to love him, and when on their third date he proposed that they get married, she agreed, and when he kissed her, she kissed him back hopefully.

They married and took an apartment in Tokyo and Kazuko was happier than she had thought she could be. But she soon found that he had to be absent a good many evenings entertaining clients. Then she began to notice he was away more and more often, and stayed later. Then the twins came and fully occupied her time and attention.

On their second wedding anniversary she prepared a celebration. He had said nothing about it, and she planned a surprise, happily preparing his favorite dishes.

He did not come.

She waited anxiously while the food got cold. By nine she was impatient. By ten she was worried. By twelve she was cried out. Then certain suspicions, that she now began to realize had been gradually taking shape in the back of her mind, emerged like evil spirits and confronted her, and she wept anew.

When he finally came at three she was relieved, but felt she could hardly forgive him for being so late on this special day.

"I have been worrying about you, terribly," she told him.

"I am very sorry," he said, and went on to explain that he had been entertaining an important client from out of town who had wanted to go to a night club.

"I was tired and didn't want to go," he concluded, "but I had no choice."

"Why not?" she asked.

"Please understand my situation," he said. "He would not have liked it if I had refused and we might have lost his business."

"All right," she said, "but how about your understanding my situation. I hope you are man enough to say no once in a while."

"It isn't done in business circles," he retorted. "You do not understand."

A few weeks later he received an official appointment and they moved to a small city to the north that was almost a suburb of Tokyo. They had a house and garden and for a while things went happily. Then he began to be absent more nights, and was often decidedly tipsy, and the amount of money he turned over to her for the household decreased month by month.

Then she learned that he had become a crony of another official in the next block who was notorious as a lavish patron of the local geisha establishment, and she knew that what she had been secretly fearing had come to pass. It came to a climax one evening when this man came and called for him.

"You are not going out again tonight, are you?" Kazuko burst out. "And with that man?"

He looked at her half-drunkenly.

"Come and wish me a happy evening," he ordered with maudlin courtesy.

Without a word she came and bowed him out formally at the door, repeating the required polite formula.

For a long time she remained thus, on her hands and knees, her forehead almost to the matting. She heard their voices die away down the street. She followed their steps in her imagination. She pictured the girls in the geisha house pouring sake for them. . . .

Next morning she put her house in order. She walked to the shore of a little lake just outside the city. She filled the long sleeves of her kimono with stones. She found a place where the bank of the lake was high enough. She stood on the edge and looked down at the peaceful water. One convulsive movement and it would be over. She gathered herself for the plunge.

Suddenly a rush of thoughts and images flooded through her mind. She saw herself falling. She saw herself drowned. She thought wildly of the twins. Who would care for them? She pictured her empty home. Who would look after it? But of course the solution was simple. He would marry again. All this was a situation that could not be escaped. It had to be endured. If she dropped out, another woman would be brought in and would have to bear it. But they were *her* children. It was her home. After all, he was her husband. These were her responsibilities.

She started taking the stones out of her sleeves, and when one rolled down and splashed into the lake she shuddered.

She told Yoko that she had really died at that time.

What remained was the stereotype of an individual, stamped out by the relentless pressure of Japanese society—the conventional, obedient wife, serving her husband; the fond mother of her children, meticulous in every detail of their welfare; the good neighbor, observant of the local folkways, saying and doing the right thing at the right time, smiling with just the right degree of cordiality; selfless.[23]

However, even if defeats are suffered on many sectors of the front, the enlightened women of the East do not intend to give up the struggle for the goal of a comradeship marriage. Increasingly, too, their husbands are also enlightened, and ready to work with them for the attainment of the same goal.

It seems inevitable, therefore, that in the East the future may be expected to bring an increasing emphasis on the interpersonal implications of the marriage relationship.

*   *   *

Happiness in marriage is closely related to expectation. It would be possible for two married couples to live next door to each other, and to undergo identical experiences, and yet for one couple to consider themselves happy, while the other rated their marriage as unhappy. Their judgment would be based on what they had anticipated that marriage would be like.

This is what is actually happening in Eastern and Western marriages today. In the East, as we have seen, expectations of what marriage would bring, in terms of interpersonal fulfillment, have been very low. Looking for little, the Asian husband and wife have been easily satisfied. The husband asked for sex and sons, the wife for security and sustenance. It was as simple as that.

In the West, expectation in marriage has become complex and elaborate. The romantic conception of marriage has pictured it as the panacea for all life's ills, an idyllic state into which harassed men and women might withdraw from life's struggles to find solace and healing. With the increase of secularism and the hushing of the apocalyptic note in religion, dreams of bliss in heaven hereafter have been replaced by dreams of bliss in marriage here and now.

Marriage is a good, and a rewarding, relationship. But it cannot deliver goods matched to this kind of anticipation. Moreover, what it delivers is strictly dependent on what husband and wife bring to it in terms of enlightened understanding and sustained effort. This, however, has been an unpopular theme, and it has been suppressed. The desire to get "something for nothing" has been a stubbornly persistent hope in human history. The dream of romantic ecstasy, effortlessly sustained in marriage, has supplanted in our time the age-old quest for the philosopher's stone, which, it was believed, would transform base metals into gold.

Consequently marriage, in the West, has been grossly oversold. Expecting more than was reasonable, young people have been doomed to disillusionment from the start. Their inflated hopes, incapable of fulfillment, were bound to be shattered.

This has had both bad and good effects. The bad effects appear in needlessly high divorce rates. Baffled and frustrated, husbands and wives who hoped to find paradise in the married state put the blame on their partners, and conclude that they have made a mistaken choice. Sometimes, no doubt, they have. But at least as often they have asked more than was reasonable of an average human being. This they finally discover, and accept, when the experience of a second marriage brings them to terms with reality. Meanwhile the community has suffered, as a result of the exaggerated expectations it has allowed these unhappy people to nourish, a good deal of social dislocation that might have been avoided.

The good effects have been the development of services to help people to succeed in marriage—educational programs to teach what marital adjustment involves, so that the rewards could be reaped; counseling programs to help those already in difficulties, so that the mistakes could be corrected. These services, virtually unknown as yet in the East, have been greatly extended in the West in recent years. No doubt they have contributed to the fact that Western divorce rates, which had reached disturbingly high levels, seem to have stopped rising and are now slowly going down.

These Western experiences have important implications for the East. A rise in expectation will soon bring new discontent with marriage as it is. This is already happening. In a program arranged for us by Lady Rama Rau, and sponsored by the Ministry of Health of the Indian Government, we conducted early in 1957 a series of two-day seminars for professional leaders in major Indian cities. In the following year we followed this up with a three-week training program in marriage counseling in Bombay. As a result of these extended discussions with leading Indian professional men and women, we became convinced that already, behind the apparently unruffled exterior, Indian wives and husbands are becoming increasingly discontented with the low levels of satisfaction in their marriages and are reaching out for something better. We have formed the same impression, on the basis of similar discussions, concerning other countries in Asia.

As these rumbling discontents begin to find more forthright

a steady increase in divorce rates seems inevitable in
~~nds~~. In our opinion it will be some years yet before
increases appear, but sooner or later this will happen.
planning ahead, and the provision of well-established marriage guidance services, could circumvent some of the resulting social dislocation. We are not at present very hopeful, however, that much will be done in this direction. Asia is so burdened with present remedial tasks of great urgency that it is not easy to generate interest in preventive programs designed to avoid troubles in the future.

While levels of marital expectation are progressively rising in the East, it is to be hoped that they will be scaled down in the West. This seems likely to happen. Sound knowledge about the marriage relationship, based on scientific research, is slowly percolating out and reaching the general public. Books, magazines, radio and television, college and high school life-adjustment courses, religious and secular organizations—all are focusing increasing attention upon a realistic appraisal of the nature of the man-woman relationship. As validated facts replace romantic illusions, the tendency to oversell marriage should in time be corrected.

The ideal at which to aim is clear. As Eastern expectations rise and Western expectations are scaled down, they should meet as they come into correspondence with attainable reality. When people throughout the world enter the marriage relationship with realistic anticipations and can rely on competent help to enable them to reach their goals, it can reasonably be hoped that many marriages will turn out happily. Other factors may, of course, intervene to prevent this desirable result. But it is certainly the goal toward which, in East and West alike, we should strive.

*   *   *

The West has already traveled a long way toward the democratization of the family. The question is even being raised whether it has not traveled *too* far in this direction.

The focus of attention, in this respect, is the position of the husband and father. The wife has gained increasing freedom and autonomy. So has the child, especially the adolescent. As their status has steadily risen, that of the man in the home has, rela-

clined. If the traditional East was a man's
...orary West has been becoming increasingly a
...l a child's world.

...is process has been to change deeply the role
...ers of the family. Under the patriarchal system
...was unquestionably the male family head. The
fath... the symbol of authority.

The de... ... idea was to place the seat of authority in the family group itself, by distributing the power among all the members. In theory this is an excellent idea. But evidence is accumulating that in practice it will not work, because differentiation of roles is essential to good family functioning. All cannot be treated as equals, because in fact they are not so. A man and a woman may be equal as persons in society. But as husband and wife, acting out their masculine and feminine roles in marriage, they are different and complementary; the concept of equality is meaningless here. A parent and a child simply cannot be equal, because the child needs the protective authority of his parents to give him the security without which he cannot grow healthily into an adult.

We are coming to see in the West, therefore, that by undermining the authority of the man in the family we are not only damaging him, but hurting everyone else as well. The wife cannot function in her feminine role if her husband's masculine role is taken from him. The family group cannot function as a family if its natural head is dethroned.

In Western marriage many troubles are arising because the reciprocal husband-wife interaction pattern is out of kilter. If the husband can no longer play his part as leader and initiator, the wife is paralyzed in her responsive function. She may retaliate by developing resentful, hostile attitudes and trying to tear him down. She then becomes the so-called demasculinizing female. The more she succeeds in destroying her husband's masculinity, the more she deprives herself of the potential source of her own feminine fulfillment.

The wife may also try to compensate for her husband's inadequacy by taking over his traditional position of leadership in the home. She "wears the pants," as we say. This also makes her miserable, because she is not being herself. She finds herself in a relationship that is unnatural, not only toward her husband, but toward her children as well.

In the traditional family group the roles of father and mother were clearly defined. Gibson Winter, using the studies of group functioning of R. F. Bales, shows how they are being confused in the West today:

"The mother who takes over the whole family will be killed in the crossfire, and deep down she knows it. A look at the real nature of parental authority reveals the ambiguity of woman's position in the home today.

"Anyone who exercises leadership can expect to be disliked. This is the price one pays for being a leader. He may be respected for his ideas; the group may even follow his suggestions; but he will not be liked.

"Groups need a leader with good ideas who will make suggestions, but they also need a member who is well liked and can keep everyone together. We have all seen such people in groups. They pat people on the back, encourage them to get in a word, and generally help knit people together. A strong and effective group develops when this best-liked person allies himself with the leader. If the best-liked person will support the leader, the group can move ahead and work out its problems. Without such an alliance, the leader can easily become so isolated by the resentment of the group that he loses his power. If this happens, the leadership dwindles and the group ends up bickering.

"The mother should fill the role of best-liked person in the family. She should become the member who supports the weak, encourages the crestfallen, and holds the family together as a group. This, at least, seems to be the proper fulfillment of her feminine role. As she lends support to her husband's leadership, the family is knit together."[24]

However, when the father's prestige is undermined by his having been scaled down to the status of "equal," he is in a poor position to assume leadership. He is not accepted as an authority figure. Why, then, should he trouble to assume a position of unpopularity?

"Few modern men are willing to accept the resentment of the children against his leadership. They come home looking for encouragement rather than responsibility. As parents, they tend to take to the best-liked role in the home. They may bring presents, they may give money; whereas mother is more demanding, since she is trying to build up responsibility in the children. So mother too often finds herself in the crossfire. She should be in the role of best-liked, but she ends up as a leader."[25]

This is only one aspect, given by way of illustration, of the confusion that results when traditional family roles are tampered with. When the authority in the home is displaced, divided, or absent, the children inevitably suffer. Children need consistent law and order in their home as much as citizens need responsible government in their country. Without it, they are restless and confused, and may ultimately become delinquent.

So the breakdown of authority in the family, and the giving to young people of more freedom than they can responsibly exercise, conspire to repeat the errors of one generation in the next. We do not wish to exaggerate this picture. But it would be foolish to suggest that our experiments with equality and democratization in family life are proving to be an unqualified and resounding success. If we rightly discern the present trends, they point decidedly toward the need to recover masculine-feminine reciprocity in marriage and parental authority in the family.

In short, at this point the West is having serious second thoughts about its own wisdom in abandoning aspects of marriage and parenthood that the East has still preserved intact.

What is needed is not, of course, a return to patriarchalism as such. A husband can play the dominant role toward his wife without being domineering. A father can exercise authority in the home without being authoritarian. It is not power that the Western man needs to recover, but the exercise of his proper function in the home.

Nor is anyone in the West recommending a return to the oppression and subjugation of the young by the old. There are signs, however, of a disposition to believe that the ancients may after all have been right in contending that youth can better prepare for life's responsibilities, including family responsibilities, by disciplined self-restraint than by uninhibited self-indulgence.

* * *

Marriage, in East and West alike, is changing. That, however, is not by itself an adequate description. Marriage is all the time undergoing a process of evolution.

"The marriage system of every society," said Tagore, "belongs to an age when, in the Parliament of Life, man was sitting on the opposite benches against Nature's government. And Nature has ever retaliated against his obstructive tactics. Thus far they have nowhere come to any satisfactory agreement."[26]

This statement could be interpreted in two ways. It could mean that marriage will never be as it should be until we have come to terms with Nature's plan and purpose. Or it could mean that we have to continue, until final victory, the struggle to establish our human ideals of marriage at a level above those served by the elementary forces of the subhuman creation.

The meaning does not matter. Whichever way we interpret it, the important point is that marriage is an institution for which we must, in our human communities, accept responsibility. It is far too important, far too basic to the well-being of society, to be trifled with. We must plan and toil to make marriages healthy and happy, because only so can family life, which emerges out of marriage and is the foundation-stone of human society, be healthy and happy.

This task will require our best thinking and our best effort. We shudder when we think of some of the grave abuses which marriage in the past has permitted. Happily we have left many of these—foot-binding and suttee, for instance—behind. But in the future lie possibilities of abuse as real as those that have existed in the past. A reading of Aldous Huxley's *Brave New World* will suggest a few of these to the reader with any imagination.

Marriage is, after all, the basic adult human relationship. At its best it brings together, reconciles, and unites in fruitful harmony the two different kinds of human being, male and female. It generates the outflowing love that gives the helpless infant the warmth and protection he needs in order to flourish. It sets before the growing child, for good or ill, a working model, a microcosm, of the greater human community in which he will later take his place. It knits two people together in an enduring comradeship that provides a bulwark against man's deepest fear—the fear of being unloved, rejected, alone.

Marriage has not always achieved these ends. But these are its functions and its possibilities. It must be our continuous effort to realize them more completely.

In the vast cultural transition of today we are all caught up on a moving conveyor belt. In different parts of the world we are at different stages of the journey, moving at different speeds. But we are all involved, or will soon be involved, in a journey that carries mankind we know not whither.

On this journey we may idly drift, declaring that we have no power to decide the course we shall take. Or we may plan and work to understand, to interpret, to exercise wisdom in discarding what is no longer of value and in preserving that which is essential to our highest well-being.

The breakup of the old type of family life, which has served the human race for countless ages, is now inevitable. It cannot be preserved intact—in East or West, or anywhere else. It is a tremendous responsibility to be involved in such a process, to be witnessing the end of a form of institution that has been the foundation of all the great civilizations since the dawn of human history. We may well ask, in fear and trembling, what we are to put in its place.

The answer is that we do not know and that we cannot know as yet. But what is important is not the institution, but the values that the institution expresses and enshrines. The loss of the institutional form is inevitable. It can be replaced in time by another, more suited to the strange new life that will be the destiny of our children and our children's children. But the loss of the values—the true values that stand for man's dignity and worth—would be disastrous.

So, as we move into the uncharted future, we must not fail to keep our bearings. This we can do only by looking back into the past. There is a danger today that we should be haughty in our self-sufficiency, dismissing our ancient traditions as of no worth. This is folly. The past represents the agelong struggle that has brought us to where we now stand. It is the worst kind of arrogance to ignore the lessons that this struggle can teach us. "The chief trouble with modern man's thinking," say Bossard and Boll, "is that he has not read the minutes of the last meeting."[27]

What we have tried to do in this book has been, so far as the marriage relationship is concerned, to examine the minutes of some

evious meetings and try to relate them to our present
-to safeguard the well-being of the family in the future.
done this in an attempt to bring East and West together
in a co-operative enterprise. The East is in close touch with the
past, the West with the future. Neither one can be sufficient in
itself. Up to now, in some measure, they have traveled separately
and alone. This is no longer possible. East and West must abandon
their separateness, and do what Kipling said they never would do.
They must meet, join hands, and move forward into the future
together.

Appendix

MARRIAGE IN COMMUNIST CHINA

We have been in a dilemma as to how to approach the significant changes in marriage and family life that have been taking place in China under the Communist regime. In a book on the East, we clearly could not ignore the vast and far-reaching events that, for a decade, have been shaping the lives of a considerable proportion of the inhabitants of Asia.

On the other hand, we were in the difficult position of knowing very little about the impact of these events upon the family relationships of the Chinese today. From China come plenty of contradictory rumors, but little enough of validated facts. In any case, the events themselves are so recent that their final outcome cannot at this stage be clearly determined.

What we have written in the main part of this book consists of impressions gained from three sources—from our study of the literature, from firsthand personal experience, and from many discussions with well-informed persons in the countries concerned. We do not claim, even on this basis, that our opinions are free from error or misinterpretation. But at least we have had considerable resources upon which to draw.

We have lacked comparable resources concerning Communist China. In the first place, much of the available literature is full of disparities and contradictions, reflecting the conflicting ideological views of the writers. This makes a student of the situation very unsure of his ground. We can only regret such lack of reliable information, and echo the opinion of a reviewer in the London *Times* who says, "We must hope that the period of polemical writing can soon end and we can begin to consider the century of change through which China is passing."[1]

Beyond the varied points of view expressed in writing, we have had virtually nothing to work on. We have looked into Communist China from Kowloon but never crossed the frontier. So our firsthand knowledge is nil. Moreover, we have had no opportunity to discuss the subject with people who could inform us. The few Chinese Communist officials we have met in India lacked sufficient acquaintance with this field to be able to answer our questions.

So what we know of this subject is quite inadequate. We hope that one day we may have an opportunity to visit China and see for ourselves what is happening to family life there. Until then, we must remain ignorant and confused on many matters.

What we have decided to do, therefore, is to deal with this subject not in a chapter of the book, but in an Appendix. In doing so we wish it to be clearly understood that the information we supply here cannot be vouched for in the same way as we have tried to ensure the accuracy of the material in the rest of the book. Our views are based on the limited materials available to us.

In our selection of these materials we have tried to concentrate on documents published in China itself and intended for Chinese readers. We acknowledge gratefully the help of our friend, Dr. Francis P. Jones, Editor of the *China Bulletin* of the Far Eastern Office of the Division of Foreign Missions of the National Council of Churches in the U.S.A. An able Chinese scholar who lived in the country for many years, he now spends a good part of his time scanning written materials that are coming out of Communist China. He was kind enough to put aside for us, over a period of time, some press reports relevant to marriage and family life, and to make translations for our use. In this way we have had access to data not otherwise available in the West.

In our other reading, we tried deliberately to listen to both sides. To balance the considerable amount of sensational anti-Communist material (some of it on a level with the outpourings of the late Dr. Goebbels) that some organs of the American press take pleasure in serving up to their readers, we studied such pro-Communist accounts as the carefully written chapter in Simone de Beauvoir's *The Long March*.

We offer the results of these efforts for what they may be worth.

*   *   *

When the Communists took over in China, their purpose was to carry out a revolution.

The main objective was to make the country strong and prosperous. To achieve this end, they wished to bring food production, then industry, up to the highest possible levels of efficiency. Nothing that seriously blocked the way to these goals was to be tolerated. Once the goals were achieved, they promised a better life for all. But on the way, they warned, toil and hardship would have to be endured.

It is in this setting that everything in China today must be seen in order to be understood.

Mao Tse-tung had promised his peasant soldiers that, when he came to power, he would break up the holdings of the hated landlords, and give every farm worker a piece of land of his own.

This promise was kept. As soon as the Communists were in control the land was parceled out to the peasants. It seemed that all their dreams had come true. Each man saw himself settled, with his family, on his own holding—his own personal property.

But this policy did not work. Resources were inadequate, farming methods inefficient, co-operation lacking. And taxes, to maintain the regime, had to be high.

A crisis resulted. There was only one way out—to unite groups of separate peasant farmers into efficient organizations for better production; in short, to form co-operatives. Attempts were made to persuade groups of farmers to join together, pooling their tools, their labor, their animals. The idea was not received with enthusiasm. Then pressure was applied. For a time confusion reigned.

"The Communists made mistake after mistake, resentment piling up against them. The dam waters of their mismanagement finally broke, and misery flooded Shanghai. Refugees from the country poured into our city. They carried their babies in their arms and their elders on their backs. Apart from this they had little resemblance to the emigrants who, only a short time previously, were passing out of Shanghai in a steady stream on the way to 'land division.' Wild-eyed, dishevelled, cheeks too bright for health, swollen-stomached from eating grass, they were sullen and slow to speak. 'Land taxed beyond its yield capacity' . . . 'crops commandeered by the Party until no grain of rice was left for us' . . . 'driven like slaves, spied upon. Then strange young men and women came among us, urging that we join together our time and our animals. If we refused, we would be tried as counter-revolutionaries' . . . 'first the tools, the animals, and then the land would be all thrown in together. And so we fled. . . .' By bamboo wireless, these hapless people already knew about the misery of collective farms in Russia. People uprooted, their spirit of individual endeavour broken are people weakened, their morale lowered."[2]

The co-operatives were, however, finally established. By 1956, seven years after the Communists had taken over, it was claimed that almost all the farmers had been organized into groups of about 350 families each. They retained some kind of legal title to their land. But for all practical purposes it was merged in the joint enterprise.

The work output demanded of the co-operative farms was such that all available labor had to be employed. The men worked day after day to the point of exhaustion. To help out, the old, the disabled and the young had to be mobilized. The women helped, too, although it had not been the Chinese custom, except in the South, to make extensive use of female labor.

At this point individual families were still living separately in their own homes. But as the work demands continued relentlessly to be made, some of the traditional functions of the home began to be given up. It was considered inefficient to have each wife and mother staying at home to cook meals and take care of her children, when by pooling these tasks many women could be released for field labor. So, here and there at first, and then on an increasing scale, nursery centers were established where mothers might leave their children in the daytime while they were out at work; and communal feeding centers provided meals so that individual families did not have to cook separately.

The result was greater efficiency and increased output. Fulsome praise was given to those who met their work quotas, pressure exerted upon those who failed to do so. The people, hard pressed as they were, began to catch the enthusiasm of achievement.

It is not really surprising that many of these peasants, despite the hard treatment meted out to them, began to believe in the new regime. What else had they ever experienced but hard treatment? "We should remember how the contrast must seem to the Chinese peasant. In the lifetime lived between 1875 and 1950, for example, how many perished from famine, flood, war, and misgovernment? Eighty million? A hundred million? Possibly even more than a hundred and fifty million. That is the true context of their present vexations for most Chinese."[3]

Against that kind of background, the vexations of the co-operatives were not so grievous. And the plan was succeeding. There was food to eat. The standard of living was rising. Truly, nothing succeeds like success.

The logical next step was the commune. Many in the West have seen this as a radical new departure, a sudden and unexpected switch from one policy to another. In point of fact, the commune simply carries to its logical conclusion what the cooperative is trying to achieve. If communal feeding and communal child care released more labor for the all-important task of increasing production, why not go all the way and introduce completely communal living?

It is the Communist claim that the communes were in the first place suggested by the workers themselves, as a means of achieving greater efficiency during the period of advance designated as The Great Leap Forward. That may or may not be. But whatever its origin, the idea of communal living fits in very neatly with Communist doctrine in general.

From the point of view of the primary Communist aims, the commune represents a highly desirable arrangement for securing maximum efficiency from the workers and maximum control over their lives.

* * *

Quite apart from achieving their economic goals, it was a definite objective of the Communists, as part of the process of taking over China, to break the power of the traditional family system.

"One man passed unobtrusively down our back alley-way, shabbily dressed, but I recognized him as Feng, a landowner's son from the Wong farmstead district. . . . Cautiously, in tiny groups, I learned, the large Feng family had fled from their farm holdings to take refuge in safe British-controlled Hong-Kong. 'I, the last one out, now go to join the others,' he explained. 'Heavier taxes are being extracted from us, and there are rumors that our land is to be no longer ours. The next order may be for patriarchal families to be *forcibly* broken up. The family group, like the land, is to be done away with, that a family called the State may be created."[4]

First the landed estates, then the patriarchal family groups. These were rightly seen as obstacles to Communist advance. The old system of working the land had to be replaced by the new. These were essential steps in the progress of the revolution.

It was not the Communists, however, who first declared the traditional Chinese family system obsolete. This had already been done in the earlier nationalist revolution. In 1931, the Kuomintang promulgated its new "Code of the Family." This embodied sweeping changes. Here are some of them:

Women could inherit property.

Marriage could take place only by the free consent of the parties.

Marriage must not be a commercial transaction, and the broker must not be paid a fee.

No betrothal must take place until the girl was fifteen, the boy seventeen.

Concubinage was no longer permitted.

The wife was granted the right to divorce.

These were far-reaching reforms. The Nationalist Code did not, however, go all the way. It retained patriarchal elements. For example, when a child was orphaned, his guardians were to be chosen only from his father's relatives. When a wife secured a divorce, her husband retained the children.

All the same, this code was a tremendous step in the right direction. Consequently several writers hotly deny the Communist claim of having done away with the abuses of the traditional family system, on the ground that this had already been done by the Nationalist government.

This is perfectly true—on paper!

The intentions of the Kuomintang were no doubt excellent. But it would seem that the new law was only halfheartedly carried out. "Most of the different articles of the Code," according to Simone de Beauvoir, "remained dead issues. It had been drafted for the bourgeoisie's use. It was given no undue publicity: even in the cities it was ignored. In the rural areas no one so much as heard mention of the new code; it would have implied an emancipation of the peasants, which was the last thing the regime wanted."[5]

Even when it was applied, the Code's objectives could be circumvented. Though it required marriage to be by free consent, for instance, there was no effective way of safeguarding this, since the signatures of the couple were not legally required.

And although the Code aimed at the liberation of the woman from her ancient thralldom, it was reported in 1937, after it had been in operation for six years, that there were still two million girl slaves in China.[6]

Thus, even if some needed reforms had been laid down in principle before the Communists came to power, most of them still had to be implemented. Into this task the Communist regime threw itself wholeheartedly.

The Marriage Act, promulgated in 1950, plainly declared the full equality of man and wife. There are no exceptions and no loopholes. Communism has never compromised on the status of women, and it did not do so in China.

The Act went further than the Nationalist Code by insisting on the *signatures* of the marriage partners as evidence of their consent. It also left no bias of any kind in favor of the husband. Children of a divorced couple were to be awarded to either parent according to what was best for their (the children's) well-being.

The Communists meant business. If anything, they were *too* zealous in putting the Act into effect. This led to some unhappy results. Concubines were dragged forcibly from their homes and, finding themselves without support or protection, committed suicide. Husbands who ill-treated their wives were so heavily censured that Simone de Beauvoir relates the story of a belligerent wife who beat up her husband and father-in-law, the miserable men not daring to retaliate for fear of being accused of "feudal brutality"![7]

Trouble soon broke out. It was little wonder that the Nationalists had hesitated to insist that their Family Code be taken seriously. The new ideas challenged thousands of years of deeply ingrained tradition. When the Communists applied pressure, they

met stubborn resistance. Some of their officials, trying to enforce
the new regulations, were set upon and murdered. When in 1952
the influence of the Marriage Act brought the total of divorces up
to nearly four hundred thousand, it was derisively nicknamed the
"Divorce Act."

The Communists did not give up. But they changed their tactics.
The government issued orders that the Marriage Act should be
explained by "a long and patient process of education." Its objectives were carefully expounded in the schools; in special lec-
tures; in the classes for political education. In this way, it
gradually became accepted as an integral part of the new order.

The evidence seems to indicate that the provisions of the Marriage Act of 1950 are now in operation throughout Communist
China. If this is true, it means that the power of patriarchal tradition, which had dominated Chinese culture for at least twenty-
five centuries, has been shattered in the space of a few years.

That is a remarkable achievement. How was it done?

*   *   *

Gandhi once said that the only way to break down the caste
system in India was to focus one's efforts upon its nerve center,
which he considered to be the condition of the untouchables.

In China the Communists, in their determination to destroy the
patriarchal family system, have focused their efforts on the status
of the woman.[8] The shock troops, in the campaign to apply the
Marriage Act, have been the members of the women's organizations. The propaganda attacking the old order has ruthlessly exposed the indignities and hardships to which it submitted the
wife. This has been a favorite theme for plays and stories. The
women of Communist China have been taught to regard the past
as an era of horror and humiliation for womanhood, the new regime as the attainment at last of their full status as persons. There
is enough truth in this to make it sound convincing.

The desire of the Communists to liberate the Chinese woman,
and their desire to enroll her labor in the task of the country's
reconstruction, have gone along very nicely together. All that was
necessary was to convince the woman that her full emancipation
would come only as she was freed from her household chores and
found her place in the economic life of her country. This is good

Communist doctrine. Said Lenin, "As long as women restrict themselves to household duties their relative position in the family will be limited. To bring about true liberation, to put the woman on an equality with the man, she must share in family finances and in production. Only thus will she be on a level with her husband." And Engels, in the same vein, declared, "The primary condition for the liberation of women is their full participation in economic production."

This theme has been elaborated in the propaganda aimed at the Chinese woman. Here are some excerpts from an article published in the magazine *Chinese Youth* on December 19, 1958. The article is by Che Hsiang-tung and was translated for us by Dr. Francis Jones.

"Communist life liberates woman, it strikes off the shackles of household work and makes it possible for her to enter into socialistic production. Without the liberation of women and the equalization of the sexes there can be no true Communism.

"In the periods of slavery and feudalism, the family was the productive unit. The family founded upon the basis of private ownership was distinguished by inequality of the sexes; the husband was the income producer, and the wife was either put in a subordinate position, or dismissed from economic production altogether. Thus in society and in the family she was entirely dependent upon her husband.

"The separate family system kept women tied to the home, wasted the labor of one half of the population, and prevented the development of socialistic production. If, when private ownership and the class system have been destroyed, this individual family system were preserved, most women would still spend their time in cooking and sewing and caring for children; they would have no share in economic production or national life; they would not be able to learn a trade, or to work to improve the level of culture. Thus, in production and in the conditions of life generally, they still would not be able to take a position of full equality of power with men."

Notice the continuous repetition here of the idea that the woman who stays in her home, and is content to be a housewife, is failing to pull her weight in the great tasks the community has to perform and at the same time is being cheated out of her full rights. The double appeal, to her duty and to her desire to gain status, would obviously have a powerful effect on the Chinese woman.

However, in getting the woman out of the home, resistance from the men also has to be reckoned with. This is handled by suitable propaganda:

"If you analyze the nostalgic feeling which some people have for the old family system, you will find that what they want is for the woman to be busy around the house, taking care of the children. This so-called joy of family life sacrifices the liberation of women, and requires them to continue to live a miserable existence.

"Some young men do not want their wives to engage in work for society; they complain and say, 'There is no one to wait upon me'; 'Home is not like home any more'; 'From now on I will be left all alone.'

"There is, of course, a reason for his feeling unhappy. In the past when he returned home, there was someone there to wait on him, household matters had been taken care of and he could relax. But now both he and his wife have their work, and the household chores must be divided between the two of them. That is why he feels, 'My wife isn't mine any more.' But that is only a reflection of the idea of male superiority.

"To look upon the wife as one's own property, that is the sin of the exploiting class. Women have been liberated, and are now equal to men in both privilege and responsibility."

*   *   *

This propaganda was effective. The following news items from the Chinese Communist press are typical.

Chin Yueh-fang, Secretary-General of the Municipal Women's Federation of Harbin, is reported to have said in a speech on July 8, 1958: "At present more than 3,000 factories have been established in the streets of the city, with approximately 24,000 women participating. The participation of women in social production not only enables their ingenuity and wisdom to be fully developed, but at the same time improves family life and achieves a closer unity among the family members."

From Heilungkiang comes this report, dated August 19, 1958:

"The province has greatly developed the labor potentialities of the women, and paved the way for mothers representing 50–60 per cent of the women's labor power to be freed from household chores. As a result more and more women have participated in industrial and agricultural production and various construction undertakings, and their labor enthusiasm is running higher and higher. After the child care organizations were set up in the countryside, 225,363 mothers have taken up production tools to work on the farm. They are full of working spirit."

Peng Yu, a Shanghai mother with five children, was a delegate to the National Conference of Active Women Builders of Socialism, held in Peiping in December 1958. She reported:

"Every housewife under 45 in my district who wants to work has been given a job. Every possible effort is made to enable husbands and wives to work in the same plant or on the same shift, in the interests of family life. The husbands are pleased to work with their wives and find that their marriages are happier now that they share more common interests with them."

She concluded, "As a woman I can say from the bottom of my heart that I and other women who are not members of the Communist Party are grateful to the Party for the happy new life we now have."

Another mother of five children, Chao Shu-lan, from Yuehchi, stood out at first against the idea of going to work. The result was that life was "difficult" for her for seven years. Finally, in 1958, she changed her mind. "This year she has entrusted her two youngest children to the nursery, and participates in production. She plans to earn 800 work points and pay for the food consumed by the entire family during the whole year." The moral of this story is: "The participation of women in productive labor has not only created wealth for the state, but has also increased their family income and raised their standard of living."

It can easily be seen that continuous stimulation of this kind is bound in time to persuade wives and mothers that their proper place is not in the home, but in the field or factory. Chao Shu-lan came round after seven years. We can imagine her situation. She sees more and more of her friends and neighbors joining the labor force. She hears them praised for their devotion to their country, while she is made to feel unpatriotic. She is aware that their families have a better standard of living than her own. Perhaps her children reproach her because they cannot have privileges which the Wongs or the Lins enjoy. Even her husband may show embarrassment because his wife is officially ranked as a "parasite." Against this pressure she holds out as long as she can. But finally, feeling more and more isolated and out of step with other wives, she "voluntarily" takes the decisive step.

By doing so she has, according to the Communist view, broken the confining shell and become a true woman. As Madame Cheng explained to Simone de Beauvoir, "So long as the village woman confines herself to domestic chores, she will remain, in the family's eyes and in her own, a semi-parasite. But on the other hand, the moment the cooperative pays a young woman a salary which she has earned entirely by herself and which belongs entirely to her, no one feels he has any prerogative over her; the autonomy she has won is meaningful."[9]

Thus the way is paved for the gradual transfer of the normal functions of the family to their more efficient performance as communally organized services.

First come feeding and child care. Then comes the making and mending of clothes. Hot baths and haircuts, weddings and funerals, care in maternity, sickness, and old age—these and other facilities follow. And, of course, at whatever point is most appropriate, housing of the type and character determined by the state. Dr. Sripati Chandrasekhar, in an article in the New York *Times* on February 22, 1959, listed sixteen services which the Chinese Communists ultimately intend to provide free to all workers.

So, step by step, the women of China have "voluntarily" marched to the communes. And if the women lead the way, what alternative have the men but to follow?

*   *   *

Next to the emancipation of women, in the Communist program to destroy patriarchalism, comes the emancipation of youth.

Communism does not favor the arranged marriage. It wants young people to be free to choose for themselves. This is an essential factor in their "liberation" from the domination of authoritarian parents. Simone de Beauvoir describes an opera she saw in China, which she considers to be typical, which portrayed a despotic father who forbids his daughter to marry the boy with whom she is deeply in love. Instead, she is forced to marry a stranger. The boy dies of grief, and on her wedding day the girl commits suicide.[10]

Revolt against parental tyranny was a popular theme with Chinese youth, and rallied them to the Communist cause. But putting the new patterns of freedom into practice has not been so easy. Girls who refused to marry the men chosen for them by their parents have been confronted by mothers who threatened to hang themselves in protest. Boys and girls in the rural areas who embarked on courtship, and had the effrontery to go out together, were severely censured by the village elders.

The young people themselves have had their difficulties. The Communists have had to rebuke scheming girls who tried to capture well-to-do husbands who could support them, so that they would no longer have to work in the factory. Boys have been so shy of approaching girls, and girls so confused when they were approached, that Communist leaders have had to step in and act as encouraging Cupids. In rural areas it was sometimes found impossible to induce the young people to get acquainted, and with the prospect of the marriage rate dropping to zero, the party members have had to act as go-betweens and arrange matches.

But with their usual zeal the Communists have persisted in their efforts. They have organized mixed social evenings and dances, put steady pressure on the young people to have dates, and applauded couples who took walks in the moonlight. This has been a somewhat unusual role for earnest Communist workers.

Freedom as interpreted by the Communists does not, however, include sexual freedom. Their standards of sex morality are uncompromisingly strict. "It is a strange fact that liberation from the old sex traditions has not by any means resulted in a leap into libertinism and promiscuity. The awakening of individual love by choice still has, among the young Chinese, something tremendously shy and pure about it. In point of fact, the number of illegitimate births has not only not gone up following the liberation of the sexes, but has even declined."[11]

After attending a dance at the Railway Men's Club in Peiping, Peter Schmid made this comment:

"The entire new sexuality is still very much in the embryonic

stage, and the trade-union secretary flung up his arms in horror
when I told him that in the decadent capitalist West this kind of
contact would occasionally be followed by greater intimacy. In
China this is entirely out of the question, not only because nobody
is ever alone anywhere, but also because there is a puritanical
atmosphere pervading the whole country.

"This atmosphere is in part a continuation of the old Confucian
tradition, and in part has now received a new content by political
propaganda. In the old days libertinism had been the privilege of
the rich: with their money and their power they had been able
to bend the daughters of the lower orders to their will. Hence, in
today's Communist China all free love is tainted with the political
odium of 'feudalism.' That, at least, is the theory; but I honestly
believe that it applies also in practice. It makes a colossal difference not having the continuous erotic stimulation provided in the
West by loudspeakers, cinema posters, and Heaven knows what
else."[12]

Simone de Beauvoir also comments on the attitude of sexual
restraint that characterizes the Chinese under Communism:

"Love does not appear to play a major role in the life of the
young Chinese. For the Chinese woman the bed for so long
signified a slavery so odious that her foremost preoccupation is to
have no more of that constraint; it is not socialist enthusiasm
that prevents her from dreaming of men, but she enthusiastically
welcomes a socialism which frees her from men's clutches.

"For every Chinese woman, from the top to the bottom of the
social scale, physical love has a negative coefficient. She must be
entirely delivered from the weight of the past before she will be
able to adopt a positive attitude when, instead of feeling pleased
with herself for having escaped love, she will be free to love as
she pleases."[13]

The Communists claim to have virtually abolished prostitution.
"Prior to the Communist 'Liberation' Shanghai had been the sinful Babylon of the Far East, a city thick with brothels and kept
women. . . . It took the Red Government two years before it decided to wield the iron broom in Shanghai. In 1951 all brothels
were closed down and their inmates taken to that very Reforma-
tory, which occupied the premises of a former retraining centre
for vagrants. . . . In the courtyard a board proudly proclaimed

the aims of the institution in big Chinese letters: 'We are fighting against the degradation of womanhood and are striving for the creation of a new human being.' . . . In the workshops the former prostitutes were sitting behind their machines as tightly packed together as sardines, knitting socks and gloves. Packed just as tightly, the night shift were dozing through the afternoon in their dormitories."[14]

Chinese Communism has set youth free. But Chinese young people have not been permitted to use their freedom for self-indulgence. As Schmid sums up, "Even Cupid has to register his shafts as weapons liable to endanger the security of the State. Virtue is marching on, with step firm and unfaltering."[15]

*　　*　　*

"In the sunny Pei Hai Park nursery the children were aglow with health and gaiety in their brightly colored little outfits; but the most remarkable thing of all was the exuberant confidence they evinced in adults, their forwardness, their unconstraint. Their teachers told me that not only are spankings forbidden but the idea of corporal punishment does not even exist any more; the wrong-doer is scolded, his misconduct explained to him: in really difficult cases expert advice is consulted. The result is that children are growing up in ignorance of fear and constraint.

"As for the 'indoctrination' of the children, they are, certainly, taught to love their country, to want to serve it, to respect the current ethic, and they are educated in the ideology that corresponds to the regime under which they live. Is it not the same in every other country?"[16]

Some may consider Simone de Beauvoir a biased witness. But when a delegation from the Society of Friends visits Communist China, with no political axes to grind, their report is likely to be taken as a more detached evaluation.

"Among the things we saw, the most delightful was the programme of child welfare work. There has been a tremendous burgeoning of crèches, nurseries and kindergartens. To a certain extent the motive of the programme is to enable more mothers to go to work, but it would be wrong to attribute it to material considerations alone. Everybody loves Chinese children, espe-

cially the Chinese. National sentiment and party ideology therefore combine happily to give the children a better deal."[17]

There has been a good deal of critical comment, especially
among the disciples of Dr. John Bowlby, of the "dumping" of babies by Chinese mothers as they go out to work. Evidently the
report that Dr. Bowlby made to the World Health Organization,
on the perils of "maternal deprivation" in children, has not been
closely studied in China. The Communists do not seem to be unduly perturbed as to what will happen to their children under the
new system.

As a matter of fact, it is not really a new system. In China children have often been passed around freely from one mother
substitute to another. Servant girls, aunts, grandmothers and other
female members of the household were accustomed to taking over
and performing maternal functions for any child in need of a
little attention. Children were even shared out on a more permanent basis. Where there was a shortage in the family, the parents
of several children might spare one or two for a childless couple.
Where there was a surplus, the grandparents would take up the
slack. The children belonged, as it were, to everybody, so that all
adults were regarded as properly qualified to exercise parental
functions. This traditional attitude has no doubt made it relatively
easy for Chinese parents to hand over their children to communal
care.

Child care provided by the state is definitely part of the Communist policy. Che Hsiang-tung, in the article already referred to,
expounds the party line thus:

"On the one hand the individual will care for his children, and
on the other hand, society will share the responsibility, and so the
life of children will be guaranteed, for they will be the high
concern of the whole of society. This will be a blessing such as
the world has never seen before. It is only under a Communist
society that such a high social order can appear. The contrast between this social order and the orphanages which we see in the
so-called civilized capitalistic nations of England and America,
is like the contrast between heaven and earth. It can be seen that
the charge which some people make, that we are lacking in hu-
mane feelings, that we do not care for children, is not worth
consideration."

However, there have evidently been some doubts among the Chinese themselves concerning the new pattern. These can be gathered from the reassurances that Che Hsiang-tung goes on to give:

"For children to live in nurseries or schools is not as terrible as some people foolishly or perversely imagine, as though parents and children were no longer to see each other or to have any affection for each other. In the early days of Liberation, when the workers put their children in nurseries, they enjoyed each other's company all the more when on days of rest they could be together.

"It is true that some people are unwilling to be separated from their own children; for the sake of their children they neglect their work, they are afraid that other people will not take good care of their children, and consider 'mother-love' to be above all, 'something for which there is no substitute,' and consider their own children to be more precious than other people's children. But this is all wrong. Of course everybody and especially mothers love their own children, but while loving their own children they should also be ready to believe that in a society such as ours today, where the level of Communist understanding has been raised so high, other people will treat their children well, they do not need to worry about them and thus neglect their work for social construction."

He repeats that only by the communal care of children can the mothers be set free for necessary work. But that is not the only reason for the vast child-care program.

"For the children to live in nurseries or schools is necessary for production, for the liberation of women, and also necessary for the education of the next generation."

What this "education" means is suggested in a press report, dated July 13, 1958, from Heilungkiang:

"After the child care organizations have been universally established, the 601,031 children in the province are given reasonable education, and they have built a fine character. They have learned to sing and dance, and pay attention to hygiene and propriety. The children of Leap Forward Cooperative in Shaochow, after two months in the kindergarten, have learned not to quarrel and fight, and greet the people politely. They can perform eight dances and sing more than ten songs. They dance and sing before their

parents when the latter return from work, and so in the homes
children have become little actors in the cultural and recreational
evening meetings."

So the program goes on apace. In the era of the co-operatives,
the percentage of children involved in this process of indoctrination was rising rapidly. All that the establishment of the communes
has done is to bring it up to a hundred per cent.

*   *   *

"The Communist Party has stepped in to replace the intracta-
ble, hard-hearted father and the testy, dogmatic mother-in-law of
the old Chinese family system. In every family affair, from marriage consent to the upbringing of the children, the Party has assumed direction. The Party is now marriage broker. The Party is
now the child's keeper. The Party is now one's father and mother.
Family life is replaced by Party loyalty; the love of a man and
woman is supplanted by obeisance to the Party machine."[18]

This statement was not made by a Communist sympathizer.
How far does it represent the true state of affairs in China today?

We wish we were in a position to answer this all-important
question. All we can say is that the statement seems to conform
in general to basic Communist principles. These have been well
summarized by Elton and Pauline Trueblood:

"The official Marxist doctrine all along has been that the home,
when it is given social priority and real importance, involves
parasitism. The unemployed woman is declared to be a parasite.
. . . Of course it follows, if the unproductiveness of home life can
be demonstrated, that families, as ordinarily organized, represent
economic waste. Since there are fully as many females as males,
the 'emancipation of women' practically doubles the labor power
at one stroke. At the same time the state wins a great victory of
another kind, in that the task of propagandizing all minds is made
easier when the center of education becomes public rather than
private. Education which is 'an instrument of propaganda for the
communist regeneration of society' is made easier if the family
does not compete or interfere."[19]

What is crystal clear is that the Communist state will only tolerate the family if it conforms to the prescribed pattern. This is
tacitly conceded by Simone de Beauvoir. "In its modern form," she

says, "the family is respected by the State."[20] Naturally, because the modern form of the Chinese family is tailor-made for the Communist regime. However, she continues, "where conflict arises between family and country allegiances, country must be chosen: but the same applies to the West, when similar conflicts arise."[21]

This is indeed true. In time of war, men are torn from the bosom of their families and sent to fight. If a mother is found guilty of a serious crime, she is sent to prison, and her family have to manage without her. But these are extreme and isolated instances. Is it fair to compare them with the demands of the state in China, which takes one by one from the family, for the sake of national efficiency, its age-old functions? Even if the difference is only one of degree, the degree of difference is surely considerable.

From the way Communists themselves describe their aims, it seems that they desire the family to exist only as a particular and limited relationship between individuals who are pledged first and foremost to the direct service of the state, which will make most of life's major decisions for them. The family is in effect to be stripped of all functions other than the reproductive and the emotional. This at least is what Che Hsiang-tung seems to be saying.

"In Communistic society the family will no longer exist as the unit of consumption. But the family as a blood connection will still continue, and will develop into a new and beautiful type of family life. Then the relation of family members to each other will be one of complete equality and mutual love, and people will at the same time be living and working as a part of the happy family of Communism. Our Chinese family has now begun to change in this direction.

"In the old society, laboring men, with wives and children always hungry, fundamentally lacked the conditions for joy in family life. But in the new society conditions are fundamentally changed; fellowship within the family has been improved as both the old and the young are properly cared for. Under the communes the family life of the workers will take a great step forward; with the change of relationships in economic production, mutual help and love within the family will have a new development.

"We are in the process of hastening the establishment of a socialist society, and positively preparing for the transition to Communism, and of course we want people to have a happy family life. But this happy family must be founded on the basis of abundance and happiness for all; if one tries to secure his own individual happiness apart from this, apart from the establishment of socialism, that is both improper and impossible of accomplishment."

*　　*　　*

The establishment of the communes in Communist China made sensational headlines in the West. An article in *Life* was headed "Misery, Oppression, Fear." It described a horror of regimentation lasting nineteen hours a day. It portrayed China as a land of blazing villages. It described husband and wife parading in line to have about half an hour of strictly rationed time alone together on alternate Saturday evenings. It quoted a member of a commune who said that in two months he had never had more than three hours' sleep a night.

Reports elsewhere were equally sensational. They declared that the brutal bosses of Communist China were planning the annihilation of the family. This inhuman plan, it was implied, had been suddenly put into operation, without preparation or warning.

Even if we impute the worst possible motives to China's present rulers, to imply that they are acting without intelligence is seriously to mislead the people of the West. We ourselves have met Chinese Communist officials. They appeared to us to be anything but irresponsible morons.

It requires only elementary common sense to realize that a whole nation cannot be made to function effectively if kept in a continual state of fear, oppression, and misery, given only three hours' sleep per night, and denied the fulfillment of elementary human needs. If we think the Chinese Communists know no better than that, we are gravely underestimating the ideology that is contending with ours for world leadership. We may wish to tell the man in the street that all Communists are knaves. But woe betide us if we deceive him by telling him that they are fools also.

In short, we cannot begin to take the measure of what Chinese Communists are doing to the family if we begin with the assumption that they are crazed lunatics. We must, in order to make sense of what is happening, give them the credit for having a carefully thought-out plan that they consider to be workable. And that plan was evolved after nine years of experience of what the Chinese people could be persuaded to accept.

A better approach for us to take, we submit, is to try to understand how the idea of the communes fits into the Eastern way of living and thinking. To try to imagine how we as Westerners would feel in such circumstances is to start at the wrong end.

We have tried to show how the communes developed naturally and logically out of what has been happening to family life in China since the Communists took over. It is no violent innovation. Most of its features already existed, in one form or another, in the co-operatives. And they seem on the whole to have proved workable.

There is no doubt that Communists are always ready to use force if necessary to gain their ends. But a long record of human experience has demonstrated that force is effective only in limited circumstances and for limited periods of time. Since the early violence of the Revolution, the Communists in China have gone to great lengths, by persuasion and encouragement, to win the good will of the people. There would be no sense in now throwing away all they have gained and antagonizing the whole nation overnight.

It seems, therefore, to be inescapable logic that the Chinese people are not averse to the communes in the sense that we in the West would be. For long centuries Chinese peasants have lived circumscribed lives, endured great hardship, worked hard for long hours. These are not new experiences. Moreover, they have not been accustomed to privacy. In the East people live more or less in public, and they like it that way. Frequently also, as we have seen, the men and women occupy separate quarters, and find their fellowship with members of their own sex. Communal living is certainly nothing new or strange to them.

What *is* new and strange, to the majority of Chinese peasants, is to be sure of having food to eat in exchange for their toil, to have their children well nourished and in good health, to be delivered from the ravages of famine and pestilence and marauding armies.

Life in the communes, in short, represents for the average Chinese citizen not a nightmare of horror, but a way of life superior in many respects to anything he has known before. If this were not so, we submit, the leaders of Communist China would never have taken the colossal risk that would have been involved in making this experiment.

We would emphasize the word "experiment." All the available information about the communes indicates that the Communists are feeling their way. This means that mistakes have been made, and will be made. Plenty of mistakes were made in organizing the co-operatives, but they have attained their objectives and greatly increased China's agricultural and industrial production. The likelihood seems to be that the communes, likewise, will fulfill the purpose for which they were planned.

Instead of indulging in sensationalism, we in the West would be better employed in trying to understand what the Chinese plan is, and what its fulfillment will mean to the position of China as a growing world power.

* * *

Because we have so little reliable information about what is happening in Communist China, we are obliged to end this discussion not by drawing conclusions, but by asking questions.

Have the Communist leaders set up the communes merely as a means of achieving the Great Leap Forward, or do they contemplate retaining them as a permanent basis for life in China in the future?

Available information gives us no clear indication of the answer. There are, of course, many statements declaring that this is the final goal of a Communist state, and that China has carried it further than any other community has dared to do. But this may merely be propaganda. Obviously the Chinese people would not co-operate willingly in an upheaval of this radical nature if they were led to believe that it was only a temporary measure. So it must be presented to them, in grandiose terms, as a new and permanent way of life.

Full-scale communal living does fit, of course, into the Communist ideology. The idea of the whole nation as one big happy family, all sharing the benefits of the prosperity attained by their common effort, is directly in line with the teaching of Marx and Engels. But the Russian Communists have never carried the principle to the extent of putting the whole nation into barracks, presumably because they believed it wouldn't work. It seems highly probable that Russian and Chinese leaders have been in consultation about the latest development in China, and that the Russian point of view has been fully considered.

On the whole it seems likely, therefore, that the communes in China are viewed officially as a temporary measure. As such, they can obviously achieve some very important ends. The total labor resources of the entire nation can be mobilized for an all-out effort to forge ahead economically. The patriarchal family tradition can be broken up completely, leaving no surviving strongholds. The emancipation of the women can be thoroughly achieved. The children of the next generation can be fully indoctrinated.

These are, from the Communist point of view, goals of the greatest importance. The leaders may well feel that a radical reorganization of life within the country is not too heavy a price to pay for such an advance. And this would seem to be a good time to make such a venture. China is forging ahead. Standards of living are rising. Serious internal opposition to the Communist regime has virtually been eliminated. The people are in good heart, optimistic, and ready to accept sacrifices in exchange for the promise of better things to come.

To put the Chinese into communes is asking no more of them than is asked of any nation in a time of great emergency. In wartime, people have to accept a very unnatural way of life so that they may strive together for victory. As long as tangible gains are being made, people can display great patience and endurance. And no people in the world have shown greater capacity for patience and endurance than the Chinese.

Is it not possible, therefore, that the communes may represent a total mobilization of the Chinese people for the tasks immediately ahead, rather than an attempt to replace the family with a new kind of communal living?

Whatever purpose the Chinese leaders have in mind, the experiment promises to be a very interesting one. Will the women of China continue to accept a way of life that deprives them of the age-old functions of homemaking? Will the children, raised communally, develop into emotionally healthy and stable adults? Or will China find, as Russia did in her early experiments along this line, that there is no substitute for home life for the nurturing of the child's personality? Will the young people continue to use their new freedom with restraint? Or will there be a decline in moral standards as novelty and inhibition recede into the background?

What will happen to China's new marriages? Will the freedom from anxiety and responsibility indeed enable husband and wife to concentrate attention on the development of deep and mutually satisfying interpersonal relationships? Or will the link between them become shallow and superficial when they are no longer united in the daily duties and responsibilities of running a home and raising a family?

Looking further ahead, what will happen when the major task of making China an industrially efficient nation is completed, and machines begin to replace human labor? During the present expanding phase every hand is needed for the task. But the time will come when this will no longer be so. China has an enormous population—an estimated 650 million, about a quarter of whom are said to be children of seven years of age and under. When the labor of women ultimately is no longer needed, will they be content to return to their ancient tasks as homemakers?

These and many other questions arise in our minds as we contemplate the future of marriage and family life in China. Time alone will reveal the answers.

REFERENCES

In order to keep references down to reasonable proportions, we have not identified quotations from such frequently used sources as, for example, the Laws of Manu. We considered that the interested reader could find these for himself without much difficulty.

In the case of books which have appeared in many editions, we have sometimes judged it to be most convenient to the reader to give the chapter from which the reference comes, rather than the page in the particular edition which we used.

In one instance—Tsao Hsueh-chin's *Dream of the Red Chamber*—we used two different versions, published by Doubleday in 1929 and 1958 respectively. We have distinguished these by the numerals (1) and (2).

The publishers and dates of the publications quoted will be found either in the Bibliography or in the list of Additional Sources.

CHAPTER 1

THE REIGN OF THE PATRIARCH

1. Nora Waln, *The House of Exile*, p. 84.
2. Ibid., p. 32.
3. N. S. Phadke, *Sex Problems in India*, pp. 87–88.
4. Waln, op. cit., p. 109.
5. Ibid., p. 197.
6. William Chase Greene, *The Achievement of Rome*, p. 93.
7. Pearl S. Buck, *The Good Earth*, Chap. 34.
8. Article written in 1947 by Professor Kawashima on "Authority and Obedience in the Japanese Family," quoted by E. H. Cressy in *Daughters of Changing Japan*, pp. 202–3.
9. Olga Lang, *Chinese Family and Society*, p. 16.
10. K. M. Kapadia, *Marriage and Family in India*, p. 71.
11. Lang, op. cit., p. 31.
12. S. C. Dube, *Indian Village*, Chap. 5.
13. Buck, op. cit., Chap. 20.
14. James Legge, *The China Review*, Vol. 6, p. 156.
15. E. H. Cressy, *Daughters of Changing Japan*, p. 32.
16. Savitri Devi Nanda, *The City of Two Gateways*, p. 29.

CHAPTER 2

CHANGE OF MODEL IN THE WEST

1. Frieda Hauswirth, *A Marriage to India*, p. 162.
2. Hilda Wernher, *My Indian Son-in-Law*, p. 81.
3. James H. S. Bossard and Eleanor Boll, *Why Marriages Go Wrong*, p. 12.
4. Ibid., p. 12.
5. George Bernard Shaw, Preface to *Getting Married*.

CHAPTER 3

WHAT IS A WOMAN WORTH?

1. Allen K. Faust, *The New Japanese Womanhood*, p. 17.
2. Olga Lang, *Chinese Family and Society*, p. 44.
3. Shingoro Takaishi, Introduction to Kaibara Ekken, *Greater Learning for Women*, p. 15.
4. Margaret Macnicol (ed.), *Poems by Indian Women*, p. 71.
5. Frieda Hauswirth, *Purdah: The Status of Indian Women*, pp. 66, 94.
6. Mary I. Bryson, *Home Life in China*, pp. 100–3.
7. Lin Yu-tang, *Moment in Peking*, p. 46.
8. Translated by Isaac T. Headland, *Home Life in China*, p. 77.
9. J. A. Dubois, *Hindu Manners, Customs and Ceremonies*, p. 210.
10. Nora Waln, *The House of Exile*, p. 55.
11. Hauswirth, op. cit., p. 147.
12. Shingoro Takaishi, op. cit., p. 16.
13. E. H. Cressy, *Daughters of Changing Japan*, p. 77.
14. Faust, op. cit., p. 21.
15. Lang, op. cit., p. 54.
16. Kang Won-Yong, *A Study of the Family System in Korea*, p. 35a.
17. P. A. Thompson, *Lotus Land*, p. 69.
18. Millicent M. Pommerenke, *Asian Women and Eros*, p. 238.
19. American Tract Society (published by), *Conditions and Character of Females in Pagan and Mohammedan Countries*, p. 7.
20. R. H. Charles, *The Apocrypha and Pseudepigrapha of the Old Testament in English*, Vol. 1, p. 470.
21. W. E. H. Lecky, *History of European Morals from Augustus to Charlemagne*, Vol. 2. Chap. 5.
22. Tertullian, *De Cultu Feminarum*, i. I.
23. Lecky, op. cit., Chap. 5.
24. Ibid., Chap. 5.
25. Henry Maine, *Ancient Law*, p. 170–71.
26. Vera Brittain, *Lady into Woman*, p. 41.
27. Lang, op. cit., p. 54.

28. Hilda Wernher, *My Indian Son-in-Law*, p. 203.
29. Hauswirth, op. cit., pp. 3–5 (abridged). When we discussed this incident with Mrs. Mehta personally, she explained that men as well as women participated, under her leadership, in this demonstration of non-violence.
30. Ibid., p. 10.
31. Ashley Montagu

CHAPTER 4

SEX IN THE ORIENT

1. Millicent M. Pommerenke, *Asian Women and Eros*, p. 102.
2. *The Times Literary Supplement*, March 15, 1928.
3. J. A. Dubois, *Hindu Manners, Customs and Ceremonies*, pp. 602–3.
4. Dalip Singh Saund, *My Mother India*, p. 62.
5. Tsao Hsueh-chin, *Dream of the Red Chamber* (1), pp. 43–49.
6. Olga Lang, *Chinese Family and Society*, p. 34.
7. John F. Embree, *A Japanese Village—Suye Mura*, p. 145.
8. Santha Rama Rau, *This Is India*, p. 51.
9. Rai Bahadur Dinesh Chandra Sen, *History of Bengali Language and Literature*, quoted by Lord Ronaldshay, *The Heart of Âryâvarta*, p. 148.
10. Vidhyapati, *Bangiya Padabali*, p. 76.
11. Ibid., p. 132.
12. Lord Ronaldshay, *The Heart of Âryâvarta*, p. 148.
13. Ananda Coomaraswamy, Introduction to Vidhyapati, op. cit.
14. Swami Vivekananda, *Bhakti Yoga*, quoted by Ronaldshay, op. cit., p. 146.
15. Dubois, op. cit., pp. 713–14.
16. N. S. Phadke, *Sex Problems in India*, pp. 173–74.
17. M. K. Gandhi, *Self-Restraint versus Self-Indulgence*, pp. 106–7, 111, 180.
18. P. H. Prabhu, *Hindu Social Organization*, p. 81.
19. M. K. Gandhi, *An Autobiography*, Part 3, pp. 174–75.
20. Pearl S. Buck, *East Wind, West Wind*, pp. 15–16.
21. Phadke, op. cit., p. 293.
22. E. H. Cressy, *Daughters of Changing Japan*, pp. 40, 42.
23. *The Book of Odes*, Part 1, Book 2, Ode 12.
24. Phadke, op. cit., p. 296.
25. Eleanor McDougall, *Lamps in the Wind*, p. 144.
26. Nora Waln, *The House of Exile*, p. 23.
27. Florence Ayscough, *Chinese Women Yesterday and Today*, pp. 271–90.
28. *The Book of Odes*, Part 1, Book 5, Ode 4.
29. Pearl S. Buck, *The Good Earth*, Chap. 18.
30. W. E. H. Lecky, *History of European Morals from Augustus to Charlemagne*, Vol. 2, p. 119.

31. Peter Schmid, *In the Shadow of the Dragon,* p. 100.
32. A. K. Faust, *The New Japanese Womanhood,* p. 60.
33. Kamala Markandaya, *Nectar in a Sieve,* pp. 137–38.
34. Pommerenke, op. cit., p. 140.
35. Ibid., p. 257.
36. Dubois, op. cit., pp. 592–93.

CHAPTER 5

ROMANCE IS TOO DANGEROUS

1. Margaret Macnicol (ed.), *Poems by Indian Women,* p. 59.
2. Ibid., p. 85.
3. Olga Lang, *Chinese Family and Society,* p. 32.
4. Johann Meyer, *Sexual Life in Ancient India,* p. 277.
5. Tsao Hsueh-chin, *Dream of the Red Chamber* (1), p. 46.
6. Pearl S. Buck, *The Good Earth,* Chap. 1.
7. N. S. Phadke, *Sex Problems in India,* p. 116.
8. Shingoro Takaisha, Introduction to Kaibara Ekken, *Greater Learning for Women,* pp. 17–18.
9. Meyer, op. cit., p. 277.
10. *The Book of Odes,* Part 1, Book 7, Ode 3.
11. Rabindranath Tagore, "The Indian Ideal of Marriage," in H. Keyserling (ed.), *The Book of Marriage,* pp. 108, 112.
12. James Legge, Commentary on *The Book of Odes,* Part 1, Book 4, Ode 7.
13. James H. S. Bossard and Eleanor Boll, *Why Marriages Go Wrong,* p. 59.
14. Ibid., p. 111.
15. Rabindranath Tagore in Keyserling, op. cit., p. 113.
16. Kang Won-Yong, *A Study of the Family System in Korea,* p. 86.
17. Nora Waln, *The House of Exile,* p. 117.
18. Quoted by Lang, op. cit., p. 32.
19. Tsao Hsueh-chin, op. cit. (1), Chap. 9.
20. Waln, op. cit., pp. 115–16.
21. Donald H. Shively, *The Love Suicide at Amijima,* p. 25.
22. Francis L. K. Hsu, *Magic and Science in Yunnan,* p. 5.
23. John F. Embree, *A Japanese Village—Suye Mura,* p. 194.
24. Mi Mi Khaing, *Burmese Family,* p. 121.
25. Ibid., pp. 98–99.
26. Savitri Devi Nanda, *The City of Two Gateways,* p. 268.

CHAPTER 6

WHO PICKS YOUR PARTNER?

1. Quoted by Isaac T. Headland, *Home Life in China,* pp. 293–95.
2. N. S. Phadke, *Sex Problems in India,* pp. 95–96.

3. Nora Waln, *The House of Exile*, pp. 120–21.
4. Maurice Freedman, *Chinese Family and Marriage in Singapore*, p. 18.
5. M. K. Gandhi, *Self-Restraint versus Self-Indulgence*, p. 72.
6. Vatsyayana, *Kama Sutra*, 3:1:11–12.
7. P. H. Prabhu, *Hindu Social Organization*, pp. 160–61.
8. *The Book of Odes*, Part 1, Book 15, Ode 5.
9. Headland, op. cit., p. 143.
10. Bryce Ryan, *Sinhalese Village*, p. 75.
11. Simone de Beauvoir, *The Long March*, p. 140.
12. Frieda Hauswirth, *A Marriage to India*, p. 57.
13. New York *Times Magazine Section*, April 3, 1955.
14. Waln, op. cit., p. 131.
15. Genesis 29:16–26.
16. Headland, op. cit., p. 143.
17. Olga Lang, *Chinese Family and Society*, p. 199.
18. Ryan, op. cit., p. 64.
19. *The Book of Odes*, Part 1, Book 2, Ode 6.
20. Yang Ping-yu, *The Love Story of a Maiden of Cathay*, p. 74.
21. Savitri Devi Nanda, *The City of Two Gateways*, p. 225.
22. E. H. Cressy, *Daughters of Changing Japan*, pp. 123–24.
23. Savitri Devi Nanda, op. cit., p. 255.
24. *The Book of Odes*, Part 1, Book 2, Ode 9.
25. Cressy, op. cit., p. 53.
26. Waln, op. cit., p. 69.
27. Ryan, op. cit., p. 72.
28. Frieda Hauswirth, *Purdah: The Status of Indian Women*, pp. 7–9.
29. Eleanor McDougall, *Lamps in the Wind*, p. 156.

CHAPTER 7

GETTING MARRIED, EASTERN STYLE

1. Quoted by N. S. Phadke: *Sex Problems in India*, pp. 92–93.
2. Dalip Singh Saund, *My Mother India*, pp. 59–61.
3. Pearl S. Buck, *Letter from Peking*, p. 125.
4. Bryce Ryan, *Sinhalese Village*, p. 75.
5. Tsao Hsueh-chin, *Dream of the Red Chamber* (2), p. 250.
6. Savitri Devi Nanda, *The City of Two Gateways*, p. 257.
7. P. A. Thompson, *Lotus Land*, p. 133.
8. Chandrakala A. Hate, *Hindu Woman and Her Future*, pp. 46–47.
9. Olga Lang, *Chinese Family and Society*, p. 37.
10. Ryan, op. cit., p. 70.
11. Mabel Waln Smith, *Springtime in Shanghai*, p. 170.
12. Ryan, op. cit., p. 71.
13. Chandrakala A. Hate, op. cit., pp. 12–13.
14. Phadke, op. cit., p. 97.

15. Frieda Hauswirth, *Purdah: The Status of Indian Women*, p. 57.
16. Hilda Wernher, *My Indian Son-in-Law*, p. 177.
17. Frieda Hauswirth, *A Marriage to India*, p. 55.
18. Dalip Singh Saund, op. cit., pp. 47–48.
19. Kumut Chandruang, *My Boyhood in Siam*, pp. 125–33 (abridged).
20. Hyontay Kim, *Folklore and Customs of Korea*, p. 102.
21. Savitri Devi Nanda, op. cit., p. 103.
22. Wernher, op. cit., p. 186.
23. The descriptions which follow attempt to summarize the heart of the Hindu marriage ritual. Details are omitted and the prayers are abridged. The account is based on P. H. Prabhu, *Hindu Social Organization*, pp. 164–74.
24. Mary I. Bryson, *Home Life in China*, p. 116.
25. Kamala Markandaya, *Nectar in a Sieve*, pp. 11–12.
26. Nora Waln, *The House of Exile*, p. 138.
27. Savitri Devi Nanda, op. cit., p. 15.
28. Yang Ping-yu, *The Love Story of a Maiden of Cathay*, p. 57.
29. Ryan, op. cit., p. 88.
30. Maurice Freedman, *Chinese Family and Marriage in Singapore*, p. 137.
31. Lang, op. cit., p. 126; and Freedman, op. cit., p. 137.
32. Herbert Feldman, *The Land and People of Pakistan*, p. 49.
33. John F. Embree, *A Japanese Village—Suye Mura*, p. 131.
34. Ibid., p. 156.
35. Savitri Devi Nanda, op. cit., p. 104.
36. Frieda Hauswirth, *A Marriage to India*, p. 245.
37. Sidney D. Gamble, *How Families Live in Peiping*, p. 199.

CHAPTER 8

CHILD WIVES OF INDIA

1. Santha Rama Rau, *Home to India*, p. 1.
2. N. S. Phadke, *Sex Problems in India*, p. 92.
3. Katherine Mayo, *Mother India*, p. 58.
4. Ibid., pp. 95, 98.
5. Ibid., p. 81.
6. Phadke, op. cit., pp. 74–75.
7. Ibid., p. 73.
8. Hester Gray, *Indian Women and the West*, p. 19.
9. Johann Meyer, *Sexual Life in Ancient India*, p. 54.
10. Hermann Keyserling (ed.), *The Book of Marriage*, p. 112.
11. Quoted by Phadke, op. cit., pp. 80–81.
12. Frieda Hauswirth, *A Marriage to India*, p. 203.
13. Phadke, op. cit., p. 66.
14. Eleanor F. Rathbone, *Child Marriage: the Indian Minotaur*, p. 61.
15. Ibid., p. 24.

16. Mrs. P. K. Roy, Report in Calcutta *Statesman,* July 26, 1928.
17. Rathbone, op. cit., p. 26.
18. Gertrude Marvin Williams, *Understanding India,* p. 248.
19. For most of the details in the following account we are indebted to Eleanor F. Rathbone, op. cit.
20. Rathbone, op. cit., p. 43.
21. S. C. Dube, *Indian Village,* p. 119.
22. Olga Lang, *Chinese Family and Society,* p. 36.
23. James Legge, Commentary on *The Book of Odes,* Part 1, Book 1, Ode 7.
24. Kang Won-Yong, *A Study of the Family System in Korea,* pp. 25–26.
25. Ibid., p. 23.
26. John Gerhard, *Loci Theologici,* VII, p. 100.
27. R. H. Bainton, Article on "Christianity and Sex" in Simon Doniger (ed.), *Sex and Religion Today,* p. 44.
28. *Encyclopædia Britannica,* Article on "Knighthood and Chivalry," Vol. 13, 1957 edition.
29. Williams, op. cit., p. 248.

CHAPTER 9

WHO KEEPS CONCUBINES?

1. Olga Lang, *Chinese Family and Society,* p. 221.
2. Isaac T. Headland, *Home Life in China,* p. 117.
3. Genesis 16:1–4.
4. Nora Waln, *The House of Exile,* p. 132.
5. J. A. Dubois, *Hindu Manners, Customs and Ceremonies,* pp. 210–11.
6. Genesis 16:4.
7. Headland, op. cit., pp. 117–18.
8. Ibid., p. 120.
9. Ibid., pp. 114–15.
10. Kumut Chandruang, *My Boyhood in Siam,* p. 62.
11. Pearl S. Buck, *The Good Earth,* Chap. 20.
12. Book of Esther 2:12–14 (Revised Standard Version).
13. *The Book of Odes,* Part 1, Book 2, Ode 10.
14. George Ryley Scott, *Far Eastern Sex Life,* pp. 54, 56.
15. Ibid., pp. 43–44.
16. Tsao Hsueh-chin, *Dream of the Red Chamber* (1), p. 111.
17. Ibid., p. 120.
18. Edward Thompson, *Suttee,* p. 46. The reference is to burning on the husband's funeral pyre.
19. Lang, op. cit., p. 51.
20. Ch'en Tung-yuan, *History of the Life of Chinese Women,* p. 74.
21. C. Ryder Smith, *Bible Doctrine of Womanhood,* p. 33.
22. Lang, op. cit., p. 50.
23. Pearl S. Buck, *Letter from Peking,* p. 137.

24. Kumut Chandruang, op. cit., p. 138.
25. Confucius, *Analects*, 17; 25.
26. Lang, op. cit., pp. 27–28.
27. Ibid., p. 219.
28. *The Book of Odes*, Part 1, Book 4, Ode 2.
29. Hilda Wernher, *My Indian Son-in-Law*, p. 79.
30. Eleanor McDougall, *Lamps in the Wind*, p. 133.
31. Hester Gray, *Indian Women and the West*, p. 18.
32. Maurice Freedman, *Chinese Marriage and Family in Singapore*, p. 32.

CHAPTER 10

MARRIED LIFE AND MARRIED LOVE

1. Allen K. Faust, *The New Japanese Womanhood*, p. 29.
2. American Tract Society (published by), *Conditions and Character of Females in Pagan and Mohammedan Countries*, p. 8.
3. Ruth Benedict, *The Chrysanthemum and the Sword*, p. 208.
4. Bryce Ryan, *Sinhalese Village*, p. 42.
5. M. K. Gandhi, *Women and Social Justice*, p. 110.
6. Quoted by Katherine Mayo, *Mother India*, p. 73.
7. Frieda Hauswirth, *A Marriage to India*, p. 100.
8. Savitri Devi Nanda, *The City of Two Gateways*, p. 31.
9. Mary I. Bryson, *Home Life in China*, p. 111.
10. This was the opinion of Choo, one of the interpreters of *The Book of Odes*.
11. Setsuko Hani, *The Japanese Family System—as Seen from the Standpoint of Japanese Women*, p. 17.
12. Margaret Macnicol (ed.), *Poems by Indian Women*, p. 95.
13. Savitri Devi Nanda, op. cit., p. 16.
14. Isaac T. Headland, *Home Life in China*, p. 87.
15. Hyontay Kim, *Folklore and Customs of Korea*, p. 89.
16. Quoted by Florence Ayscough, *Chinese Women Yesterday and Today*, pp. 14–15.
17. Albert Richard O'Hara, *The Position of Woman in Early China*, p. 260.
18. Nora Waln, *The House of Exile*, p. 78.
19. Savitri Devi Nanda, op. cit., p. 203.
20. *The Book of Odes*, Part 1, Book 10, Ode 5.
21. Waln, op. cit., p. 166.
22. Savitri Devi Nanda, op. cit., p. 255.
23. Ayscough, op. cit., p. 38.
24. Savitri Devi Nanda, op. cit., p. 17.
25. Shingoro Takaishi, Introduction to Kaibara Ekken, *Greater Learning for Women*, pp. 19–20.
26. Macnicol, op. cit., pp. 65–66.
27. Ayscough, op. cit., p. 39.

28. Quoted by Millicent M. Pommerenke, *Asian Women and Eros*, pp. 103–4.
29. M. K. Gandhi, *Self-Restraint versus Self-Indulgence*, p. 111.
30. Quoted by Kumut Chandruang, *My Boyhood in Siam*, p. 141.
31. Quoted by Shingoro Takaishi, op. cit., p. 20.
32. Kumut Chandruang, op. cit., p. 43.
33. Ryan, op. cit., p. 42.
34. Headland, op. cit., p. 270.
35. Ibid., p. 270.
36. Hyontay Kim, op. cit., pp. 20–21.
37. Mi Mi Khaing, *Burmese Family*, p. 77.
38. Savitri Devi Nanda, op. cit., p. 25.
39. Kang Won-Yong, *A Study of the Family System in Korea*, p. 30.
40. Quoted by George Ryley Scott, *Far Eastern Sex Life*, p. 51.
41. Ibid., p. 183.
42. Faust, op. cit., p. 25.
43. P. Thomas, *Women and Marriage in India*, pp. 87–88.
44. Waln, op. cit., p. 133.
45. Benedict, op. cit., p. 185.
46. E. H. Cressy, *Daughters of Changing Japan*, pp. 119–20.
47. *The Book of Odes*, Part 1, Book 3, Ode 10.
48. Hilda Wernher, *My Indian Son-in-Law*, p. 231.
49. Kumut Chandruang, op. cit., p. 149.
50. James H. S. Bossard and Eleanor Boll, *Why Marriages Go Wrong*, pp. 12–13.
51. Kiplinger Magazine, "Changing Times," September 1958.
52. *The Book of Odes*, Part 1, Book 2, Ode 3.
53. Mabel Waln Smith, *Springtime in Shanghai*, p. 172.
54. Kumut Chandruang, op. cit., pp. 146–47.

CHAPTER 11

THE WIDOW'S FIERY SACRIFICE

1. K. M. Kapadia, *Marriage and Family in India*, p. 160.
2. American Tract Society (published by), *Conditions and Character of Females in Pagan and Mohammedan Countries*, p. 5.
3. Kapadia, op. cit., p. 97.
4. Frieda Hauswirth, *A Marriage to India*, p. 65.
5. Olga Lang, *Chinese Family and Society*, p. 40.
6. *Record of Rites*, 1:457.
7. Lang, op. cit., p. 203.
8. Kang Won-Yong, *A Study of the Family System in Korea*, pp. 31–32.
9. Setsuko Hani, *The Japanese Family System—as Seen from the Standpoint of Japanese Women*, p. 13.
10. James H. S. Bossard and Eleanor Boll, *Why Marriages Go Wrong*, p. 12.

11. Kumut Chandruang, *My Boyhood in Siam*, p. 224.
12. Chandrakala A. Hate, *Hindu Woman and Her Future*, pp. 148–49.
13. Hilda Wernher, *My Indian Son-in-Law*, p. 167; and Hester Gray, *Indian Women and the West*, p. 21.
14. Johann Meyer, *Sexual Life in Ancient India*, p. 417.
15. Katherine Mayo, *Mother India*, p. 82.
16. Chandrakala A. Hate, op. cit., pp. 52–53.
17. Ibid., p. 258.
18. J. A. Dubois, *Hindu Manners, Customs and Ceremonies*, p. 312.
19. P. Thomas, *Women and Marriage in India*, p. 68.
20. Kapadia, op. cit., p. 173.
21. Hauswirth, op. cit., pp. 49–52.
22. M. K. Gandhi, *Young India*, August 5, 1926.
23. Gray, op. cit., p. 22.
24. Savitri Devi Nanda, *The City of Two Gateways*, p. 263.
25. Kapadia, op. cit., p. 160.
26. Nora Waln, *The House of Exile*, pp. 128–29.
27. James Legge, *The Chinese Classics*, Vol. 4, Part 2, p. 76.
28. Florence Ayscough, *Chinese Women, Yesterday and Today*, p. 290.
29. *The Book of Odes*, Part 1, Book 4, Ode 2.
30. Waln, op. cit., p. 128.
31. Kang Won-Yong, op. cit., p. 33.
32. Allen K. Faust, *The New Japanese Womanhood*, p. 26.
33. W. E. H. Lecky, *History of European Morals from Augustus to Charlemagne*, Vol. 2, p. 136.
34. Jerome, *Contra Jovin*, i.
35. Gertrude Marvin Williams, *Understanding India*, p. 277.
36. W. H. Sleeman, *Rambles and Recollections of an Indian Official*, Vol. 1, pp. 23–28.
37. Edward Thompson, *Suttee*. We are indebted to this source for much of what follows in this discussion.
38. Meyer, op. cit., p. 413.
39. Thompson, op. cit., p. 47.
40. Dubois, op. cit., p. 172.
41. Thompson, op. cit., pp. 50–51.
42. William Ward, *A View of the History, Literature and Mythology of the Hindoos* (1822), Vol. 3, pp. 316–17. Quoted by Thompson, op. cit., p. 146.
43. Kapadia, op. cit., p. 163.
44. Savitri Devi Nanda, op. cit., p. 268.
45. Mary I. Bryson, *Home Life in China*, pp. 118–19.
46. Ayscough, op. cit., pp. 31–34.
47. Hyontay Kim, *Folklore and Customs of Korea*, p. 29.
48. George Caiger, *Tojo Say No*, p. 46.

CHAPTER 12

ABOVE ALL, GIVE US CHILDREN!

1. Quoted by Nora Waln, *The House of Exile*, p. 130.
2. Allen K. Faust, *The New Japanese Womanhood*, pp. 52–53.
3. Waln, op. cit., pp. 137–38.
4. David R. Mace, *Hebrew Marriage*, pp. 202–3.
5. Millicent M. Pommerenke, *Asian Women and Eros*, p. 126.
6. Kamela Markandaya, *Nectar in a Sieve*, pp. 70–72.
7. Pommerenke, op. cit., p. 144.
8. J. A. Dubois, *Hindu Manners, Customs and Ceremonies*, p. 601.
9. Edward Westermarck, *History of Human Marriage*, Vol. 3, pp. 208–9.
10. Mace, op. cit., p. 206.
11. W. E. H. Lecky, *History of European Morals from Augustus to Charlemagne*, Vol. 2, Chap. 5.
12. Waln, op. cit., p. 212.
13. Ibid., p. 102.
14. Ibid., p. 82.
15. Quoted by Eleanor Rathbone, *Child Marriage: the Indian Minotaur*, pp. 38–39.
16. Malcolm Smith, *A Physician at the Court of Siam*, p. 58.
17. Kumut Chandruang, *My Boyhood in Siam*, p. 60.
18. Waln, op. cit., p. 212.
19. Pearl S. Buck, *The Good Earth*, Chap. 3.
20. Hilda Wernher, *My Indian Son-in-Law*, p. 195.
21. Lucy H. Crockett, *Popcorn on the Ginza*, p. 32.
22. Hyontay Kim, *Folklore and Customs of Korea*, p. 53.
23. Isaac T. Headland, *Home Life in China*, pp. 14–15.
24. Kumut Chandruang, op. cit., p. 37.
25. Buck, op. cit., Chap. 3.
26. Headland, op. cit., pp. 260–61.
27. Eleanor McDougall, *Lamps in the Wind*, p. 38.
28. Quoted by Eleanor Rathbone, op. cit., p. 34.
29. Quoted by Eleanor Rathbone, op. cit., p. 66.
30. *The Book of Odes*, Part 2, Book 4, Ode 5.
31. E. H. Cressy, *Daughters of Changing Japan*, pp. 14–15.
32. Pommerenke, op. cit., p. 237.
33. Maurice Freedman, *Chinese Family and Marriage in Singapore*, p. 36.
34. Margaret Macnicol (ed.), *Poems by Indian Women*, p. 88.
35. Quoted by Kumut Chandruang, op. cit., p. 141.
36. McDougall, op. cit., p. 122.
37. Bryce Ryan, *Sinhalese Village*, p. 44.
38. Emily H. Mudd, "Pinpoint Impressions of Family Living in Japan," in *Population Bulletin*, August 1955.

39. Faust, op. cit., p. 63.
40. Ryan, op. cit., p. 44.
41. *Record of Rites*, 29:29.
42. Waln, op. cit., p. 45.
43. Ryan, op. cit., p. 41.
44. Savitri Devi Nanda, *The City of Two Gateways*, p. 53.
45. Ryan, op. cit., p. 61.
46. P. Thomas, *Women and Marriage in India*, p. 39.
47. Olga Lang, *Chinese Family and Society*, p. 27.
48. Tsao Hsueh-chin, *Dream of the Red Chamber* (2), Chap. 20.
49. Mi Mi Khaing, *Burmese Family*, p. 2.
50. Buck, op. cit., Chap. 17.
51. Quoted by Kumut Chandruang, op. cit., p. 141.
52. John H. Gubbins, *The Making of Modern Japan*, p. 285.
53. Wernher, op. cit., p. 70.
54. Kang Won-Yong, *A Study of the Family System in Korea*, p. 40.
55. Marion J. Levy, *The Family Revolution in Modern China*, pp. 63, 66.
56. Waln, op. cit., p. 197.
57. Lang, op. cit., p. 231.
58. Gubbins, op. cit., pp. 288–89.
59. Buck, op cit., Chap. 34.

CHAPTER 13

THE FUTURE OF MARRIAGE

1. International Missionary Council (published by), *The Christian Family in East Asia*, p. 14.
2. Edward Thompson, *Suttee*, pp. 143–44.
3. Quoted by Setsuko Hani, *The Japanese Family System—as Seen from the Standpoint of Japanese Women*, pp. 33–34.
4. Savitri Devi Nanda, *The City of Two Gateways*, p. 270.
5. Djang Hsiang-lan, "New Womanhood in Old China," in Chester S. Miao (ed.), *Christian Voices in China*, pp. 95, 109.
6. Sumie Seo Mishima, *The Broader Way*, p. 238.
7. Hyontay Kim, *Folklore and Customs of Korea*, p. 103.
8. E. H. Cressy, *Daughters of Changing Japan*, pp. 284–85.
9. Ibid., p. 53.
10. Shingoro Takaishi, Introduction to Kaibara Ekken, *Greater Learning for Women*, p. 25.
11. Cressy, op. cit., p. 195.
12. *Time*, January 26, 1959.
13. Ernest W. Burgess and Harvey T. Locke, *The Family. From Institution to Companionship*, p. 367.
14. Ralph Linton, *The Study of Man: An Introduction*, p. 175.

15. James H. S. Bossard and Eleanor Boll, *Why Marriages Go Wrong*, pp. 131, 134, 136.
16. Jessie Bernard, *Remarriage: A Study of Marriage*, p. 119.
17. Dalip Singh Saund, *My Mother India*, pp. 37, 39.
18. Quoted by Hilda Wernher, *My Indian Son-in-Law*, p. 203.
19. Bossard and Boll, op. cit., p. 44.
20. James Boswell, *The Life of Samuel Johnson*, p. 705.
21. E. S. Turner, *A History of Courting*, p. 269.
22. Sumie Seo Mishima, op. cit., pp. 221–23.
23. Cressy, op. cit., pp. 300–5 (abridged).
24. Gibson Winter, *Love and Conflict*, pp. 43–44.
25. Ibid., pp. 45–46.
26. Rabindranath Tagore, "The Indian Ideal of Marriage," in H. Keyserling (ed.), *The Book of Marriage*, p. 117.
27. Bossard and Boll, op. cit., p. 124.

APPENDIX

MARRIAGE IN COMMUNIST CHINA

1. *The Times*, London, July 31, 1958.
2. Mabel Waln Smith, *Springtime in Shanghai*, p. 198.
3. Review article in *The Times*, London, July 31, 1958, "Communism and Change in China."
4. Smith, op. cit., p. 198 (abridged).
5. Simone de Beauvoir, *The Long March*, pp. 141–42.
6. Ibid., p. 155.
7. Ibid., p. 146.
8. Ibid., p. 143.
9. Ibid., p. 149.
10. Ibid., p. 129.
11. Peter Schmid, *The New Face of China*, p. 107.
12. Ibid., p. 108.
13. de Beauvoir, op. cit., pp. 153–54.
14. Schmid, op. cit., p. 110.
15. Ibid., p. 114.
16. de Beauvoir, op. cit., pp. 157–59.
17. Society of Friends (published by), *Quakers Visit China*, p. 18.
18. Edward Hunter, *The Black Book on Red China*, Chap. 8.
19. Elton and Pauline Trueblood, *The Recovery of Family Life*, pp. 15–16.
20. de Beauvoir, op. cit., p. 153.
21. Ibid., p. 160.

BIBLIOGRAPHY

The following is not a selected bibliography on our subject. Rather it is a fairly complete list of the books we used in our quest of material about the East. All were not of equal value to us for our particular purpose; but we would like to acknowledge our gratitude to the authors for the mine of information which, taken as a whole, these volumes furnished. The authors to whom we owe a particular debt can be distinguished by the frequency with which we have quoted them.

The alphabetical listing of Eastern names, concerning which there appears to be no generally accepted rule, has posed a problem for us. Some of these cannot be divided into surnames and given names as in the West, and cannot therefore be listed alphabetically under surnames.

We have discussed this problem with nationals of most of the countries concerned. Acting on their suggestions, we have listed a Burmese author's name as a complete unit under the first letter of the name concerned; and Indian, Thai, and Japanese names in Anglicized form under the first letter of the last name (or names). In the case of Chinese and Korean names, in both the References and the Bibliography, we have used the customary form employed in translation of always putting the family name first, and treating the whole name as a unit.

Ayscough, Florence, *Chinese Women Yesterday and Today*. Houghton Mifflin Company, Boston, 1937.

Barbour, Katherine H., *Women of Japan*. National Board of the Y.W.C.A. of the U.S.A., 1936.

Benedict, Ruth, *The Chrysanthemum and the Sword*. Secker and Warburg, Ltd., London, 1947.

Bryson, Mary I., *Home Life in China*. American Tract Society, New York, no date.

Buck, Pearl S., *East Wind, West Wind*. The World Publishing Co., New York, 1943.

Buck, Pearl S., *The Good Earth*. John Day Co., Inc., New York, 1931.

Buck, Pearl S., *Letter from Peking*. Pocket Books, Inc., New York, 1958.

Caiger, George, *Tojo Say No*. Angus & Robertson, Ltd., Sydney and London, 1943.

Chandruang, Kumut, *My Boyhood in Siam*. John Day Co., Inc., New York, 1940.

Ch'en Tung-yuan, *History of the Life of Chinese Women*.

The Christian Family in East Asia, International Missionary Council, New York, 1958.

Conditions and Character of Females in Pagan and Mohammedan Countries. American Tract Society, no date. (Pamphlet)

Cressy, Earl Herbert, *Daughters of Changing Japan*. Farrar, Straus & Cudahy, Inc., New York, 1955.

Crockett, Lucy Herndon, *Popcorn on the Ginza*. Victor Gollancz, Ltd., London, 1949.

Dawson, Miles Menander, *The Ethics of Confucius*. G. P. Putnam's Sons, New York and London, 1915.

de Beauvoir, Simone, *The Long March*. The World Publishing Co., New York, 1958.

Dube, S. C., *Indian Village*. Routledge and Kegan Paul, Ltd., London, 1955.

Dubois, Abbé J. A., *Hindu Manners, Customs and Ceremonies*. 2 Vols., Clarendon Press, Oxford, 1897.

Embree, John F., *A Japanese Village—Suye Mura*. Kegan Paul, Trench, Trübner & Co., London, 1946.

Faust, Allen K., *The New Japanese Womanhood*. George H. Doran Company, New York, 1926.

Feldman, Herbert, *Land and People of Pakistan*. The Macmillan Co., New York, 1958.

Freedman, Maurice, *Chinese Family and Marriage in Singapore*. H. M. Stationery Office, London, 1957.

Gamble, Sidney D., *How Chinese Families Live in Peiping*. Funk & Wagnalls Company, London and New York, 1933.

Gandhi, M. K., *An Autobiography*. Phoenix Press, London, 1949.

Gandhi, M. K., *Self-Restraint versus Self-Indulgence*. Navajivan Publishing House, Ahmedabad, 1947.

Gandhi, M. K., *Women and Social Justice*. Navajivan Publishing House, Ahmedabad, 1942.

Gray, Hester, *Indian Women and the West*. Zenith Press, London, no date. (Pamphlet)

Gubbins, John H., *The Making of Modern Japan*. Seeley, Service and Co., London, 1922.

Hani, Setsuko, *The Japanese Family System—as Seen from the Stand-point of Japanese Women*. International Publishing Co., Ltd., 1948. (Pamphlet)

Hate, Chandrakala A., *Hindu Woman and Her Future*. New Book Company, Ltd., Bombay, 1948.

Hauswirth, Frieda, *A Marriage to India*. Vanguard Press, Inc., New York, 1930.

Hauswirth, Frieda, *Purdah: The Status of Indian Women*. Kegan Paul, London, 1932.

Headland, Isaac Taylor, *Home Life in China*. The Macmillan Co., New York, 1914.

Highbaugh, Irma, *Family Life in West China*, Agricultural Missions, New York, 1948.

Hsu, Francis L. K., *Magic and Science in Yunan*, Institute of Pacific Relations, New York, 1943.

Hunter, Edward, *The Black Book on Red China*. The Bookmailer, New York, 1958.

Kaibara Ekken, *Greater Learning for Women* (Introduction by Shingoro Takaishi), in *Women and Wisdom of Japan*. John Murray, London, 1905.

Kang Won-Yong, *A Study of the Family System in Korea*. Unpublished S.T.M. Thesis at Union Theological Seminary, New York, 1956.

Kapadia, K. M., *Marriage and Family in India*. Oxford University Press, London, 1955.

Kearns, J. F., *Marriage Ceremonies of the Hindus of South India*. Higginbotham and Co., Madras, 1868.

Kim Hyontay, *Folklore and Customs of Korea*. Korea Information Service Inc., Seoul, Korea, 1957.

Lang, Olga, *Chinese Family and Society*. Yale University Press, New Haven, 1946.

Legge, James, *The Chinese Classics*. 7 Vols., Trübner and Co., London, 1861–72.

Levy, Marion J., *The Family Revolution in Modern China*. Harvard University Press, Cambridge, Mass., 1949.

Lin Yu-tang, *Moment in Peking*. John Day Co., Inc., New York, 1939.

McDougall, Eleanor, *Lamps in the Wind*. Livingstone Press, London, 1940.

Macnicol, Margaret (ed.), *Poems by Indian Women*. Oxford University Press, London, 1923.

Malabari, Behramji M., *Infant Marriage and Enforced Widowhood in India*. "Voice of India" Printing Press, Bombay, 1887.

Manava Dharma Sastra, or *The Institutes of Manu*, verbally translated from the original with a Preface by Sir William Jones. Third Edition, J. Higginbotham, Madras, 1863.

Markandaya, Kamala, *Nectar in a Sieve*. John Day Co., Inc., New York, 1954.

Mayo, Katherine, *Mother India*. Harcourt, Brace & Co., New York, 1927.

Mayo, Katherine, *Slaves of the Gods*. Harcourt, Brace & Co., New York, 1929.

Menon, Lakshmi N., *The Position of Women*. Oxford University Press, 1944. (Pamphlet)

Meyer, Johann, *Sexual Life in Ancient India*. Barnes & Noble, Inc., New York, 1953.

Miao, Chester S. (ed.), *Christian Voices in China*. Friendship Press, New York, 1948.

Milam, Ava B., *A Study of the Student Homes of China*. Teachers College, Columbia, New York, 1930.

Mi Mi Khaing, *Burmese Family*. Longmans, Green & Co., Bombay, India, 1946

Mishima, Sumie Seo, *The Broader Way*. John Day Co., Inc., New York, 1953.

Mukerji, Dhan Gopal, *A Son of Mother India Answers*. E. P. Dutton and Co., Inc., New York, 1928.

Nanda, Savitri Devi, *The City of Two Gateways*. George Allen & Unwin, Ltd., London, 1950.

O'Hara, Albert Richard, *The Position of Women in Early China*. Catholic University of America Press, Washington, D.C., 1945.

Phadke, N. S., *Sex Problems in India*. D. B. Taraporevala Sons and Co., Bombay, 1929.

Pommerenke, Millicent M., *Asian Women and Eros*. Vantage Press, Inc., New York, 1958.

Prabhu, Pandharinath H., *Hindu Social Organization*. Popular Book Depot, Bombay, 1958.

Quakers Visit China, Society of Friends, London, 1955. (Pamphlet)

Rama Rau, Santha, *This Is India*. Harper & Brothers, New York, 1954.

Rama Rau, Santha, *Home to India*. Harper & Brothers, New York, 1944.

Ranga Iyer, C., *Father India: A Reply to Mother India*. Louis Carrier & Co., New York, 1928.

Rathbone, Eleanor F., *Child Marriage: the Indian Minotaur*. George Allen & Unwin, Ltd., London, 1934.

Ronaldshay, Earl of, *The Heart of Āryâvarta*. Constable & Co., London, 1925.

Ryan, Bryce, *Sinhalese Village*. University of Miami Press, 1958.

Sastri, A. Mahadeva, *The Vedic Law of Marriage*. Government Branch Press, Mysore, 1908.

Saund, Dalip Singh, *My Mother India*. Pacific Coast Khalsa Duvan Society, Stockton, California, 1930.

Schmid, Peter, *The New Face of China*. George C. Harrap & Co., Ltd., London, 1958.

Schmid, Peter, *In the Shadow of the Dragon*. George Weidenfeld & Nicolson, London, 1957.

Scott, George Ryley, *Far Eastern Sex Life*. Gerald G. Swan, Ltd., London, 1943.

Shively, Donald H., *The Love Suicide at Amijima*. Harvard University Press, Cambridge, Mass., 1953.

Sleeman, Major General Sir W. H., *Rambles and Recollections of an Indian Official*. Constable, London, 1893.

Smith, Mabel Waln, *Springtime in Shanghai*. George C. Harrap & Co., Ltd., London, 1957.

Smith, Malcolm, *A Physician at the Court of Siam*. Country Life, Ltd., London, 1947.

Snedegar, Dorothy M., *The "Mother India" Controversy*. Unpublished M.A. Thesis at Duke University, North Carolina, 1938.

Sorabji, Cornelia, *Love and Life Behind the Purdah*. Fremantle and Co., London, 1901.

Thomas, P., *Women and Marriage in India*. George Allen & Unwin, Ltd., London, 1939.

Thompson, Edward, *Suttee*. George Allen & Unwin, Ltd., London, 1928.

Thompson, P. A., *Lotus Land*. T. Werner Laurie, London, 1906.

Tsao Hsueh-chin, *Dream of the Red Chamber*. Translated by Wang Chi-chin, Doubleday and Co., Inc., New York (1) 1929, (2) 1958.

Vatsyayana, *Kama Sutra*. Printed under the supervision of Professor H. S. Gambers, Amritsar, 1930.

Vaughan, Kathleen Olga, *The Purdah System and its Effect on Motherhood*. W. Heffer and Sons, Ltd., Cambridge, 1928. (Pamphlet)

Vidhyapati, *Bangiya Padabali*. Old Bourne Press, London, 1915.

Waln, Nora, *The House of Exile*. Little, Brown & Company, Boston, 1933.

Wernher, Hilda, *My Indian Son-in-Law*. Doubleday and Co., Inc., New York, 1949.

Wilkinson, H. P., *The Family in Classical China*, Macmillan & Co., Ltd., London, 1926.

Williams, Gertrude Marvin, *Understanding India*. Coward-McCann, Inc., New York, 1928.

Yang Ping-yu, *The Love Story of a Maiden of Cathay*. Fleming H. Revell Co., New York, 1911.

ADDITIONAL SOURCES

We have listed here, for the purpose of identification, further sources from which we have quoted, but which, since we did not read them as part of this project, are not included in our bibliography.

Bernard, Jessie, *Remarriage: A Study of Marriage.* Dryden Press, New York, 1956.

Bossard, James H. S., and Boll, Eleanor S., *Why Marriages Go Wrong.* The Ronald Press Company, New York, 1958.

Boswell, James, *The Life of Samuel Johnson.* Oxford University Press, 1953.

Brittain, Vera, *Lady into Woman.* Andrew Dakers, Ltd., London, 1953.

Burgess, Ernest W., and Locke, Harvey T., *The Family, from Institution to Companionship.* American Book Company, New York, 1945.

Charles, Robert Henry (ed.), *The Apocrypha and Pseudepigrapha of the Old Testament in English.* Clarendon Press, Oxford, 1913.

Doniger, Simon (ed.), *Sex and Religion Today.* Association Press, New York, 1953.

Greene, William Chase, *The Achievement of Rome.* Harvard University Press, Cambridge, Mass., 1938.

Keyserling, Count Herman A. (ed.), *The Book of Marriage.* Harcourt Brace & Co., New York, 1926.

Lecky, W. E. H., *History of European Morals from Augustus to Charlemagne,* 2 Vols., Longmans, Greene & Company, London, 1911.

Linton, Ralph, *The Study of Man: An Introduction.* D. Appleton-Century Co., Inc., New York, 1936.

Mace, David R., *Hebrew Marriage.* Epworth Press, London, 1953.

Maine, Sir Henry Sumner, *Ancient Law*. John Murray, London, 1930.

Mill, John Stuart, *Subjection of Women*. Appleton, New York, 1869.

Smith, C. Ryder, *Bible Doctrine of Womanhood*. Epworth Press, London, 1923.

Trueblood, Elton and Pauline, *The Recovery of Family Life*. Harper & Brothers, New York, 1953.

Turner, E. S., *A History of Courting*. Michael Joseph, Ltd., London, 1954.

Westermarck, Edward, *The History of Human Marriage*, 3 Vols., Macmillan & Co., Ltd., London, 1925.

Winter, Gibson, *Love and Conflict*. Doubleday and Co., Inc., New York, 1958.

INDEX

Abraham, 185, 186
Acton, William, 93–94
Aden, 15
Adoption, 252; Japan, 227
Adultery, 40, 214–18; Japan, 227; punishment for, 217
Affection: demonstrations (East), 206–7; expressions of, 125
Africa, 15, 263; bride-price, 153; women's inferiority, 81
Age: status, 271, East-West differences in, 271
Age of chivalry, 183
Alexander the Great, 239
Alexandre, Clement, 12
Allegory of Love, The, 111
Amazons, 60
American men, preference in women, 280
Ancestors, Buddhism and, 30
Ancestor worship, 29–30, 82
Anthony, Susan B., 77, 80
Aquinas, St. Thomas, 81, 111, 254
Aristotle, 247
Artha Shastra, 198
Asia, 21, 276, 279, 295; railway travel, 13–14; revolutionary movements, 282
Asian Christians, 17; training program, 17–18
Asians, 278–79; attitude toward Western family life, 43–44; interdependence, 19; involvement, 19; on marital relationships, 207
Astrology, 132–34
Aung San, 80
Australia, 17, 77; aborigines, 49
Ayscough, Florence, 208

Bainton, R. H., 183
Bales, R. F., 298
Bangkok, 13, 14, 18, 110, 188; *Krung Thep,* 14
Begam, Raziyya, 120
Benedict, Ruth, 197, 215–16
Bentinck, Lord William, 242
Berkeley, Thomas, Lord of, 183
Bernard, Jessie, 284
Betrothal, 151–53; child, 152; East-West difference, 151; infant, 152–53; medieval Europe, 183; -wedding, relationship (East), 157 ff.
Birth, of son (East), 25
Birth control, 81
Blake, William, 54
Boadicea, Queen, 60
Boll, Eleanor, 284, 287, 301
Bombay, 37, 70, 107, 250, 295; Hanging Gardens, 126
Book of Odes, 111
Bossard, James, 46, 284, 287, 301
Bowlby, Dr. John, 318
Brahma marriage, 118
Brahmins, exploitation of *devadasis,* 109
Brave New World, 300
Bride-price, 153–54
Britain, 15; *see also* England
British: child marriage controversy, 178; marriage bureaus, 290; matriarchy, 60
British Government, *suttee* and, 241, 242
Bryson, Mary, 69, 70, 200
Buck, Pearl, 98, 193
Buddha, 62
Buddhism, 10, 63, 209; ancestor worship, 30; celibacy, 94; female con-

B1